What They Said

This study of the trek between the Customs House and Howth Head minutely covers the area in all its facets, angles and aspects. The finished product from this mammoth undertaking is both informative and entertaining. Its wide and varying reach throughout the Dublin North Bay catchment area is panoramic and includes standout events, places, buildings, people, the area's topology, flora and fauna and, its customs and traditions. Sport, clubs, institutions, churches and schools all feature. Indeed, the scope of this work often goes far beyond the Dublin North Bay area with, for example, a very insightful chapter on many notable writers associated with the area. The book is copiously illustrated with a well-chosen selection of images. – **K. McM.**

This 'History and Guide to Dublin's North Bay Area' is a most insightful treatise of the expanse of territory covered. It is a marvellously detailed tome that escorts the reader through the socio-cultural backdrop of the region in a very easy-to-follow, unrushed style. The book goes to the soul of the North Bay area, examining and detailing its rich historical lore and its large cultural scope. And the author's research illustrates just how deep our mine of local and social history is. The minute detail in the text clearly shows the author has a love of the area, which he has obviously passionately embraced. His multi-faceted account of the terrain covered is surely a treasury of its historical riches. – **J.K.**

This most welcome book is a companion/information guide to the North Dublin Bay locality for the walker, trekker, cyclist, tourist, visitor. But it is much more. If ever the statement, "it's all about the journey" was true, then it could have been coined for this comprehensive, all-embracing volume. It has detail and range above and beyond the usual local history publications. Every step of the trek has an engaging history and story. – **A.B.F.**

This is not just a local history but rather, a series of local histories covering the Customs House area, Docklands, North Strand, Summerhill, Ballybough, Fairview, Marino, Donnycarney, Clontarf, Killester, Raheny,

Continued >>>

Kilbarrack, Bayside, Donaghmede, Baldoyle, Sutton and Howth. Everyone living in these areas and, far beyond, should arm themselves with a copy of this outstanding publication. It is in keeping with the author's reputation for detailed output in his other publications, especially the bestselling, *The Meadow of the Bull: A History of Clontarf.* "He has an eye for detail that many a sleuth would love to possess.– **C. McE.**

Bar being taken by the hand and walking along the trail from the Customs House to Howth Head, you will not find a better or more detailed guide book. The author has surely used a fine toothcomb in going through the records. It has everything that local history should have – and that bit extra. – **A. O'T.**

This is a very comprehensive history of and guide to the entire North Dublin Bay area, from the stately Customs House in the city centre to wild and charming Howth Head. It is packed with much fascinating information, the research for which clearly was exhaustive and exhausting. It makes a fascinating read and an even better reference book. It is mana and a 'must have' for general readers, residents, teachers, tourists and students at all levels. – **O.M.**

Customs House to Howth Head:

A History and Guide to the Dublin North Bay Area

Dennis McIntyre

Le gach dea ghuí

Denny McIntyre

*Customs House to Howth Head: A History and Guide to the
Dublin North Bay Area*
Copyright © Dennis McIntyre, 2023
The author has asserted his moral rights

First published in Ireland, in 2023 by The Shara Press, 32 Howth Road,
Clontarf, Dublin 3
e-Mail: dublinnorthbaytourism@gmail.com

ISBN: 978-0-9527311-6-0
A CIP catalogue record for this book is available from the National
Library

Typesetting, page design and layout, cover design by
DocumentsandManuscripts.com

Published with the assistance of The Manuscript Publisher, publishing
solutions for the digital age – www.TheManuscriptPublisher.com

Published, printed and bound in Ireland

Also by Dennis McIntyre

- *The Meadow of the Bull: A History of Clontarf* (The Shara Press. First published in 1987. Second edition published 2014)

- *Bram Stoker and the Irishness of Dracula* (The Shara Press, 2013)

- *Irish Nationalism, Irish Republicanism and the 1916 Easter Rising* (The Shara Press, 2016)

- *The Principal Brathadóir* (The Shara Press, 2018)

- *Gaysa, the Spoiled Priest* (The Shara Press, 2020)

Available from Dublin North Bay Tourism
e-Mail: dublinnorthbaytourism@gmail.com

See inside back cover for further information

Preface

There is little doubt but that tourism in Dublin, in the main, is concentrated in, on and around the city centre and the immediate south side of the city. The northside appears to be the poor relation! Dublin North Bay Tourism (DNBT) promotes the Dublin North Bay area from the classic Customs House to the rugged wilds of Howth Head.

History often, and especially in our school days, is brought to us as events and happenings in other places, far away and long ago. However, history is all around us – on our own street or road. With the help of this volume, we invite you to discover or rediscover the Dublin North Bay Way (and experience) with us. You will be pleasantly surprised at its depth, general riches, charms and contrasts.

Our route or trail takes us from the Customs House through Ballybough, the North Strand, Fairview, Marino, Clontarf, Raheny, Kilbarrack, Sutton to Howth, with many other neighbouring or adjoining areas visited as well. For some, parts of our route may seem or look unattractive but, to paraphrase Ralph McTell's song –

Let us take you by the hand and lead you
Through the North Bay streets.
We will show you something
To make you change your mind.

For example, many who encounter the North Bull Island for the first time dismiss it as a desert-like, barren, bleak wilderness, inhospitable and isolated! We will help you to see rather than just look... and discover a fascinating place meriting its declaration as a biosphere reserve by UNESCO!

Likewise, parts of the north inner city may appear cold, uninviting even forbidding! However, we will encourage you to dig a little deeper than what your first impressions might convey to you! While many north inner-city residents have been and are, socio-economically disadvantaged, you will become engrossed and realise that what you thought was an ugly duckling is really a beautiful swan! You will uncover a wonderful history and heritage and above all, a proud, loyal, close-knit people who were never found wanting, especially in troubled times, when the chips were down for our capital city and our country.

The Dublin North Bay Way and trail is very different and very representative of both old and modern Dublin and Ireland. It is a cross section (a microcosm) of all aspects and areas of Dublin and Ireland's history.

The water of the North Bay is a constant companion along our route. That water is twice daily reinvigorated by millions of barrels of water from the Irish Sea. Indeed, the diverse North Bay area is a littoral wonderland, is of tremendous natural beauty and a great resource. It is most accessible for many activities, including sailing, kayaking, surfing, swimming, fishing, nature walks and field trips and its beaches are there for all beach related activities. And we encounter many examples of 'Rus in Urbe', where the countryside harmoniously blends with the city.

The route embraces our national historical story in all its facets, angles and aspects. It is a treasury of history. It covers our very engaging political, literary, social, cultural and sporting history, including heritage, customs and traditions. Like all other areas the identity of the Dublin North Bay area is defined firstly by its people and secondly by its natural and built heritage. We recall the area's lore and legend as well as recollecting famous events, outstanding personalities and standout places and buildings. We talk about schools, churches, burial grounds, clubs, institutions, not forgetting monuments and memorials.

Our natural history – flora, fauna and wildlife in general – surrounds us as we travel. Our tour winds its way along the North Bay shoreline (UNESCO declared all of Dublin Bay a biosphere reserve in 2015) with all its biodiversity. And right in the eye of Dublin Bay is the unique jewel that is the North Bull Island, which is a bird sanctuary and is flanked by the renowned Dollymount Strand. The Tolka Estuary, Baldoyle Estuary, Ireland's Eye Island and Howth Head are also very significant sites in the whole Dublin Bay biosphere. Indeed, such is the variety of our trail that, you could say, there are several Dublin Bays!

We invite you to enjoy the North Bay experience with all its charms, traditions and its heritage. Discover the real Dublin, the real Ireland to grasp fully and understand the events that created our city and our country. As well as being informatively educational, you will find the North Bay experience very engaging and most entertaining... with some spectacularly wonderful sightseeing.

A special feature of our trek is that practically all of our route, from the Customs House to Sutton Cross is, in fact, on land reclaimed from the sea. Take advice from Robert Frost's wonderful poem and travel with us on

THE ROAD NOT TAKEN

Much of this publication is based on a very popular series of Dublin North Bay history programmes presented by the author on NEAR FM radio.

Because of the nature of a work such as this there will be some unavoidable repetition of names, events, etc. For example, there are many references to the 1916 Easter Rising. North Dublin Bay writers, its churches and graveyards, its public houses, transport and Bloody Sunday are given individual chapters.

Introduction

The original coast road from Dublin city (then centred around Christ Church and Church Street) to the northside and the sea ran via Parnell Street, Summerhill, Summerhill Parade, Ballybough Road (formerly Ballybough Lane) and crossed the Tolka river at Luke Kelly Bridge – better known, perhaps, as Ballybough Bridge. The coastline then ran from Clontarf through Ballybough Bridge, the North Strand, Amiens Street, Beresford Place, and Strand Street to the site of today's Grattan Bridge, which was named after the politician, Henry Grattan (1746-1820) in 1875. Since it was built in 1697, it was known as the Essex Bridge, recalling Arthur Capel, Earl of Essex who was Lord Deputy from 1672 to 1677.

Both the Liffey (named after the female deity Anna Livia) and Tolka rivers are tidal and it was the controlling, containment and embankment of their large delta areas and subsequent reclamation works that totally changed the entire landscape and aspect of the northeast area of Dublin City, the approach to Clontarf and beyond. And all this took place less than three hundred years ago. The original South Bull Wall was built between 1715 and 1730. Its construction was an early effort to control serious silting in the Dublin harbour and docks area. It can be taken as the initiative that began the major reclamation works that took place in the eighteenth and nineteenth centuries and, indeed, carried on into the twentieth century.

The embankment of the Liffey began in 1717 and was completed in 1721, when the North Wall was built. A huge portion of what is today's north inner city was earmarked for reclamation – roughly the area enclosed by the North Wall, the East Wall, the North Strand Road and Amiens Street. It included today's large Catholic Parishes of St Laurence O'Toole and St Joseph. It was called the North Lotts as, early in 1717, corporation officials drew lots as to how the reclaimed land would be shared – among themselves! Newfoundland was its other title!

The reclamation allowed Annesley Bridge to open in 1793 and a new route to the northside came into existence. Beginning at the Customs House, it ran through Amiens Street and the North Strand Road and became the new gateway, through Fairview, to the northside areas of Clontarf, Raheny, Baldoyle, Portmarnock, Howth and Malahide. It quickly became the more popular thoroughfare, as the old Ballybough route had a reputation as being somewhat unsafe and inhospitable! The 'old' and 'new' routes converge into one at the spot known as Edge's Corner in Fairview.

Itinerary

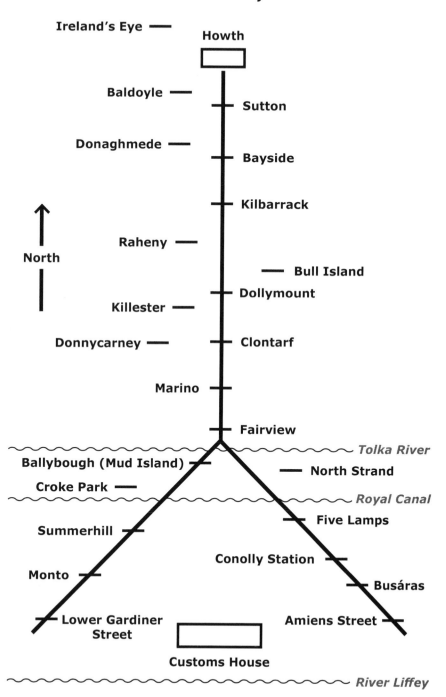

Ireland's Eye —

Howth

Baldoyle —

— Sutton

Donaghmede —

— Bayside

— Kilbarrack

Raheny —

— Bull Island

↑
North

Dollymount

Killester —

Donnycarney —

— Clontarf

Marino —

Fairview

Tolka River

Ballybough (Mud Island) —

— North Strand

Croke Park —

Royal Canal

— Five Lamps

Summerhill —

Conolly Station —

Monto —

— Busáras

Lower Gardiner Street

Amiens Street —

Customs House

River Liffey

Contents

CHAPTER ONE

Customs House. Lower Abbey Street, Beresford Place, Eden Quay, Liberty Hall, Butt Bridge, Loop Line Railway Bridge, Matt Talbot Bridge, Famine Memorial, Eternal Flame, Financial Services Centre

The classic, serene Customs (or Custom) House is, arguably, Dublin's, if not Ireland's, most beautiful building. It was designed by the world-famous architect, London-born James Gandon (1742-1823), and opened on 7 November 1791.

It has an island setting, hard by the River Liffey, being surrounded by Custom House Quay (so named in 1791, after the Customs House), Beresford Place and Memorial Road. Beresford Place, dating from 1791, is called after John Beresford (1738-1805), a powerful government official who actually brought Gandon to Ireland and, on whose advice, the Customs House was built. Memorial Road commemorates all sailors who died at sea after sailing out of Dublin. However, some sources suggest that it was named, in 1922, in memory of the Dublin Brigade of the IRA.

The design of the elegant edifice is Palladian in the neo-classical style. The building is portal and has four fronts – a Portland stone facade facing the Liffey, while the other three sides are of granite. The exterior of the Customs House displays sculptures and coats of arms by Thomas Banks, Agostino Carlini and Edward Smyth. Smyth's series of fourteen keystones depict thirteen faces of river gods of Ireland and one face for the Atlantic Ocean. All are men except Anna Livia, representing the River Liffey. Images of these godheads were later used to decorate the backs of Ireland's first currency notes. The dome of the Customs House has a statue of commerce on its crown.

Today's building replaced the original Customs House, which opened in 1707 on the site of the present Clarence Hotel on Wellington Quay, which had become unsound and not fit for purpose. Matters concerning customs and excise are no longer dealt with in the Customs House. The nerve centre of Dublin Port had moved to today's Alexandra Quay area, in the latter half of the nineteenth century. The 'new port' of Dublin came to be in the area east and north of the East Wall Road and south of the Liffey, between Ringsend and the area around the old Pigeon house, with the Alexandra Basin at its centre. The Alexandra name is derived from Alexandra, Princess of Wales, who formerly opened the basin in 1885, in the company of her husband, the future King Edward VII.

The first authority to manage the affairs of the port of Dublin was the Ballast Board, established in 1707. The Corporation for Preserving and Improving the Port of Dublin took over in 1786. This latter body was replaced by the Dublin Port and Docks Board in 1868. In modern times, Dublin Port Company (established as a corporate entity in 1997) manages all matters in relation to Dublin Port.

The Customs House became the headquarters of the Local Government Board of Ireland and remained so until Irish independence in 1922. With Dublin Castle, it was central to the administration of British rule in Ireland. During the 1916 Rising, the British army used it as a base.

On 25 May 1921, during the War of Independence, and with the full backing of the IRA Ard Comhairle, the Dublin Brigade of the IRA attacked the Customs House, to effectively destroy all records in the building and cripple it as an administrative centre. In what became known as the Battle of the Customs House, the IRA, led by Oscar Traynor (1886-1963) with Tom Ennis (a member of O'Toole's GAA Club) commanding officer on the day, burned the building to just about total destruction. In terms of propaganda this act gained worldwide publicity for the rebels. Sadly, in the process, records going back hundreds of years were destroyed. The fire was actually the third on the site. The first happened in 1789, before the building was completed and the second occurred in 1833.

About 270 members of the IRA took part in this burning and five of them died in the ensuing fighting. The building burned for five days, with temperatures reaching up to 1,300 degrees Fahrenheit. To commemorate this event, a memorial garden, designed by Daithí Healy, was built in the grounds of the building in 1956. The garden contains a fountain monument, designed by Yann Renard Goulet, with a bronze figure, representing Ireland, protecting a wounded soldier. The monument depicts Ireland's fight for freedom and remembers all members of the Dublin IRA Brigade who gave their lives for Irish freedom and, especially recalls the five IRA volunteers who died that day – Sean Doyle (from North Richmond Street), Daniel Head (from Seville Place), Patrick O'Reilly, Stephen O'Reilly and Edward Dorrens.

Beginning in the 1920s, the Customs House was rebuilt as closely as possible to resemble the 1791 building. The rebuilding went on right up to the 1990s. Nowadays, the Customs House is home to the Department of Housing and Planning (Local Government) and to those entrusted with the upkeep and general overseeing of our national monuments (Heritage).

Situated in city centre territory, the Customs House, which houses a visitor centre, is surrounded by some landmark buildings and places. At the junction of Beresford Place with Lower Abbey Street (Abbey Street is so called, since 1728, after the old St Mary's Abbey) is the New Irish Life building. On its forecourt is *The Chariot of Life* statue group by Oisín Kelly, put in place in 1982, which depicts reason overcoming emotion.

Standing on the corner of Beresford Place with Eden Quay, which dates from 1796 and recalls William Eden, Chief Secretary for Ireland 1780-82, is the sixteen-storey high Liberty Hall, built in 1964 to a design by Desmond Rea O'Kelly. It was the headquarters of the Irish Transport and General Workers Union and replaced an earlier building destroyed in the course of the 1916 Rising.

Originally the Northumberland Commercial and Family Hotel occupied the site. It was from here, at the front of Liberty Hall – which then fronted onto Beresford Place not the quays – that Pádraic Pearse (1879-1916) and James Connolly (1868-1916) led Volunteers and Citizen Army members (about 1500 in all) on Easter Monday, 24 April 1916, to occupy the GPO and formally declare the birth of the Irish Republic.

Across the road from Liberty Hall, on Beresford Place in the shadow of Butt Bridge, is a bronze statue of James Connolly, sculpted by Éamonn O'Doherty and unveiled by President Mary Robinson on 13 May 1996, to mark the 80th anniversary of Connolly's execution. Connolly actually lived in Liberty Hall in the period just before the Rising began. The starry plough flag design behind the statue is the flag of the Irish Citizen Army and also represents ownership of Ireland – earth to sky – by the working-class people. It is also symbolic of the present and future of the working class.

The original Butt Bridge was opened in 1879. It crosses the Liffey joining Custom House Quay with Burgh Quay and recalls Isaac Butt (1813-1879), who founded the Irish Home Rule movement and party in 1870. The present bridge dates from 1932, when it replaced the old 1879 bridge.

The towering Loop Line Railway Bridge, opened in 1891, takes its name from the fact that it connected what were two separate railway terminals – today's Connolly (Amiens Street) and Pearse Street (Westland Row) stations. The bridge totally ruins the view of the Customs House from the western side.

The Matt Talbot (1856-1925) Memorial Bridge across the Liffey was opened in 1978. It joins Custom House Quay with George's Quay – named, in 1821, after King George IV. The bridge recalls the pious and saintly, the Venerable Matt, noted for reforming from extremely drunken ways to a life of self-denial, self-punishment, servitude and prayer. Born at 13 Aldborough Court, Matt worked in a number of jobs in the Dublin port area.

At the southern end of the Matt Talbot Bridge, at City Quay, is a limestone statue of Matt by Albert Power, put in place in 1988. A bronze head of Matt can be seen on the site of his last address, 17 Upper Rutland Street (now Sean O'Casey Avenue). It is beside a block of flats named Matt Talbot Court. A cross on railings at Granby Lane marks the spot where the Venerable Matt died and, across the street is a marble wall tablet with the inscription, *Matt Talbot collapsed and died on Trinity Sunday June 7th 1925*.

Beside Matt Talbot Memorial Bridge on Custom House Quay is the Famine memorial statue sculpture group by Rowan Gillespie. Simply titled *Famine* and put there in 1997, to commemorate the 150th anniversary of The Great Famine (or An Gorta Mór) the statues are surely one of Ireland's most haunting and poignant memorials, recalling what are arguably the country's darkest hours. The scene depicts desperate people, clinging on to frugal belongings as they attempt to escape the fate of a multitude of their fellow people – starvation and death.

At the confluence of Beresford Place, Memorial Road and Amiens Street stands the *Eternal Flame*. It is spherical in shape and made of interlocking chains (representing prisoners everywhere) with an everlasting flame (fed by natural gas) at its centre. Its accompanying message reminds us that we should not forget all the people 'whom we failed to rescue from prison, who were tortured, who were kidnapped, who disappeared'.

Across the road is the International Financial Services Centre, which breathed new life into the Custom House Docks area, where re-development began in 1987. However, many locals viewed the great changes it and other programmes of 'modernisation' brought in bitter terms. They felt that economic change heralded great hardships for locals. While the port of Dublin remained active in the old working ways (so vividly described by James Plunkett in his epic book, *Strumpet City*) there was work for locals that sustained them and the local economy. Many are convinced that all the new ventures, while good for Dublin, simply do not belong in dockland territory.

Over many years, in an area with a strong seafaring tradition, thousands of men, generation following generation, were involved as carters and labourers, all too often in grim, austere and dreadful conditions. But, time and again, the coming together of the community has proved that just about any obstacle, dilemma or tragedy can be overcome.

Many were aggrieved and pointed out that cosmopolitan buildings, high-rise apartment blocks and 'big business' generally were simply alien to

Customs House

James Gandon

**Famine Memorial
(Custom House Quay)**

Matt Talbot

Oscar Traynor

The Chariot of Life

Eternal Flame, Memorial Road

Liberty Hall and Customs House

James Connolly

traditional dockland activity and would end a way of life ingrained in the locality. However, regular industries in the docks area, such as coal, fertiliser, flourmills, sugar-refining, bottle-making and joinery were petering out, with dereliction setting in, so change was inevitable. And the reality was that the daily activities in docklands moved to the Alexandra Basin area, as the old Customs House Docks, which first opened in 1796, became antiquated early in the twentieth century and there was a real need for a 'new departure' in the area.

In any case, when the Financial Service centre arrived in 1987, it went ahead only on the proviso that the distinctive character of the locality would be preserved as far as possible, particularly its very own and unique engineering and architectural features. The entire area – expanded to include the Amiens Street locality, the North Strand, the East Wall, Summerhill and Ballybough – had a reputation of life being lived lustily, by a people embedded in place. The area was characterised by a woven-routed oneness and a deep-rooted sense of community. And that community, where many people faced many cultural and economic difficulties, have always exhibited a rich historical heritage and an enviable cultural and sporting heritage, with long celebrated customs and traditions.

As time passes, it is evident that all the challenging and exciting new developments and new people have blended excellently with the more traditional aspects of the region. A bond has evolved between the new and the old and the area now supports many hundreds of businesses.

CHAPTER TWO

Lower Gardiner Street, "Monto", Summerhill, Ballybough and "Mud Island", Clonliffe Road, Richmond Road, Philipsburgh Avenue

As we begin our journey towards Howth, we will first follow the old route, to where the two routes become one, in Fairview. Indeed, so entwined is the whole area that old and new routes are joined together by several streets – Lower Gardiner Street, Buckingham Street, Portland Row, North William Street, Charleville Avenue, Bayview Avenue, Spring Garden Street, Poplar Row and Cadogan Road, with Fairview Passage as a connecting laneway.

Lower Gardiner Street is a wide Georgian Street that runs from Beresford Place at the Customs House to the junction of Parnell Street with Summerhill. It replaced the route called Old Rope Walk. The street dates from circa 1787 and, is named after the second Luke Gardiner (1745-98), who became Lord/Viscount Mountjoy. He was a property developer from a family of property developers. The street surely vies for the title of 'accommodation centre of Dublin', with the many guest houses, small hotels and B&Bs to be found there. Actor, playwright and theatre manager Dion Boucicault (1820-1890) lived at 47 Lower Gardiner Street.

The streets between Gardiner Street and Buckingham Street were at the heart of the area colloquially known as 'Monto' or 'Nightown', a notorious red-light district and a very unsavoury part of Dublin. While there were no definite boundary lines on the 'Monto' area, the general acceptance is that it was contained by Talbot Street, Gardiner Street, Amiens Street and Gloucester Street. It was in the vicinity of Montgomery Street, a brothel and tenement area, where poverty and prostitution prevailed. One local described Monto as a place "where young ladies shared their favours with lonely but cash laden young men". Monto is the Nightown of Joyce's *Ulysses* and the setting for the 'circle' scene.

Lower Seán McDermott Street was named in 1933, in memory of the 1916 patriot who also has a plaque in his memory at 12 D'Olier Street. The patriot, Sean Heuston (1891-1916), who led the Volunteers at the Mendicity Institute on the River Liffey during the 1916 Rising, was born in Seán McDermott Street (then named Gloucester Street). He is commemorated by Heuston mainline railway station, with a wall plaque within the station, Sean Heuston Bridge over the Liffey and a monument by Lawrence Campbell at the People's Gardens in the Phoenix Park. Seán McDermott Street had been known as Gloucester Street since 1772, after William Henry, the Duke of Gloucester (1743-1805).

On Seán McDermott Street is the building that housed one of the ten so-called Magdalene Laundries in Ireland. Its correct title is 'The Monastery of the Sisters of Charity and of Refuge'. They operated since the foundation of the Irish Free State in 1922 and the sisters of Our Lady of Charity ran this one since 1886, in their convent originally founded in 1821 at 106 Mecklenburgh Street (now Railway Street). It is in today's location since 1836. The notorious laundries were cruel and punitive institutions, where socio-economically vulnerable girls were held against their will and ruthlessly exploited to undertake unpaid laundry work and other manual labours. The Seán McDermott Street Asylum of Our Lady was the last of the ten to close, in September 1996.

At the meeting of Seán McDermott Street with Gloucester Place, the Lourdes parish primary schools are located. There is a plaque to Sean Connolly of the Irish Citizen Army at 58/59 Seán McDermott Street, the old Connolly homestead and off Seán McDermott Street is the interestingly named Champions Avenue. It was so named in 1986, after the champion boxers who lived here in the 1930-40 era.

The Monto area included the road junction near Our Lady of Lourdes Church, known as the Gloucester Diamond, as well as James Joyce Street, formerly named Corporation Street and before that, Mabbot Street, remembering a Gilbert Mabbot who organised a watermill nearby, in 1670. The area still has a Mabbot Lane. Monto also encompassed Railway Street and Foley Street. Railway Street is so named since 1911 but it was once known as Great Martin's Lane. In 1775 it became Mecklenburg Street, after King George III married Princess Charlotte of Mecklenburg, then a province in northeast Germany. It became Tyrone Street too, for a while.

Foley Street, since 1908, was first known as World's End Lane but became Montgomery Street in 1776, after Elizabeth of Sir William Montgomery's family, who have the dubious honour of having their name shortened to give us the place and 'action' name 'Monto'! John Henry Foley (1818-1874), the renowned sculptor, was born at 6 Montgomery Street. His most famous Dublin works are the Daniel O'Connell monument on O'Connell Street and the statues of Edmund Burke, Oliver Goldsmith and Henry Grattan on College Green.

Architect, James Gandon lived at 7 Mecklenburg Street and later resided at 39 Upper Gloucester Street. The well-known stonemason, Edward Smyth resided at 36 Montgomery Street and 101 Mecklenburgh Street was home to Patrick Heeney (1881-1911), who composed the music for Peadar Kearney's *The Soldier's Song*, our national anthem. Heeney is well-commemorated by a plaque on Railway Street and Patrick Heeney House and Crescent at 28 Gloucester Place (lower), opened in November 2016.

An unusual aspect of the 'Monto Scene' was the fact that 'business' was permitted to operate without interference from the police. Recognised as one of Europe's darkest pits of immorality, it is on record that from 1800-1900 the area had 1600 'active' prostitutes. Prostitution was not regulated by the police anywhere in Dublin, quite unlike Britain. The prostitutes were organised by procurers, modern brothel keepers, pimps and bullies. However, all this changed (and rapidly) when the Irish Free State came into being in 1922, and with the zealous work of the Legion of Mary to close down the area. This latter apostolic movement was founded in Francis Street, Dublin in September 1921 by Frank Duff, Fr Michael Toher and Mrs Elizabeth Kirwan. Within a few short years, Monto was no more and very little of 'Monto' is identifiable today, due to the replacement of houses and changing street and street names. The final death knell come in 1925 when, at the behest of the Legion of Mary, Gardaí arrested 120 people in the area. It is now mainly remembered by George D Hodnett's song, *Monto*, written in 1958 the chorus of which is:

> Take me up to Monto, Monto, Monto,
> Take me up to Monto,
> Lan-ge-roo
> To you!

It is also recalled in the Dublin ballad, *The Waxies' Dargle*:

> I went down to Monto Town to see young Kit McArdle,
> But he wouldn't lend me half a crown to go to the Waxies'
>   Dargle

At the top of Lower Gardiner Street, we turn right onto Parnell Street (near its junction with Summerhill) named in memory of Ireland's 'uncrowned king', Charles Stewart Parnell. It was formerly Great Britain Street since 1728 but was renamed on 1 October 1911, on the occasion of the unveiling of the Parnell Monument (at its junction with O'Connell Street) by John Redmond MP. The 'Great Britain' name was coined by King James I who, in 1604, titled himself 'King of Great Britain.'

Shortly on the right is (Lower) Rutland Street, named after the fourth Duke of Rutland and Lord Deputy from 1784-87. The street is famous for its imposing building, the now closed Pro-Cathedral Boys and Girls National Schools, commonly known as Rutland Street schools. The domineering edifice is unmistakably Victorian in style although it dates from 1910, nine years after the death of Queen Victoria. A plaque on the school recalls Andy 'The Dazzler' Mulligan, who fought in the GPO during the 1916 Rising. He was subsequently imprisoned in Knutsford Prison in England.

As we move along Summerhill and Summerhill Parade (once known as Farmers Hill), on our left is Sean O'Casey Avenue, named after the writer but formerly Upper Rutland Street. Thomas Caffery, a member of the Invincibles, lived at 45 Upper Rutland Street. He was betrayed by the informer, James Carey and hanged on 2 June 1883 for his part in the Phoenix Park murders of Irish Chief Secretary, Frederick Cavendish and Under Secretary, Thomas Burke on 6 May 1882.

Just off Summerhill Parade and the North Circular Road and, close to the Royal Canal on North Richmond Street stands the celebrated O'Connell Schools. The street name (along with Richmond Road, Avenue, Estate, Cottages, Crescent, Lane and Parade, all of which are in the vicinity) commemorates Charles Lennox the fourth Duke of Richmond, Lord Deputy 1807-13. There was also, at one time, a Richmond townland here. A school and novitiate were established here by Blessed Edmund Rice (1762-1844), who founded the Irish Christian Brothers in Waterford, in 1802.

The foundation stone for the schools was laid by Daniel 'The Liberator' O'Connell (1775-1847), after whom the schools are named – although first officially opened in 1831 as The Catholic Model School. Rice lived in a monastery beside the school for seven years and is commemorated by a lovely museum there. He was beatified in Rome in 1996.

Famous past pupils include Captain Sean Connolly of the Irish Citizen Army and an Abbey Theatre actor. He was the first rebel to kill an opponent when fighting broke out in 1916. That was Dublin Metropolitan Police Constable James O'Brien, who was on duty at the gates of Dublin Castle when Connolly and his troops arrived there at the outbreak of the Rising. Ironically, Connolly himself was the first rebel to die when he was killed in action at City Hall, on 24 April 1916. He lived at 108 Philipsburgh Avenue, Fairview.

Former President of Ireland, Seán T Ó Ceallaigh; former Taoisigh, John A Costello and Sean Lemass; Fenian/Clan na nGael leader in America, John Devoy; writers, James Joyce, John D Sheridan, Oliver St John Gogarty; poet, Thomas Kinsella; the Venerable Matt Talbot; athlete and Olympic gold medal winner, Ronnie Delaney; folk singer, Luke Kelly; sports commentator, Michael O'Hehir; actors, Colm Meaney and Brendan Cauldwell and, broadcaster, Pat Kenny all attended O'Connells School. Many republicans also attended, of whom, the best known is Ernie O'Malley. Sports commentator Mícheál Ó Muircheartaigh was a teacher at O'Connell's.

Nearby, on the other side of the North Circular Road on Fitzgibbon Street is Fitzgibbon Street Garda Station. Fitzgibbon Street dates from 1795 and recalls John Fitzgibbon (later Earl of Clare) who was Lord Chancellor in 1789. Victorian in style, the russet brick Garda station was originally built in 1910. It was closed in 2011 for major refurbishment and re-opened in 2022 as a 'modern, state-of-the-art' Garda station. It points the way for future community-based policing in Ireland, being complete with a community response (Garda) team, a crime victim support suite, an events officer and a community hub suite.

James Joyce's time at O'Connells was short, as his father did not want him associated with 'Paddy Stink and Mickey Mud'! Joyce lived, for a time, at 17 Richmond Street and among his myriad of Dublin addresses were four in Fairview – 29 Windsor Avenue, Convent Avenue, 13 Richmond Avenue and 8 Royal Terrace (now Inverness Road).

Next, we cross the Royal Canal just before Ballybough Road at Clarke's Bridge, named after Edward Clarke, a canal company director. The Royal Canal dates from 1780 and joins the River Liffey with the River Shannon in County Longford. The canal begins at Spencer Dock at Guild Street/North Wall and ends at Cloondara, County Longford, where it connects to the River Shannon at Termonbarry via the Carlin river at Richmond Harbour. At one time it represented the northern boundary of Dublin's north inner city. Along the canal, you walk on the towpath, which recalls the days when horses towed barges along in the canal water.

The Royal Canal was built, in the first place, due to the obstinance of a certain 'Long' John Binns (hence Binns Bridge in Drumcondra) and his determination to outdo and outstrip the older and established Grand Canal on the south side of Dublin, which had been completed in 1804. He disliked what he perceived as the snobbish attitude of the board members of the Grand Canal. The Royal Canal came to be known as the 'Rival Canal' or 'the Cobblers' – Mr Binns had been a shoemaker.

The purpose of the canal was to transport passengers and goods. The actual building of the canal began in 1789, laboriously with spade, shovel, wheelbarrow and horse and cart. It became fully operational in 1817. The Royal Canal Way incorporates the National Famine Way, which recalls the sad and weary journey of 1,490 people from the Mahon Estate in Strokestown, County Roscommon in 1847, making their way on foot to avail of 'assisted emigration' on emigrant ships departing from Custom House Quay.

Both the Royal and Grand Canals were taken over by CIE in 1944. The canals ceased to carry passengers in 1952 and all commercial undertakings ended in 1961. The canals have been managed by the Office of Public Works since 1981.

The brutally dismembered remains of Kenyan, Farah Swaleh Noar (real name Sheilila Salin) were found under Clarke's Bridge in March 2005. Investigations proved that two sisters, Charlotte and Linda Mulhall (who came to be known as the 'Scissors Sisters') had killed Farah with a knife and a hammer at Flat 1, 17 Richmond Cottages, Summerhill – a five-minute walk away. It remains one of the most violent, grotesque and brutal murders in the history of the state. Four years earlier, in July 2001, a group of children came across a suitcase in the same stretch of the Royal Canal. The suitcase was found to contain the body of a 23year-old Romanian named Adrian Bestia, who had been murdered.

On the left are Sackville Gardens and Sackville Avenue, dating from about 1815 and named after Rev Sackville Usser Lee, a one-time property owner in the area. Sackville Avenue leads to the GAA National Handball Centre beside Croke Park, at Ardilaun Square. A little further on is Foster Terrace (with Foster Place North across the road), which recalls the last speaker (from 1785-1800) of the old Irish House of Commons, John Foster, who later became Baron Oriel – hence, Oriel Street and Place, off Seville Place.

Ballybough Road was so named in 1854. Since 1735 it had been known as Ballybough Lane. Ballybough (earlier spelt 'Ballyboght' or 'Balliboght') is not an easily defined area, as it spills over into adjacent locations of Drumcondra, Fairview and the North Strand. There is, for example, no Mason-Dixon Line separating Ballybough from Drumcondra.

It is generally accepted that the name Ballybough is derived from the Irish *Baile Bocht*, the 'Town of the Poor' but a strand of local tradition suggests the Ballybough name (including Ballybough Avenue, Court and Lane) could stem from *Baile Buach* (or *Buachan*), the 'Town of the Victor' or the 'Victorious', recalling that the final rout of and victory over the Vikings at the Battle of Clontarf in 1014, was achieved at the weir that preceded Ballybough Bridge. Others claim that the name translates into 'The Land by the Sea'.

An area within Ballybough once known as Mud Island (or *Crinan* in Irish) can, with reasonable confidence, be marked out. Generally speaking, this locality, eternally recalled and immortalised in story and song, lay between today's Royal Canal, Ballybough Road, Spring Garden Street and the North Strand Road. Indeed, these boundaries represent the heart of Ballybough. The Mud Island village stood out in notoriety thanks to three McDonnell brothers, who came to the area as refugees from Ulster, after the British Government in its 'Order and Conditions' laid down the framework for the Plantation of Ulster in 1609. The McDonnells were able to set up residence and, indeed, 'found' the island unhindered, as most people saw the area as uninhabitable due to the nature of its terrain and its isolation. As the name suggests, Mud Island was an extensive slobland of marshy muddy pools and filthy oozy sands. It was surrounded by water and could only be reached on foot at low tide. Over time, a village of thatched mud cabins came into being on the island. The McDonnells ruled the roost and had their own King of Mud Island and only the king's laws were obeyed – today's Kings Avenue (formerly Kings Lane beside Ballybough Lane) recalls the 'kingship'.

As time went by, a King was actually elected – very often a MacDonnell family member – but the King was really the chief criminal among the notorious sorts, who abided in his 'kingdom' wrong doers of every kind and desperados of any and all types. Included were thieves, brigands, outlaws and highwaymen. Mud Island was a hiding place for such characters but above all, it became a haven for smugglers and a 'laundering centre' for smuggled goods. In the main the 'goings on' went unhindered by the authorities as even the most job conscientious police constable, exciseman or bailiff, dared not enter the area – and those who did rarely survived the experience. There were tussles however, and when wrongdoers were actually apprehended, gallows were erected beside Ballybough Bridge – and used. Corpses of law breakers were sometimes left to hang for days as a signal to outlaws that crime would not pay.

BALLYBOUGH BRIDGE – ROBBERIES

To the Editor of the Freeman's Journal.

Sir – there his scarcely a night passes that I do not hear of some robbery taking place on the road, called the Strand, which lead from the Customs House to Ballybough Bridge; and I would strongly recommend our worthy Police Magistrates to guard against those villains who generally frequent this road, and not have the public in danger of their lives. – By inserting this in your valuable Paper, you will much oblige.

Your obedient servant,

Summer-Hill   T.T.A

Freeman's Journal *16th Nov, 1810*

Thus, Ballybough's unenviable and evil reputation made Dubliners very reluctant to travel through in daylight, never mind at night. This situation went on for more than two hundred years. After around 1850, there was a marked decline in smuggling. This came about, in part because of the presence of a permanent police station in Fairview and also, as a result of the physically changing face and nature of the whole area due to reclamation.

These rather chilling lines would not entice you to visit Ballybough!

> *Isle of Ireland's brightest Stars,*
> *Of broken skulls and bodily scars;*
> *Where 'Sunday Men' might walk apace*
> *Whilst bailiffs dare not show their face;*
> *Where wakes and weddings entertained*
> *The 'boys' that bells and 'bulkies' brained;*
> *Where doors of knocks and names were reft;*
> *And numbers changed from right to left;*
> *Where bonfires blazed and boasters bragged*
> *Of crimes that might have got them 'lagged';*
> *But woe to 'stag' or 'peeler' who would attempt to lie perdue;*
> *If seized, the Mudlarks all would flock*
> *To martyr him to Ballybough;*
> *Or, perhaps with all intents*
> *A plunge bath o'er the battlements*

Ballybough has and had many well-known sportspeople. Here we recall two in particular. In an area renowned for pugilists (bare knuckle boxers) Jack Langan (1798-1846) was the most famous. Born in Clondalkin in 1798, he spent most of his life in Ballybough. Having beaten all challengers in Ireland, he twice fought Tom Spring (1795-1851), 'Champion of England and the civilised world', for the title. He lost what were two extraordinary fights. The first took place at Worcester Racecourse in January 1924 and lasted seventy-seven rounds! The second fight was at Birdham Bridge, Chichester in June 1924 and lasted seventy-six rounds!

Soccer player, Paddy Moore (1909-1951) a top class forward, was born and reared in Ballybough. He played club football for Shamrock Rovers and for Aberdeen in Scotland. He played senior international soccer under the jurisdiction of the FAI and the IFA. Undoubtedly one of Ireland's best ever players (some claim he was the country's first 'superstar' footballer) he is remembered by a plaque on the wall of the house where he was born on Clonliffe Avenue.

After Foster Terrace comes the looping Clonliffe Avenue, which encircles O'Sullivan's Avenue, named after the politician, nationalist, journalist and poet, TD Sullivan (1827-1914), who lived at 19 Richmond Place and was Lord Mayor of Dublin in 1886/87 and MP from 1880-1900. He assisted his brother, Arthur Sullivan with the publication of the nationalist newspaper *The Nation*. The name Clonliffe probably comes from the old Clonliff (no 'e') village although, some argue that it translates into 'Meadow of the Liffey'.

On the city side, at the junction of Ballybough Road with Clonliffe Road, on the left adjacent to Trinity Terrace, is the site of a 'suicide plot' for the burial of suicide victims. It is a place that was part of Bram Stoker's inspiration for his *Dracula* creation. Suicide victims were supposed to become vampires unless they got the 'stake through the heart' treatment before burial. The place is now a small, landscaped garden with seats. Directly across the road is Courtney Place, just past Ballybough Railway Bridge.

Clonliffe Road was once known as Fortick's Lane. At one time, the only house on Clonliffe Road, known as the 'Red House', was occupied by a certain Frederick 'Buck' Jones. He was a magistrate, a theatre manager and a gambler with a fearsome reputation. He had Jones' Road opened, in 1799, to create a short route to the city centre. He died in 1834 but a 'Phantom Horseman', who allegedly haunts the area at night, is believed to be Jones. In 1840, Jones' Road was officially named after him. Jones' Road becomes Russell Street – called after the former lord deputies, John Russell and John Rusell respectively – or, it could possibly be named after a builder in the area named John Rusell!

Clonliffe or Holy Cross College the Dublin Archdiocese seminary (now closed) was built on the site of Jones' Red House. It was built by Archbishop (later Cardinal) Cullen (1803-1878) and first opened in 1863. Cullen's body was later interred there. In 1890, a permanent residential palace for the Archbishop of Dublin was built on part of the site. The nearby Mater Dei Institute of Education was founded in 1966 by Archbishop JC McQuaid, for the purpose of training teachers of religion for Irish secondary schools. Affiliated to St Patrick's College, Maynooth from 1966-1999, it was then linked to Dublin City University (DCU), until it closed in 2016 and became fully incorporated into DCU.

On Jones' Road is Croke Park Stadium the headquarters of the Gaelic Athletic Association (GAA). The grounds were once owned by a Maurice Butterly and known as the City and Suburban Racecourse and also as Jones' Road Sportsground. Frank Dineen, a Gaelic games administrator and the only person ever to serve as GAA General Secretary and as GAA president, was a missionary who saw the potential of the place. He purchased fourteen acres of the site in 1908 and sold the grounds to the GAA in 1913, for €3,500. The GAA, originally founded in Thurles in 1884, named the place Croke Memorial Park, after Archbishop Thomas Croke (1824-1902) of the Cashel and Emily Catholic Diocese. He was an enthusiastic supporter and patron of the GAA. Apart from being the venue for major GAA hurling and football matches, Croke Park Stadium has hosted many other events, including the Special Olympics, a boxing match featuring Muhammad Ali as well as concerts by world-famous singing groups and singing stars, such as Neil Diamond and Garth Brooks. The stadium stands as a major landmark in the history of Ireland's development as a nation.

The bridge on the Royal Canal at the spot where Russell Street and Jones' Road meet was not named after a canal director – as all canal bridges are. It was built many years after the canal was opened and was officially named Clonliffe Bridge but oftentimes known as Jones' Road Bridge or Russell Street Bridge. It is now Bloody Sunday Bridge (see Chapter 10).

Seán McDermott (already mentioned), the 1916 patriot, lived at 16 Russell Street. He was the full-time organiser of the Volunteers and, despite being scourged by polio, he travelled all over Ireland.

Luke Kelly Bridge (better known, perhaps, as Ballybough Bridge) straddles the Tolka river between Conliffe and Richmond Roads, both of which take the traveller to Drumcondra. As already stated, this was the site or, part of the site or, close to the site known as the Fishing Weir of Clontarf, where the forces of King Brian Boru finally routed the Vikings in the famous 1014 battle.

The first actual bridge here was a timber structure built by Dublin Lord Mayor, John Decer in 1308 but was destroyed by floods in 1313. In 1489, a new, solid bridge replaced it. A large white stone marked the then city boundary and the structure included a large gate, which was securely locked at night. A toll house and turnpike gate were erected at the bridge in 1786 and remained in use until all tolls were abolished 69 years later, in 1855. A stronger, wider bridge was built on the site in 1937. This was further widened and strengthened in 1985 and renamed Luke Kelly Bridge.

Just before we cross the bridge, on the right, is Ballybough House complex. Two plaques hang on the railings of the complex, both poignant for different reasons. One remembers Kitty Donovan, who died in June 2014, as the 'Queen of Ballybough House' for 55 years. The other plaque recalls Paul McCannon, who was fatally injured here in September 1997.

The Tolka river (sometimes recorded as the Tolekan, the Tulken or the Tulcainn) is thirty kilometres long (fourteen miles). It rises near Batterstown in County Meath and flows through Clonee, Blanchardstown, Glasnevin and Drumcondra, before entering the sea at John McCormack bridge on the Alfie Byrne Road. It was originally a tributary of the Liffey but was re-routed from Ballybough Bridge during the reclamation of the North Lotts.

In 1534, at Ballybough Bridge, the forces of Silken Thomas (Lord Offaly) (1513-37) fought a skirmish with British forces that had landed at Clontarf. Thomas rebelled on being fed a false rumour that his father, Lord Deputy Garret Óg Fitzgerald (1489-1534) had been executed in London by King Henry VIII (1491-1547).

The bridge was the scene of much fighting during the 1916 Rising and the War of Independence. From 1910 until the 1916 Rising, Tom Clarke, his wife Kathleen and their family lived at 31 Richmond Avenue (now conjoined with Richmond Estate) off Richmond Road. Edward (Ned) Daly (1891-1916), Kathleen's brother, moved in with the Clarkes in 1912. He commanded the Four Courts insurgents during the 1916 Rising and was shot in Kilmainham Gaol on 4 May 1916.

Tom Clarke (1857-1916), a revolutionary throughout his life, is generally regarded as the real instigator of the 1916 Rising. Just before Ballybough Bridge on the left, on the city side, is a small residential complex known as Tom Clarke House and the former East Link Toll Bridge across the River Liffey is now called the Tom Clarke Bridge. It joins the East Wall Road, with York Road on the south side of the Liffey. There is also a plaque to his memory at 74 Parnell Street.

Kathleen Clarke (1878-1972), a republican activist served as a councillor, a TD, a senator and became Dubin's first female Lord Mayor in 1939.

Cathal Brugha (1874-1922) was born at 13 Richmond Avenue. With Éamon de Valera and Arthur Griffith in jail, he chaired the first ever meeting of Dáil Éireann on 21 January 1919. A founder member of the Irish Volunteers in 1913, he served as second in command to Éamonn Ceant (1881-1916) during the 1916 fighting at the South Dublin Union (now St James's Hospital). He became chief of staff of the IRA in 1917 and died fighting on the Republican side, in 1922, during the Civil War. Cathal Brugha Street in the city centre, then called Greg Lane, where he was shot down, was named in his memory in 1932.

A well-known institution, St Vincent's Hospital, founded by the Presentation Sisters in 1867 stands on Convent Avenue off Richmond Road. Further along, if we take a right hand turn on to Grace Park Road, we have on the right, the Ierne Sports and Social Complex. Adjacent to Grace Park Wood is St Joseph's School for the Blind, opened in 1966, which shares a site with Child Vision, run by the Health Service Executive (HSE) and a charity organisation.

Further along, at 9 Grace Park Road, is Rosmini Community School. From the school, Rosmini Gaels GAA Club was founded in 1969, to provide an outlet for Gaelic Games in the Drumcondra area. The club fields teams at adult senior level and has a base (a small edifice) at the Drumcondra Road end of Botanic Avenue.

On the left is the former missionary All Hallows College. Much of its premises is in use by Dublin City University.

Tolka Park Stadium stands between Richmond Road and the Tolka river at the Drumcondra end of the road. The park has a rich sporting tradition, in the area. Since at least 1924, it has been an integral part of Dublin's sporting life. Seven League of Ireland clubs have been based there over the years – Dolphins, Drumcondra, Dublin City, Home Farm, Shamrock Rovers, St James's Gate and Shelbourne, whose home it has been since 1989. Tolka Park can claim at least three 'firsts'. It hosted the first floodlit football game in Dublin in March 1953. It was from Tolka Park that the first televised League of Ireland game was broadcast live, in the 1996-1997 season and Tolka became the first all-seater stadium in the Republic of Ireland in 1999.

Now back to our main route and we are on Fairview Strand, once known as Philipsburgh Strand. It is a generally well-preserved street, still maintaining a number of its original edifices. Situated beside Esmond Avenue is a former Jewish caretaker's house (for details on this, see Jewish Cemetery, Fairview Strand in Chapter 8).

The area seems to have always been attractive to 'foreigners' as some Quakers, who first came to Ireland in 1654, settled in Ballybough. In the years after 1698, some Huguenots also settled in the area. Nowadays, the area is multicultural and multinational.

The place where some Jews settled here was called Annadale and the Annadale name is retained with Annadale Avenue, Crescent and Drive, all off Philipsburgh Avenue. The house beside the Jewish Caretakers House (on the city side) was an RIC police station from 1832 until 1909 – there had previously been a police station at Annesley Bridge. That old station on Fairview Strand has been replaced by a house called Fairview Mews. In 1900, the Boundaries Act incorporated Clontarf Township into Dublin City proper. New barracks were opened at Strandville Avenue East in 1909 and the DMP police replaced the RIC.

Esmond Avenue is on our left as we reach Philipsburgh Avenue, which was once called Ellis Lane and dating from the middle of the 18th century but, it is uncertain as to where the name originated. Some authorities suggest that it recalls the siege of Philipsburg, a small habitation of the River Rhine, where the Duke of Berwick was killed in 1734. Others variously claim that the name recalls Michael Phillips or Chichester Philips who, in 1718, made a plot of land here available to the Jewish community.

Off Philipsburgh Avenue are two sites very central to the story of the 1916 Easter Rising. The first is a secluded three-acre site at Windsor Villas, once known as Fr Matthew Park. The Capuchin Order has owned the site since 1908 and it is now occupied by St Mary's National School. This is surely one of the most historic settings of any school in the country because the 2nd Battalion of the Irish Volunteers drilled openly and practised rifle fire here in the run up to the 1916 Rising.

It was from here, too, that 1,000 Volunteers marched to Howth, on 26 July 1914, to accept the rifles and ammunition brought ashore by Erskine Childers in the yacht, *Asgard*. (This very significant event is dealt with elsewhere in this publication). The bulk of the rifles were hidden here and deployed from here to the insurgents who marched on the GPO, on 24 April 1916. Two plaques – one at the school gate, the other at the school doorway – record the happenings here.

The second site is at the junction of today's Casino Road, with Croydon Terrace/Croydon Park Avenue. Here stood Croydon House and Estate. The house was first built in 1772, by a Dublin merchant named William Lynham. The Jim Larkin/James Connolly led ITGWU took over the entire premises a few years before the 1916 Rising. It served many purposes, including use as a recreation centre. It was here that the Irish Citizen Army (founded by Connolly at Liberty Hall to defend workers against the brutality demonstrated by the DMP to workers, especially during the infamous 1913 lockout) drilled and trained under Captain Jack White (1879-1946) who lived at 10 Summer Street, North Circular Road. In the absence of guns, like the Volunteers, they used hurley sticks.

A socialist, James Connolly came to Dublin from Scotland in 1896 and organised to secure the national and economic freedom of the Irish people, making his name as a journalist and a lecturer. He was commandant in charge of the GPO during the 1916 Rising. His execution at Kilmainham Gaol, on 12 May 1916, was proceeded with while he was tied to a wheelchair. Connolly mainline railway station commemorates him.

'Big Jim' or James Larkin (1876-1947), a socialist, a persuasive orator and passionate demagogue founded the ITGWU in 1909, mainly to fight for justice with proper rights and conditions from the capitalists and employers for the working class and, especially for the unskilled workers and the oppressed. His methods were very militant and forceful. He actually lived in Croydon Park House for some time and at the house, he advised the ITGWU, on 18 January 1914, to return to work after the 1913 lockout.

Croke Park

St Vincent's Hospital (Fairview)

O'Connell Schools

PÁIRC AN
ATHAR MAITIÚ
Chuaigh Óglaigh an 2ú Cathlán
FAOI OILIÚINT ANSEO

FR. MATHEW PARK
Volunteers of the 2nd Battalion
TRAINED HERE

ÉIRÍ AMACH NA CÁSCA 1916

Plaque at St Mary's NS

BUILT
IN THE
YEAR
5618

**Caretaker's House at Dublin's
Jewish Cemetery**

Blessed Edmund Rice

Luke Kelly

John Henry Foley

Tom Clarke

Kathleen Clarke

Seán McDermott

Cathal Brugha

Jim Larkin

Seán Lemass

Seán T Ó Ceallaigh

John A. Costello

Ronnie Delaney

Paddy Moore

James Carey

Larkin and his two sons, James (junior) and Denis all served as Dublin City Councillors and as TDs in Dáil Éireann. Jim represented the Clontarf constituency in the Dáil for many years, being elected first in 1927. He and James (junior) were both elected to the Dáil on the same day, in 1943, Denis Larkin (1908-87) represented Dublin North East in the Dáil for many years, being first elected in 1954. He became General Secretary of the Workers Union of Ireland and served as Lord Mayor of Dublin in 1955/56. He lived with his family at 10 Marino Park. Big Jim is immortalised by a statue of him in the middle of Dublin's O'Connell Street. It captures him in characteristic pose, demanding proper rights and conditions for workers.

Windsor Avenue (named after Windsor, a town on the River Thames in southeast England) is on the left as we reach Fairview Corner, colloquially known as Edge's Corner, after Edge's Hardware shop at that spot which, in 2017, celebrated the milestone of one hundred years in business. This is where the two routes from the city, old and new, meet and together form the road known as Fairview, which in turn becomes Marino Mart. First however, we must return to Customs House and follow the new route to Fairview.

CHAPTER THREE

Amiens Street, Connolly Station, The Docks area, The Five Lamps,
North Strand Road, East Wall Road, Old Clontarf Island

Going on to Amiens Street from the Customs House, on our left is Busáras, which literally means a house or building for buses. It is incorporated into the bigger Áras Mhic Dhiarmada, home to the Department of Social Protection. Busáras, at 22 Store Street, is enclosed by Amiens Street, Store Street and Beresford Place. Busáras was designed by architect, Michael Scott and first opened in 1953. It is the Dublin rendezvous for all provincial bus services operated by Bus Éireann. The Áras Mhic Dhiarmada building once had a nightclub on the top floor and the Eblana Theatre in the basement.

Store Street is named after the Customs House and Dockland Stores and one of the best-known buildings on the street is the very large Store Street Garda Station, probably the busiest Garda station in the entire country. It was once known as the Red Lamp Police Station. On Store Street Plaza is an unusual sculpture called *The Mirror*. The creation of Robert McColgan and unveiled in 2007, it encourages us to 'reflect the sky, the void and the soul.'

Amiens Street is so called, since 1829, in memory of Edward Stratford, Viscount Amiens who was also Earl of Aldborough (1741-1831). He built the dominant, towering Aldborough House (completed in 1796) at the junction of Portland Row and Killarney Street. The house was the last of the great Georgian or aristocratic houses to be built in Dublin and the local Aldborough Place, Square and Parade are named after it. It served only a few short years as a residence. From 1812-38 it was home to the Feinaglian School, founded by Luxembourg-born Professor von Feinaigle. It then became a military barracks until about 1870. After that, it was used as offices and stores for the post office. It finally fell into disuse.

The dominant feature of Amiens Street is Connolly railway station, which dates from 1844. It was first opened as Dublin Station and was called Amiens Street Station until 1966, when it was named after 1916 martyr, James Connolly. It was designed by William Dean Butler as a somewhat lofty, triple-tower city terminus for the Dublin and Drogheda Railway Company. Italian in style, it has a campanile or bell tower at its centre and smaller campaniles at each end.

In James Joyce's *Ulysses*, Buck Mulligan, Stephen Daedalus and a number of medical students alight from a train at Connolly Station, en route to the close-by, red-light district of 'Monto'.

Connolly Station underwent a total refurbishment in 1980/81, ahead of the introduction of the DART rail system and, incorporated into the station is the highly sophisticated computer system that centrally controls the administration of Ireland's entire rail network. It is now the starting point and terminal for trains serving Belfast, Sligo and Wexford.

The old Victorian City Morgue was at 2, 3 and 4 Amiens Street. The entrance to it and the Coroner's Court next door was from Store Street, with a back entrance from Amiens Street. The morgue was opened in 1901 and demolished in 1999.

A notable building on Amiens Street is number 55, where 1916 leader Tom Clarke opened a newsagents and tobacco shop when he returned from America in 1907. The premises doubled as an IRB haven. In 1910, Clarke moved to new premises at 75a Parnell Street.

The novelist, Charles Lever (1806-1872) was born in Amiens Street and later lived on Talbot Street.

The landmark North Star Hotel (Now named The Address, Connolly) stands on Amiens Street across from Connolly Station. Also directly across the street from Connolly Station is Talbot Street, so named, in 1921, after Charles Talbot, Lord Deputy from 1817 to 1821. It was formerly known as Moland Street and earlier as Cope Street North.

As you enter Talbot Street, there stands a large stone memorial to those who lost their lives in the Dublin and Monaghan bombings of 1974. Some of those killed were locals or had local connections:

1. John Dargle, who lived at Portland Row.
2. Concepta Dempsey, a shop assistant in Guiney's Store, Talbot Street.
3. Collette and baby Doherty. Colette was nine months pregnant and ran a shop off Sherriff Street.
4. May McKenna, who lived over O'Neill's shoe shop on Talbot Street.
5. The O'Brien family: John and Anne and their two babies, Jacqueline and Anne Marie, who lived on Gardiner Street.

Just past Connolly Station, on the right, is Sheriff Street, so named in 1773 after the office of the City of Dublin Sheriff. It eventually connects to the East Wall Road. Immediately on our right, on Sheriff Street, just past the railway bridge, was the old postal sorting office.

A well-known soccer club in this area is Sheriff YC, based in Sheriff Street. The senior team participates in the Athletic Union League and have been a very successful junior amateur team on the playing field since 2010, winning the league several times. The team has also won AUL League Cups, Nivea Cups, Liddy Cups and the Tom Hand Memorial Cup. Sheriff FC has won FAI Junior Cups, Leinster Junior Cups and competed in the FAI Cup.

Explorers who wish to meander off our route along Amiens Street/ North Strand Road and explore the greater port and docks area will find much of interest in an area originally contained by Custom House Quay, North Wall Quay and East Wall Road. Many of the places, buildings, etc encountered by trekkers give a real feel for the special character of the area, where regeneration and gentrification has left a mixture of modern ways and designs with architecture and remnants from the bygone era. And, surprisingly, the new often compliments the traditional and old. The Old Dock was situated at today's Memorial Road and was eventually filled in during the redevelopment of the entire area.

Here, alphabetically, we list some of the more notable features of the northside docks area.

Central Bank of Ireland – Situated on New Wapping Street, close to North Wall Quay. This is a modern edifice built in 2010 and used by the Bank of Ireland since 2017.

CHQ Building – This large building was erected in 1820 and was known as Stack A, acting as a wine and tobacco warehouse. On Custom House Quay, it contains the EPIC Ireland Emigration Museum.

Convention Centre – The Dublin Convention Centre opened in 2010. The carbon-neutral, international conference building, with a rather unusual design and curved glass façade, is at Spencer Dock and has been given the moniker 'The Tube in the Cube'.

Dock Hooks – The old dock hooks along the North Quay Wall, where cargo ships used to tie up are still there and used, in a similar manner, by tall ships during Tall Ship Festivals.

Dublin Harbour – You enter the harbour (as in, where the ships come in) where the East Wall Road meets Tolka Quay Road. The place is backboned by Tolka Quay Road, Promenade Road and Alexandra Road. The car ferry terminal here is of great interest to many people.

So too, is the Port Centre itself, from where the Dublin Port Authority organises port affairs. It has been at the heart of Dublin Port's centre of administration since it moved there in 1976, from the old Ballast Board premises, which was located in the city centre at the corner where Aston Quay and Westmoreland Street meet. At the Port Centre, the *Dark Night* sculpture by Michael Warren can be viewed. This wooden structure, dating from 1981, portrays the traditional materials once used around the port and the more modern architecture now on view.

George's Dock – Named after King George IV, George's Dock was opened in the 1920s and a large Triumphal Arch, dating from 1813, was taken from Amiens Street in 1998 and placed at the dock.

Harbourmasters Pub – This pub is at Fade Street, Inner Dock. The site once had The Dock Office and Harbourmaster House. Inner Dock goes back to 1824.

Jeanie Johnston – The Jeanie Johnston 'famine' or 'coffin' ship at Custom House Quay is really a museum. It is a 2002 replica of the original ship, which was built in Quebec, Canada in 1847 and which sank on a trip in 1858.

London and North Western Hotel – This striking building on North Wall Quay dates from the 1880s. It was built on the site where the Prince of Wales Hotel once stood and, it was to become known as the British Rail Hotel.

Mayor Square – At Mayor Street Lower, Mayor Square contains the National College of Ireland, a third level institution that offers a variety of courses.

Point Depot – The 'Point' was the spot where North Wall Quay met the East Wall Road. The Point Depot building was erected in 1878, as a train depot for the very busy nearby port. It was known as 'The Point Store'. In the 1980s, it was converted into a music venue and known as The Point Depot or Theatre. After extensive refurbishment in 2008, it was renamed the O2. In 2014 it became the 3Arena.

Samuel Beckett Bridge – Named after the famous author and Nobel Prize winner, the bridge is a harp-shaped, cable-stayed bridge first opened in 2009. It joins North Wall Quay with City Quay on the south side of the River Liffey. The bridge rotates horizontally to let ships go by.

Scherzer Bridges – Scherzer Rolling Lift Bridges replaced the old drawbridge in 1912, where George's Dock meets the River Liffey.

Sean O'Casey House – Well-known playwright, Sean O'Casey lived for over twenty years at 4 (now 18) Abercorn Road, which is off Sheriff Street. He also lived at nearby Hawthorn Terrace.

Spencer Dock – Spencer Dock, with Guild Street alongside, joins the Royal Canal with the River Liffey. The dock was first opened in 1873 and recalls John Spencer, the 5th Earl of Spencer (1835-1910) who was Lord Deputy in Ireland for a time. Spencer Bridge dates from about 1900, the drawbridge being almost an heirloom of a bygone age.

The Mariner – A bronze statue of a sailor and an anchor by John Behan can be viewed at Maritime House, North Wall Quay. In place since 1973, it shows the courage and dedication of all sea people.

The Oasis Centre – This centre at St Laurence Place East, Emerald Street was established, in 1882, by the Sisters of Charity in a very eye-catching, red-bricked building. It has been a refuge and resource centre for the area, especially in the fields of healthcare and education. Beside the Oasis Centre is the Presbytery: the residence of the parish priest of the St Laurence O'Toole parish since 1872.

Vallance and McGrath Old Pub – Situated at the meeting point of Castleforbes Road with North Wall Quay, the buildings colloquially known as Valence McGrath once housed a pub and a warehouse. The buildings have now been converted into apartments

Left, off Amiens Street is Buckingham Street, named in 1790 after the Marquis of Buckingham, who was Lord Deputy in 1782-3 and again from 1787-90. The family of Bram Stoker, author of *Dracula*, lived here at 17 Upper Buckingham Street from 1858-1864.

In the little island at the confluence of Buckingham Street with Killarney Street and Seán McDermott Street is a monument by Leo Higgins, to those lost to drugs.

Troy Parrott who, in November 2019, became the youngest player to represent Ireland at senior soccer level since Robbie Keane in 1998, was reared in Buckingham Street. He was actually born in nearby St Mary's Mansions on Seán McDermott Street.

A 24-year-old blacksmith named Michael Fagan from 36 Artisan Buildings, Buckingham Street, one of the 'Invincibles', was hanged on 20 May 1883 in connection with the Phoenix Park murders of Irish Chief Secretary, Cavendish and Under Secretary, Burke the previous year. Like his friend, the previously mentioned Thomas Caffrey, he too was betrayed by James Carey.

One of the four people killed in the 'Batchelors Walk Massacre' that happened in the aftermath of the 'Howth Gun Running Confrontation', in Clontarf on 26 July 1914 (more details on this below) was 18-year-old James Brennan from 7 Lower Buckingham Street.

Off Amiens Street, on the right is Preston Street, named after the Preston family, who once owned property in the city.

Next, we come to a most unique place known simply as 'The Five Lamps'. Here, on a little island where five streets meet, stands a five-branched lamp standard put there in 1880 – a lamp for each street. The streets are Amiens Street, Killarney Street, Portland Row, the North Strand Road and Seville Place.

Killarney Street is a section of Lower Seán McDermott Street (the former Gloucester Street), so named in 1908. Portland Row dates from 1809 and recalls the third Duke of Portland (1738-1809). He was Lord Deputy in 1782 and went on to become Prime Minister of Great Britain (1783) and then of the United Kingdom from 1807 to 1809. Seville Place commemorates the capture of Seville by the British in the Peninsular War of 1812. Portland Row and Seville Place are really extensions of the North Circular Road, which extends to the Phoenix Park.

Both the North Circular Road and the South Circular Road were constructed in the 1760s, following an act of parliament directing that they should follow the routes of the Royal and Grand canals respectively. At the time, the North Circular Road (actually called that since 1849) marked the most northerly boundary of Dublin City.

The Five Lamps adorn an ornate decorative column, with drinking fountains, as a memorial to the five great battles won by the British in India in colonial days. Officially known as the General Henry Hall Memorial Fountain, the Five Lamps recall Athenry, County Galway-born Hall, a British military commander with the rank of superintendent in the late 1800s. He also served with the British Raj in India. It is said that he requested the provision of a drinking fountain to discourage the consumption of alcohol.

There was a turnpike toll gate and house at the Five Lamps, which was removed in 1817. The place was a very popular venue for public meetings.

Well-known, Irish, international boxer, Kelly Harrington, who attended St Vincent's GNS, North William Street, is a native of Portland Row. She won a gold medal at the 2018 World Boxing Championships in New Delhi, India. She followed this up by winning a gold medal at the Tokyo Olympics in Japan, in 2021. She also played senior international soccer for Ireland. An Post honoured Kelly by featuring her on a postage stamp in March 2002. Kelly was also honoured with the Freedom of the City of Dublin in June 2022.

Irish senior soccer international players, Wes Hoolahan and Jack Byrne are also from the area.

This locality was the original home of the St Laurence O'Toole GAA Club. Matters concerning the club and the tragic events surrounding Bloody Sunday, 21 November 1920 are dealt with in Chapter Ten.

The very historic St Laurence O'Toole CBS Boys National School in Seville Place, which opened in 1847, has some illustrious past pupils. Among them are the Venerable Matt Talbot; Alfie Byrne (the 'shaking hand') former Lord Mayor of Dublin; Paddy Cullen, goalkeeper with Kevin Heffernan's Gaelic football revolutionary team of the 1970s (who played his club football with the local O'Connell Boys Club) and Stephen Gateley of the Boyzone musical group, who died on 10 October 2009. In September 2020, Dublin City Council voted to rename the Royal Canal Linear Park, Stephen Gately Park in his memory. The Park is alongside Spencer Dock, close to Sheriff Street, where Stephen was reared.

Thespian and ballad singer with The Dubliners folk band, Luke Kelly was another past pupil. Luke was born in Lattimore Cottages in Sheriff Street. In January 2019, President Michael D Higgins unveiled a marble bust of Luke (who was 43 years old when he died) by Vera Klute at Guild Street, Spencer Dock. For good measure there is also a bronze sculpture of Luke Kelly by artist John Coll on South King Street, off Grafton Street.

Those two well-known brothers of drama/film fame, Jim and Peter Sheridan were reared in 44 Seville Place and attended St Laurence O'Toole CBS.

Frank Cahill (1882-1957) was a teacher at that school for 50 years and a plaque there commemorates him. A republican, he was a TD for a time and was variously associated with Cumann na nGaedheal, Sinn Féin and the Nationalist Party. Dedicated to the cause of Irish independence, he was close friends with both Sean O'Casey and Arthur Griffith. He was a founder member of the St Laurence O'Toole GAA Club and Cumann na mBunscoil. The Frank Cahill Cup is competed for annually in Dublin Primary Schools GAA competitions.

Playwright, Sean O'Casey was a familiar figure in this area.

And the thriving Docklands Boxing Club has its premises at Arch 3, Seville Place.

Now we move on to North Strand Road – so called because it actually was the strand or seashore before reclamation. On De Gommes' 1673 map of the area, today's road is represented as a pathway. Up to about 1800, it was called The Strand, later The North Strand and the foreshore along here covered today's North Strand Road and Amiens Street up to Beresford Place. The name North Strand Road has been used since 1800. On our right is Connolly House, once the home of the North Strand Technical College and is now in use as a campus of the Marino College of further education. To the left of the entrance door is a plaque remembering all in the locality who served with the Irish Citizen Army between 1913 and 1923.

Ireland took a neutral stand during World War II but on the night of 31 May/1 June 1941 (June Whit Holiday) four German bombs were dropped on North Dublin in just 37 minutes between, 1:28am and 2:05am. The first exploded at the intersection of the North Circular Road (582 NCR) with North Richmond Street. Another fell in the Phoenix Park, demolishing the Dog Pond and doing some damage to Áras and Uachtaráin, the Cricket grounds and the zoo. A third bomb fell on Summerhill Parade.

The fourth was the largest and most deadly. It was a 500lb (pound) Luftwaffe bomb (or maybe a landmine) and it fell at 2:05am on the North Strand Road at its junction with North William Street. It just about obliterated the area between the Five Lamps and Newcomen Bridge opening a huge crater in the middle of the road. It actually wiped out the terrace of cottages between Seville Place and Newcomen Bridge. The scene was devastating. Some twenty-eight people were killed and over one hundred seriously injured with about 2,000 left homeless as over three hundred houses were hit. The local community was literally ripped apart and never really recovered. The youngest to die was James Michael Fitzpatrick of 15b North Strand Road, who was aged just two months. While flats were built to replace most of the little terraced houses destroyed by the blast, one small street, Synnott Street, which was totally destroyed, was never rebuilt. Many people were rehoused in Cabra.

Various theories have been suggested as to how and why the bombing happened but, the event remains one of the World War II's great unexplained mysteries. The dreadful occasion of the bombing is always recalled with the great reverence and sadness when the history of the North Strand is recalled. In a little memorial garden, situated between Connolly House and Shamrock Terrace on the North Strand Road, a granite stone memorial slab stands in memory of all who lost their lives on that awful night. The slab had two unveilings. The first was on 31 May 1991 and was performed by Dublin Lord Mayor, Michael Donnelly, to mark the 50th anniversary of the event. The second occurred on 31 May 2011, the 70th anniversary, when the unveiling was performed by Councillor Ray McAdam, with the then German Ambassador to Ireland, Busso von Alvensleben present. The garden also recalls and remembers many other events and occurrences in Irish history.

Just past the garden, on Shamrock Terrace, is St Laurence O'Toole Specialised National School, known as SLOT 2. It was first opened at 44 Seville Place.

On the left is North Great Clarence Street, dating from 1796 and North William Street, so named in 1805. Both streets recall William, Duke of Clarence (1765-1837) who became King William IV in 1830.

Bram Stoker's parents (Abraham and Charlotte) lived at 45 North William Street after they married in January 1844. They moved to The Crescent, Clontarf in 1845.

It was in an old convent on this street (no longer in existence) that Mary Aikenhead (1787-1858) founded the Irish Sisters of Charity in 1815. This is recalled by a plaque at the site of St Vincent's primary schools. For many years, the Daughters of Charity of St Vincent de Paul ran the still flourishing schools.

Next, we cross over the Royal Canal at Newcomen Bridge, which is named after Sir William Newcomen (as are Newcomen Avenue and Court on our left) who was a canal company director from 1789-1810. Clinch's Court at Newcomen Avenue recalls the celebrated highway robber, Larry Clinch who 'worked' in the Ballybough area. He was especially fond of robbing Ulster Mail Coaches!

Charleville Mall is next on the left, dating from 1836. Then we have Newcomen Avenue, beside which Newcomen Court/Clinch's Court leads us to the 'oasis' that is Mud Island Community Garden and Charleville Avenue further on (once known as Bayview Parade) dates from 1866. Some sources suggest that the name Charleville originates with the Coghill family from Yorkshire in England, who came to possess considerable property in Drumcondra. This included Drumcondra House, the site and grounds of which became All Hallows College. Hester Coghill married Charles Moore, Lord Tullamore who became Lord Charleville. Others suggest the Charleville name came to the North Strand area through Lord Monck. He owned land in the vicinity and his home, in Bray, was named Charleville. Dunne Street, which joins Portland Row with Charleville Mall, site of the local library, dates from 1840 and was named after a local landlord/builder. Pat Tobin, GAA General Secretary from 1891 to 1894, lived in Charleville Mall.

On our right, after crossing Newcomen Bridge is Ossory Road, which recalls the old Irish south midlands Kingdom of Ossory (*Osraige*), which is to this day the name of a Catholic church diocese.

A little further on, after the North Strand Post Office, is Bessborough Avenue, named in 1848 after the Earl of Bessborough, who was Lord Deputy in 1846-47. Further along, on the right, are the self-explanatory street names Strandville Avenue, Xavier Avenue, Northbrook Avenue, St Brigid's Avenue and Leinster Avenue. Northbrook Avenue (lower) has a plaque recalling 'Seamus Costello, Republican Socialist'.

Over to the left-hand side again and after Charleville Avenue comes Bayview Avenue, named in 1840 because of the great view it enjoyed over Dublin Bay at that time. Antiquarian John O'Donovan (1809-1861) lived at

55 Bayview Avenue and also at 8 Newcomen Place. He is best remembered for his translation of the *Annals of the Four Masters*.

Next is Waterloo Avenue, so called, in 1841, in memory of the defining 1815 Battle of Waterloo. The distinguished Augustinian priest, Professor FX Martin (1922-2000), historian and activist, lived at 11 Waterloo Avenue in his youth. He is especially remembered for his leadership in attempting to prevent the destruction of the world-class Viking heritage site at Wood Quay in the late 1970s and early 1980s.

After Waterloo Avenue comes Nottingham Street, a name that goes back to 1798 and recalls a Nottingham House (also called The Red House) which stood here.

Spring Garden Street was so named in 1846 and recalls the old Tea Gardens that were there once.

The North Strand Fire Station, which replaced the old station in Buckingham Street, is a landmark on the right as we come to Annesley Bridge. The bridge was built in 1792, a handsome erection of granite consisting of three semi-circular arches and straddles the River Tolka at the junction of the North Strand Road with Poplar Row and the East Wall Road. Like Annesley Bridge Road, Annesley Avenue and Place, the bridge recalls Richard Annesley, a member of the old Irish house of Parliament, chairman of the trustees of the Malahide turnpike road and a member of the Board of Directors of the Royal Canal Company. He became Lord Annesley when he succeeded his brother to the title in 1802. The opening of Annesley Bridge provided a new gateway to the sea and to the northside generally. The bridge had a toll house and turnpike gate from 1793 until 1869. In 1928, a new and widened bridge, a three-span steel-beam bridge replaced the old bridge.

On the left, off Annesley Place, after Enaville Avenue, is Taaffe's Place, named after a one-time landowner in Clontarf. Directly opposite, on the right, is Austin's Cottages dating from the 1950s and once part of Taaffe's domain.

Poplar Row has, at times, been referred to as 'Sandy Row', with echoes of that loyalist area of Belfast and the 12th of July but, maybe it derives its name from the poplar tree of the Populus genus. It was completed in 1823 to join Clonliffe Road with East Wall Road. Much fighting took place in this area during the 1916 Rising and this is generally recalled as the Battle of Annesley Bridge. Kathleen Clarke is remembered by the Kathleen Clarke block of flats at Poplar Row.

Two Henderson Brothers, Frank and Leo from 5 Windsor Villas, were captains of the F and B companies respectively, components of the 2nd Battalion of the Dublin Brigade of the Irish Volunteers whose overall commanding officer was Thomas McDonagh. The battalion drilled, paraded and trained openly at Father Matthew Park, Fairview. Oscar Traynor was a lieutenant in the F company. The members of the companies were mainly from Fairview, North Strand and Ballybough and also from Clontarf and Dollymount and included Harry Colley, Harry Boland, Arthur 'Boss' Shields and Conway McGinn.

The F company sent sixty-five members into action on Easter Monday. Both the Henderson brothers' companies – B and F – were detailed to intercept British Army reinforcements coming from its Bull Island training camp from reaching the city centre, by blocking Ballybough and Annesley Bridges. After skirmishes at the bridges and at Poplar Row, they headed for the GPO but Pádraic Pearse sent them back, with Sean T O'Kelly (aka Seán T Ó Ceallaigh) as 'overseer', to 'hold the pass' at Fairview. The insurgents attempted to blow up the twin arch bridge on the Clontarf Road and there was also fighting at Newcomen Bridge. There were casualties on both sides and also civilian casualties.

Sean Russell (1893-1940), who lived on the North Strand Road, had a troop of Volunteers in action in the Poplar Row area before they also reported to the GPO. Russell was to become director of munitions for the IRA in 1921-22 and later, Chief of Staff. A statue to his memory stands in Fairview Park, erected by the National Graves Association. The statue was first unveiled in 1951 with Brendan Behan among those in attendance. It was replaced by another statue in 1965 and the present bronze figure was put in place in 2009.

Oscar Traynor (1886-1963) – noted above in relation to the Battle of the Customs House – fought here. He went on to become a TD and a government minister and was president of the FAI from 1948-1963. At this time, he lived at Clonmore Terrace beside the Royal Canal in Ballybough. The Oscar Traynor Road in Coolock, on Dublin's northside, commemorates him.

The East Wall Road, with its dockland homes and little industrial and business units, is essentially an embankment containing and directing the flow of the Tolka river's water into Dublin Bay. The road connects the North Strand Road with the North Wall Road. It was actually once called the Wharf Road, after a spot along the road where there was a slip to the sea, for the convenience of bathers.

For many years, the view northwards from the East Wall was over open sea. Only Clontarf Island, then situated in the sea, about 140 metres from the most easterly point of the East Wall Road, impeded a sweeping, spectacular view of the North Bay area in general, including Howth Head.

The ribbon-shaped Clontarf Island, with one end facing the East Wall was, for centuries, a prominent landmark in Dublin Bay. It was used as a place of recreation, with free and easy access, especially in the late 18th century. Sometimes called 'Clontarf Isle' or 'Clontarf Head', it was some 450 metres long (east to west) and 120 metres wide (north to south).

The island was gradually eroded by locals constantly carting away its sands. Also, after the construction of the Great South Wall and later the North Bull Wall, the currents in Dublin Bay and the flow of water were affected and this gradually helped to wear away the island's sand. However, there was a sadness and genuine nostalgia among Dubliners when on the night of 9 October 1844, the island was totally washed away by the greatest storm ever to hit Dublin Bay.

The entire island site has been engulfed in the reclamation of the docks area. Part of the Bond Road area now occupies the site of the island. Many believe that the North Bull Island was a gift from the sea in compensation for the loss of Clontarf Island! However, just as the earlier reclamation of the North Lotts changed the North Strand forever, so too did the reclamation of the sprawling North Docks area, Fairview Park, the Clontarf foreshore and promenade, the building of the North Bull Wall and subsequent growth of the North Bull Island entirely transformed the view and the seashore from the East Wall to Sutton Cross.

St Joseph's Co-educational National School is situated on the site of the original East Wall Girls National School, close to the East Wall/Church Street corner. The Sean O'Casey Community Centre, on St Mary's Road, occupies the site of the Old Boys National School.

A famous soccer player, Liam Tuohy (1933-2016), was born in the East Wall. An outside left, he played mainly for Shamrock Rovers in the 1950s and 1960s. He also had a spell with Newcastle United in England. He played internationally for Ireland. As a manager, he was in charge of Dundalk, Shamrock Rovers and Shelbourne football teams and he was also manager of the Irish team in the 1970s.

Writer, political activist and Irish language enthusiast, Liam O'Briain (1888-1974) was born in Church Place. A professor at University College Galway (UCG), he made many TV and radio appearances in the 1940s and 50s. His writings (in Irish) are mainly recollections of the 1916 Rising.

The Nalty Apartment complex on the East Wall Road recalls Jack Nalty, who was born and spent his young life in the East Wall area. A republican and socialist, he fought with the International Brigade, defending Spain against the fascists led by General Franco during the Spanish Civil War (1936-1939). He was the last Irish soldier to die during the war, when he lost his life in September 1938 at the Battle of Ebra. He was just 36 years old. He had previously been a member of the IRA and had been involved, in Ireland, in the War of Independence and the Civil War. In 2018, a plaque was unveiled in his memory close to his East Wall family home.

As we head for Fairview along Annesley Bridge Road, which was at first a raised causeway over the sea, we pass two roads on our left. The first is Cadogan Road, named after the Earl of Cadogan, who was Lord Deputy from 1895-1902. On the wall of 15 Cadogan Road is a memorial plaque to Cathal Goulding (1923-1998) with the inscription 'a working-class socialist republican'. It was put there by the Workers Party. The second road, Addison Road, recalls the British Statesman and writer Joseph Addison (1672-1719).

We have again reached Edge's Corner, Fairview and from here we have an unbroken route to Howth.

The whole of our North Bay tour area is speckled with a plethora of diverse and quality food outlets, especially Fairview, Clontarf and Howth Village. Be assured our route is not wanting in the culinary field! The aroma of good and enticing 'fodder' is always wafting around you! Whatever tickles your palate can be catered for in the cornucopia of restaurants, cafes, gourmet pubs, hotel dining rooms, takeaways, delicatessens and other hostelries on the road from the Customs House to Howth Head.

The big change, over the years, has been Dublin's rapid population growth and the ensuing, ongoing need for houses. We have observed the green areas from Ballybough and the North Strand northwards disappear – farm by farm, field by field and garden by garden all replaced by buildings. The only green spots left, until we reach St Anne's Park in Clontarf, are the unique Fairview/Marino green circles and the reclaimed Fairview Park and Clontarf Promenade.

A feature of the Ballybough/North Strand area are the colourful wall murals of Dublin's famed senior GAA footballers and their managers, especially those of the two 'golden ages' of Dublin football in modern times – 'Heffo's Heroes' of the 1970s and the later history-making six-in-a-row All-Ireland winning team of 2015-2020. What better place could you pick to honour these great sportsmen than in the great heartland of GAA activities, in the shadow of Croke Park?

Busáras

Connolly Station

Dublin/Monaghan bombings memorial

Convention Centre

3Arena (previously 02) at the site of the old Point Depot

Jeanie Johnston (famine memorial ship)

CHQ Building

North Strand Bombing Memorial Garden

St Laurence O'Toole CBS

North Strand fire station

Charleville Mall library

Edge's Corner

Kelly Harrington

Liam Tuohy

Jim Sheridan

Sean Russell

Stephen Gately

CHAPTER FOUR

Fairview, Marino, Lord Charlemont, The Casino, St Mary's Christian Brothers Generalate, Griffith Avenue, Donnycarney

The Fairview and Marino area is a diverse locality, rich in history and forms a settled, mature suburb. The area is cosy and somewhat quaint in that it holds on to aspects of its original individuality, incorporating remnants of a rural, agricultural neighbourhood, combined with definite seaside characteristics.

Fairview is so called because of the fair and panoramic view it enjoyed across the open sea to the Dublin and Wicklow mountains. The reclamation, referred to earlier, drastically and dramatically changed all that.

As we proceed, Fairview Avenue is on the left. It once led to Croyden Park House. Fairview Park on the right is marked on early maps of Dublin simply as 'mud' and locals called it 'sloblands'. Up to 1800, the sea infringed on Fairview Strand and the area was a tidal mudflat. Intensive reclamation work during the eighteenth century gradually pushed the sea back. The actual reclamation of Fairview Park itself (essentially seashore slobland) began in the 1840s, after the construction of the Great Northern Railway line across the sea and the final reclamation of the park from the sea was only completed between 1920 and 1925. Until completed, the park was a landfill site – a dump! – and much of its twenty hectares was infilled with city rubbish. After the 1916 fighting, much rubble from the O'Connell Street area was dumped here.

Today's park is a truly wonderful local amenity, always well landscaped. One can truthfully observe that if anything defines and characterises an area, surely Fairview Park does. It is an urban park with playing fields and is noted for its tree-lined walks – with maple, beech and oak very noticeable throughout the park – and its colourful spring and summer flower beds. In the middle of the park is a sculpture from 1991 by Joe Moran. Entitled *Family Unit* it depicts a family of three.

The final section of the Dublin Port Tunnel, opened to traffic in December 2006, crosses beneath Philipsburgh Avenue, runs under the entire Marino housing estate and proceeds under the centre of Fairview Park as it makes its way to Dublin Port.

The shops, offices and businesses opposite Fairview Park were planned to replace the forbidding, high wall guarding the Charlemont Estate (see later). The old Fairview cinema building is still there as we move past the iconic footbridge at Merville Avenue.

As we enter Marino Mart, part of which takes us to the left, with St Joseph's Schools on the left and Marino Post Office, for many years, on the right. (The location of the post office changed in 2022 and now operates at the Spar supermarket on Fairview Strand). This was the original site of the celebrated gates at the entry to Lord Charlemont's demesne and, for a time, one entered St Joseph's schools via these gates. St Joseph's postal address is actually Merville Avenue.

St Joseph's School (affectionately known as 'Joey's') opened in 1888. First known as St Joseph's Marino, then as St Joseph's Fairview, it was purposely established as a teacher training/practice school for Christian Brothers. St Laurence O'Toole CBS on Seville Place was also used for this purpose. The role was later adopted by Scoil Mhuire, Griffith Avenue. In the 1890s, St Joseph's expanded to include a secondary school.

The school boasts a wonderful reputation in terms of educational and sporting achievements. Among its better-known alumni are two former Taoisigh, John A Costello (1891-1976) and Charles J Haughey (1925-2006). Three government ministers attended the school – George Colley (1925-1983), who also served as Tánaiste; Gerard Boland (1885-1973) and his son, Kevin Boland (1917-2001).

Gerard Boland, who was educated at the O'Brien Institute, Malahide Road, was a republican soldier who fought at Jacob's Factory, Bishop Street during the 1916 Rising. At that time, he was living at 15 The Crescent, Marino. Later, he set up home at 102 Howth Road. He was a founder member of the Fianna Fáil Party. Kevin Boland resigned as secretary of Fianna Fáil in 1970 because he did not agree with the party policy on the Northern Ireland issue. He set up the short-lived Aontacht Éireann party in 1972.

Eugene Timmons TD and Lord Mayor of Dublin from 1965-67, was a Joey's pupil, as was the previously mentioned Captain Sean Connolly.

Poet, songwriter and painter (by trade) Peadar Kearney (1883-1942), who was born at 68 Lower Dorset Street, attended Joey's. He wrote the words of our national anthem, *The Soldier's Song*, which was published in 1912. Patrick Heeney set the lyrics to music in 1916 and later, Liam O'Rian translated the song into Irish. The ballad, *God Save Ireland*, composed by TD Sullivan, in honour of the Manchester Martyrs (who were hanged in 1867), was accepted for many years as the national anthem (often referred to as the 'Fenian Anthem') but from 1916 on, the Irish Volunteers sang and played *The Soldier's Song* as their marching tune and it became the anthem of nationalists and republicans generally. It was formally adopted by the government as the Irish national anthem in 1926.

Kearney, who was also a stagehand at the Abbey Theatre, lived at two addresses in Ballybough – 3 Richmond Parade and 17 Russell Street. He fought at Jacob's Factory, alongside Thomas McDonagh, during the 1916 Rising and served time in Ballykindler internment camp, in County Down. Kearney, being a brother of Kathleen Behan, was an uncle of her son, the writer, Brendan Behan. Kathleen's husband, Stephen Behan, became part of Michael Collins' 'extended' squad when occasion demanded. Seamus de Búrca, son of Peadar's sister, Margaret, published a biography of Kearney in 1957. There is a memorial monument to Peadar Kearney at his birthplace on Lower Dorset Street, now occupied by Derrynane Square. It is situated at the junction of the square with Ennisfallen Parade. There is also a memorial, made of Kilkenny limestone, dating from 1967 and dedicated to three patriots: Peadar Kearney, Thomas Ashe and Piaras Béaslaí in Glasnevin Cemetery.

All-Ireland senior football medal winners with Dublin, who attended Joey's include Kevin Heffernan (in 1958 as captain), Des Foley (1963 as captain) and Tony Hanahoe (twice as captain, 1976 and 1977). Des Foley (1940-95), a St Vincent's clubman, has a record of achievement as a player that is hard to match. Before he captained Dublin to win the Sam Maguire cup in 1963, he had already captained the Dublin minor team to victory in the 1958 All-Ireland Minor Football Final. In 1959, he was captain of the Joey's senior team that became the first Dublin team to win the Hogan Cup (the trophy for winning the All-Ireland Post Primary Schools Senior A Championship). He played Railway Cup (interprovincial) football for Leinster before he played senior for Dublin. On St Patrick's Day in 1962, he became (and remains) the only player to win Railway Cup medals in hurling and football on the same day. In the political field, Des was twice elected to Dáil Éireann as a Fianna Fáil TD, in 1965 and 1969. He died at the early age of fifty-four.

Film actor and director, Brendan Gleeson (born 1955) attended Joey's.

During the 1890s, the Clontarf branch of the Gaelic League (founded in 1893 by Éamonn Ceannt, revolutionary and 1916 martyr) held its weekly meetings at Joey's before moving to a premises on Griffith Avenue. Ceannt lived in Fairview at the time.

On the wall outside the school is a round plaque, commemorating all those from the area who served the Irish Citizen Army between 1913 and 1923. The plaque dates from 2016. After Joey's, we pass Marino College of Higher Education, established in 1936 and the cosy Marino Public Library, dating from 1934.

In the 1940s and 50s, a certain Fairview resident called Bill Stephens had the rather unusual occupation of being a lion tamer! He often brought his lions for a walk in Fairview Park! On 11 November 1951, while many locals were watching a film in Fairview Cinema, one of Bill's troop, a lioness, escaped behind the cinema and headed down Merville Avenue, creating panic and havoc. The people were kept in the cinema until Gardaí managed to shoot the lioness before she could kill anyone.

On the 8 December 1954, a huge flood hit the Fairview/East Wall/North Strand area. It rained incessantly and heavily all day long, accompanied by strong winds. That night, the railway bridge crossing the Tolka river at East Wall Road collapsed into the river, causing the water levels to rapidly rise and the Tolka to burst its banks. This resulted in severe flooding, with the Fairview area under six feet of water. Many people had to be evacuated from their homes. Access to Amiens Street Station was blocked and overnight, the quiet Clontarf railway station (known as 'Clontarf Halt', opened on the Howth Road by the Great Northern Railway Company in 1898) became a major rail terminal as all trains from the north were routed there. The situation lasted until 5 January 1955, when a new railway bridge was opened over the Tolka. 'Clontarf Halt' was permanently closed on 3 September 1956.

Part of the overall Marino area was always known as the 'Bloody Fields'. Some sources allege that Tomar's Wood, so much associated with the 1014 Battle of Clontarf, stretched down to here from Glasnevin and that fierce, hand-to-hand fighting did indeed occur here during the monumental battle.

The name Marino is a relatively modern one, dating from 1753, when James Caulfeild, Fourth Viscount and First Earl of Charlemont (Lord Charlemont 1728-1799) first settled there. At the age of six, he had inherited the viscount title, with large estates in counties Tyrone (at Moy) and Armagh. The earl title came in 1763. He was a descendant of the Caulfeilds of Oxfordshire, England. Roxboro Castle, at Moy in Co. Tyrone, was the seat of the earls of Charlemont, along with Charlemont Fort, a garrison at Charlemont in Co. Armagh.

As a youngster and indeed, all his life, Charlemont was of delicate health. For this reason and the fact that he had a tendency to gamble and, was inclined towards the lifestyle often associated with gambling, he was sent on a tour of continental Europe. He was just 18 years of age and went with his tutor, Rev Edward Murphy, on what was known as the 'Grand Tour'. It was a rite of passage for young aristocrats of that era and in Charlemont's case, it lasted for 10 years: 1746-56. During the first few years, he visited Greece, Turkey and Egypt. Although he was laden with anti-Catholic prejudice, he spent the last five years, 1749-1754, in Italy, mainly in Rome. In later life, he opposed Catholic relief acts in 1792 and 1793. However, he seems to have accepted Catholic Emancipation before his death.

Having mixed with 'high society' in Europe's splendid courts, he returned home in his 28th year, having acquired a consuming interest in classical architecture. He had also become something of an aesthete, with a taste for fine food and drink and for witty, interesting and congenial companions. He was to become a leading figure in Dublin's political and social life in the latter half of the eighteenth century. On his return, he accepted a mansion, built in 1755 with a 300-acre estate, as a gift from his stepfather. He was Thomas Adderley, a rich linen merchant and politician. Charlemont also inherited family estates at Charlemont (hence the title) in County Armagh and Moy in County Tyrone.

The Marino mansion was built of Portland Stone and stood at the junction of today's Brian Road and Brian Avenue. The place was referred to locally as the Charlemont Demesne. It stretched from the present Collins Avenue to Fairview Strand. Charlemont proceeded to spend a fortune to make his estate one of grandeur and eloquence, equal to that of any of his artistic and aristocratic contemporaries. At the time, the building dwarfed all other buildings in the locality – its art gallery alone was sixty feet long. Charlemont added an extensive and exquisite temple beside the house, complete with a marble floored banqueting hall. Rejoicing in the name 'Rosamond's Bower', the temple had an accompanying lake. The domain also had many ornamental 'follies', in keeping with the style and tradition of such manorial ranches at the time.

Charlemont named his residence Marino, from a place of that name in Italy, near the Pope's summer residence at Castel Gandolfo on the western shore of Lake Albano. In time, the whole area came to be called Marino. At the entrance to his demesne (today's Marino Mart, which becomes Marino Park Avenue) he arranged a beautiful ornamental gateway. The actual gates (mentioned above) now stand at the approach to Marino Institute of Education, formerly St Mary's Christian Brothers' headquarters on Griffith Avenue (see below). Charlemont's town house on Parnell Square (then Rutland Square), today houses the Hugh Lane Municipal Gallery of Modern Art and is a very popular city gallery.

Many people recall Lord Charlemont as a patron of the arts, who founded the Royal Irish Academy in 1785. Others remember him as the 'Volunteer Earl', associated with Grattan's Parliament, seeking legislative independence for Ireland from Britain in the years after 1778. He was, in July 1780, elected as commander-in-chief of the Volunteers, a part-time military force first recruited in 1778-79, which grew to about 60,000 in number by May 1782.

Above all, he is remembered for the Casino or Casine, as it was first known, which still stands on the present Cherrymount Crescent, just off the Malahide Road. It is Ireland's most perfect building and surely challenges the Customs House as Ireland's most beautiful building! It is one of the best surviving examples of eighteenth-century Sicilian Doric architecture anywhere in the world. The enchanting structure, one of Dublin's most iconic landmarks, was originally built on an expansive base in an open plain. Finished in 1773, it enjoyed panoramic views all around but especially out over Dublin City and bay to the Wicklow mountains.

The building was designed by English architect Sir William Chambers (1726-1796), who never set foot in Ireland! It was actually built by Simon Vierpyl, an Italian sculptor who Charlemont met during his 'Grand Tour'. The exquisite, unique and ornate 'temple' is of Portland stone in the neo-classical style, resembling a Greek temple. Charlemont had the eloquent casino built as a showpiece, a summer house, a pleasure house for pastoral life, a rural retreat in his search for eloquence and for the lavish entertainment of his high society associates – he was a member of the House of Lords. The politicians, literati, artists and general intelligentsia who came to dine, wine and converse with him at the Casino included politicians and orators, Henry Flood and Henry Grattan; politicians and writers, Charles Lucas and Edmund Burke; lawyer and nationalist, John Philpot Curran; judge and historian, Jonah Barrington; United Irishman, Lord Edward Fitzgerald and John Wesley, the founder of Methodism. Henry Grattan, of course, owed his parliamentary seat in the Irish House of Commons to the good Lord, as he was returned, first in 1775, for the Borough of Charlemont in County Tyrone. Charlemont, with his extensive properties there, effectively decided who would be MP for the area.

Charlemont adopted the name 'casino' from the Italian word *cassino*, which means 'a small house'. From a distance, it actually looks small but on closer examination, subtly designed, it is deceptively large, being of three storeys and containing sixteen rooms. It has been described as 'architectural poetry in Portland stone'! A national monument since 1930, it has, beneath it, a series of tunnels about which, legendary yarns proliferate. However, it is a fact that many of the revolutionary, Michael Collins' foot soldiers used the tunnels for gunfire practice during the War of Independence in the 1919/1921 era.

Charlemont is recalled on our route by Charlemont Housing Estate on Griffith Avenue, Charlemont Road, which joins the Howth and Malahide Roads and Charlemont Lane, which connects the Clontarf Road with the

Howth Road. Elsewhere in Dublin, Charlemont Gardens, Hall and Place recall him in the south city centre. Charlemont Avenue and Terrace recall him in Dún Laoghaire.

When Lord Charlemont died in 1799, his successors managed the estate until 1876, when the last of the Charlemonts left Marino forever. The whole estate was actually on lease from Dublin Corporation and it now reverted to that body. All arrangements and leases with the Caulfeilds finally terminated in 1921.

The Archbishop of Dublin, Cardinal Cullen, bought the estate in 1878 and his successor, Cardinal McCabe, sold it to the Christian Brothers in 1882 – all except fifty-two acres that were reserved for the provision of an orphanage, which became known as the O'Brien Institute. The Brothers' developed their overall headquarters at Marino – Generalate, Novitiate, Teacher Training College, Practice School and Missionary College.

Blessed Edmund Rice (1762-1844) founded the Christian Brothers and Presentation Brothers at Mount Sion in Waterford, in 1802. The Congregation of the Christian Brothers got the formal blessing and recognition of Pope Pius VII in 1820. Rice moved his headquarters to O'Connell Schools CBS in 1831 and (now as Brother Ignatius) lived with the community there until 1838, when his health failed and he returned to Waterford, where he died in 1844. He was beatified by Pope John Paul II in Rome, in 1996. There is a lovely memorial museum to Rice at Edmund Rice House beside the O'Connell Schools on North Richmond Street and the Edmund Rice Heritage Centre was opened in 2008, at Mount Sion, Barrack Street, Waterford.

The brothers moved their headquarters to Belvedere House in Drumcondra (later to become St Patrick's Teacher Training College) in 1873 but found it unsuitable. So, in 1883, they again moved, this time to Lord Charlemont's former Marino House residence. Then, in 1904, they moved to their new purpose-built 'citadel', St Mary's Monastery on today's Griffith Avenue. In the past, Charlemont's mansion eclipsed all surrounding buildings but, it was itself dwarfed by this new, three-storey edifice built of Wicklow granite on high ground. It was and is a truly magnificent structure of the classic style, forming a hollow square with a very fitting 'head office'.

St Mary's initially catered for the training of teachers for both primary and second level schools. In 1929, the Department of Education recognised St Mary's (or Coláiste Mhuire) as a full and proper training college, with the right to award the National Teachers Diploma (NT).

The Christian Brothers became Ireland's largest teaching order and produced many textbooks for schools. At their peak, in the 1960s, Brothers taught in some 125 schools in Ireland and served hundreds more around the world. Membership peaked then at about 4,000 – one thousand of them in Ireland. They have had a huge impact on Irish education, at both primary and second levels. The 'four R's' in Irish education were especially associated with the Brothers – religion, 'riting, reading and 'rithmetic. They were the most fervent supporters of Gaelic games since the GAA was founded in 1884. Many well-known men spent some time as members of the Christian Brothers Congregation, such as senator Pól Ó Foighil (1928-2005) and Richard (Dick) Burke (1932-2016) both of the Fine Gael political party. Burke became a TD, government minister and European Commissioner. Writers, Críostóir Ó Floinn and Cathal Ó Sándair were members, for a time, as was Gaelic scholar, Liam Ó Caithnia. In 1962, a distinguished visitor to St Mary's was Cardinal Montini from Italy, who became Pope Paul VI the following year in 1963.

St Mary's remained the generalate until 1967, when it was moved to Rome – a reflection of the greater international membership of the Brothers. In the late 1980s, St Mary's became the Marino Institute of Education and is an associated college of Trinity College, Dublin. It offers many courses, including the four-year Bachelor of Education (B. Ed) course for primary school teaching. In the ailing days of Taoiseach Leo Varadkar's 'confidence and supply' government in conjunction with Fianna Fáil, a full cabinet meeting was held at the Institute on 9 January 2020.

The O'Brien Institute, that staid, red brick building just off the Malahide Road close to its junction with Griffith Avenue, was established in 1883 at the behest of the two O'Brien twin sisters, in whose names the title deeds were. The O'Brien Twin Sisters Educational Trust, set up in 1876, stipulated that a home and school for orphans be established for the education of the sons of businessmen "in reduced or impoverished circumstances". The institution was first known as 'the school of the twin sisters' and they also directed that it would always be used for educational purposes. The Christian Brothers were given overall control of the institute.

Among the more prominent people to attend the O'Brien Institute were the Fianna Fáil government minister, Gerard Boland (mentioned above); former President of Ireland, Erskine Childers and comedian, Dave Allen. Allen (real name – David Tynan O'Mahoney) was a native of Tallaght in South Dublin. A humourist and a satirist, many will recall him for his sketches and monologues, whiskey in hand on his trademark high stool.

The institute, being no longer viable, closed in 1976. In 1982 it became the training centre for Dublin Fire Brigade and part of the building houses a delightful museum, detailing the extraordinary history of the fire brigade.

After the closure of the old City Morgue at Store Street, it was temporarily housed on the grounds of the O'Brien Institute. The morgue is now situated in the old Whitehall Garda Station, at the junction of Griffith Avenue with the Swords Road. Nazareth House nursing home opened on the Malahide Road on an eight-acre site on institute grounds in 1970. It caters for close to one hundred elderly residents.

Griffith Avenue, named after political leader, Arthur Griffith, was built between 1924 and 1928. It connects the Malahide Road with the Swords (Airport) Road, the Ballymun Road and with Glasnevin. Beautifully and uniquely double tree lined at the time, with London plane trees, we have the legacy of the lovely boulevard it is today. The avenue is reputed to be the longest avenue in the northern hemisphere without commercial properties.

Scoil Mhuire and Scoil Uinseann De Pól on Griffith Avenue, both opened in 1928. Scoil Mhuire was purpose built as the principal teacher practice school for trainee Christian Brother teachers from St Mary's. However, it quickly became the main primary school for boys in Marino. Both Scoil Mhuire and St Joseph's (Joey's, mentioned above) became embedded in Gaelic Games and formed the real nursery and academy for GAA activities in Dublin. In 1931, the then parish priest, Fr Fitzpatrick (Fairview and Marino were one parish until 1949) and Brother Killian Fitzgerald, principal teacher at Scoil Mhuire, became the chief founders of the very famous St Vincent's GAA Club. St Vincent's clubhouse and playing fields stand close to the Marino Institute of Education.

Marino Gaels GAA Club preceded St Vincent's in the area, having been founded in 1924. That club was based in the newly reclaimed Fairview Park but expired in the mid-1930s, as St Vincent's became the dominant club in the area. From the start, the club had and has a steady supply of players from Scoil Mhuire and Joey's and, from the local Ard Scoil Rís (named after the aforementioned Edmund Rice) since it opened in 1972. In 1979 Ard Scoil Rís won the Hogan Cup, emulating Joey's 20 years earlier. With such riches of supply in terms of players, the club was almost destined to be great and successful!

No club in Ireland can claim to be a better exponent of our national games (Gaelic football, hurling, camogie and ladies' football) than St Vincent's. Indeed, for a time, especially in the 1950s, St Vincent's **was** Dublin GAA, particularly in relation to football. In terms of senior county championships won, 'Vinnys' are way ahead of the posse, having accumulated twenty-nine titles. Added to this, the club has won seven Leinster championships and three All-Ireland crowns. The club has produced three All-Ireland Dublin Senior Football winning captains: the already mentioned Kevin Heffernan,

Des Foley and Tony Hanahoe. In the National League Final of 1953, Dublin beat reigning All-Ireland champions Cavan, with a team that included 14 St Vincent's players. The exception or '15th man' was goalkeeper, Tony O'Grady from the Air Corps club. That statistic is unlikely to ever be repeated, never mind beaten. Another fact that will hardly be surpassed is that Dublin beat Derry in the 1958 All-Ireland Senior Football Final with a panel containing twelve St Vincent's players, ten on the starting fifteen and two subs.

Founded in 1931, St Vincent's remarkable success on the playing field is all the more noteworthy in that the club was without a home – nomads until they eventually settled in their present 'spiritual' home in Marino, in 1987. Never lacking in ambition, confidence, drive and ability, the club has produced thirty-three players to various Dublin senior football teams that have won 15 All-Ireland titles between 1958 and 2020, bringing 53 All-Ireland medals to Marino! They supplied the team captain on four occasions. The 33 players are; Simon Behan, David Billings, Ger Brennan, Pat Canavan, Diarmuid Connolly, Tommy Conroy, Jim Crowley, Leslie Deegan, Bobby Doyle, Des Foley, Lar Foley, Ollie Freaney, Des Ferguson, Paddy Farnan, Noel Fox, Pat Gilroy, Tony Hanahoe, Padraic Haughey, Ray Hazley, Kevin Heffernan, Johnny Joyce, Jimmy Keaveney, Mick Kissane, Críostóir Leavey, Des McKane, Brian Mullins, Gay O'Driscoll, Cathal O'Leary, Brendan Pocock, Fran Ryder, Michael Savage, Mossie Whelan and Mark Wilson.

With a few rare exceptions – such as Brian Mullins, who attended Coláiste Mhuire (Parnell Square) – all of these players attended Scoil Mhuire (Griffith Ave) or Joey's or both schools.

In 1958, Dublin won both senior and minor All-Ireland football finals and no fewer than 18 St Vincent's players took home All-Ireland medals on that day – 28 September.

St Vincent's has won the Dublin senior hurling championship on thirteen occasions. The club has won the Dublin double titles in football and hurling on five occasions. In camogie, the club has won 13 Dublin titles and two Leinster championships.

We need to give special mention to one outstanding club member, player, coach and manager, Kevin Heffernan. Kevin grew up in Turlough Parade in the heart of Marino and, in married life, lived on the Howth Road in Raheny. As a player in the 1950s, he orchestrated new tactics and innovative ideas/techniques on the field. Later, off the field, as manager of a brilliant 'breakthrough' Dublin team in the 1970s, he changed the very nature and structure of the way Gaelic football is played. His pure drive and philosophy redefined the game from a kicking/propelling one to a fast-moving, passing game. He built a team that became folk heroes, with a very attractive, even flamboyant style of play. 'Heffo' as he came to be known with his innovative and revolutionary ideas, 'sold' the game beyond its traditional rural 'cloth cap' fraternity to include all human life. A huge volume of supporters, who came to be called 'Heffo's Army', with colourful banners, with mottos and with songs enthusiastically followed their swashbuckling team! Gaelic Football became something people wanted to be involved with. He 'lifted' Dublin City and put the capital back on top of the football world, having been in the doldrums for so long. New GAA clubs sprang up, such as Naomh Barróg in Kilbarrack. On Dublin's southside, Gaelic football expanded enormously. Kevin was awarded the Freedom of the City of Dublin in May 2004.

Many will recall the lines from the song *The Likes of Heffo's Army*, written and recorded by The Memories musical group after Dublin won the 1974 All-Ireland Senior Football Final.

We'll be marching down from Ringsend,
And from Ballyfermot too.
From East Wall and Marino
To support the boys in blue.
For eleven long years we've waited
And there's nothing left to prove.
So, let's hear it now from Dublin.
Heffo's army on the loose.

The district of Marino consists, in the main, of the former Charlemont and Croyden Park Estates. In the early 1920s, Dublin Corporation bought back the southern part of the Charlemont estate and proceeded to carry out the first building programme of a native Irish government. Political events in the turbulent 1920s delayed the project. The two big mansions – Marino House and Croyden Park House – were demolished and in all, some 1,500 new homes were built. The aim was to provide social housing to alleviate Dublin's slum dwellings and the inhuman conditions in which so many of Dublin's population lived at the time.

Building began in 1923 and was finally completed in 1930. The 'Garden City' design used was borrowed from Ebenezer Howard (1880-1928), the English town planner. It was a very creative plan and scheme and left us with the distinctive Marino 'green circles' housing estate. It certainly altered the entire face and aspect of the area. Essentially a rural locality, its green fields were gone forever and replaced by rows of architecturally interestingly designed houses, with their service roads and avenues. The scheme was totally life changing for the poor and the wretched who moved in from the tenements, basements and cellars of city lanes, side streets and grimy backstreets to houses with running water and a garden. Some of the houses also had small back gardens, in which the owners were encouraged to grow vegetables.

On the opposite side of the Malahide Road, directly across from the Casino, are Mount Temple Comprehensive School and Clontarf Golf and Bowling Club. The school at 178 Malahide Road, close to its junction with Copeland Avenue, opened in the old Mount Temple mansion (built in 1860) on the former Bradshaw estate in 1949. It was essentially the transfer of Mountjoy School to Clontarf, which later amalgamated with the Hibernian Marine School (Clontarf) and the Bertrand and Rutland School (Eccles Street). It became co-educational in 1972 and is regarded as a liberal, multi-denominational school. Four of Mount Temple's most famous pupils are the members of the U2 band, formed in 1976, who rose to international fame in the early 1980s. They are Paul Hewson (Bono), Dave Evans (The Edge), Larry Mullen and Adam Clayton. The Edge adopted that name from Edge's shop and corner in Fairview!

Clontarf Golf Club, founded in 1912, originally operated from where Mount Temple School is today. It moved to its present clubhouse in 1922. This is the former Donnycarney House, first built in 1781 and once the home of the Master of the Rolls, who was responsible for all Irish Public Records.

Adjoining Clontarf Golf Course, on Cloncarthy Road off Collins Avenue (once known as Puckstown Lane), is the spiritual home of Dublin GAA, Parnell Park, obviously named after Ireland's 'uncrowned king' CS Parnell. On the same site is the clubhouse of Craobh Chiaráin GAA Club, founded in 1962, when two existing clubs amalgamated – Craobh Rua and Naomh Chiaráin. It is known mainly as a hurling club although it held senior football status for many years. The club has won the Dublin senior hurling championship on five occasions.

A little further along Collins Avenue are Donnycarney's primary schools: Scoil Chiaráin CBS and Our Lady of Consolation school. A famous family who lived on Belton Park Road off Collins Avenue in Donnycarney was that of former Taoiseach, Charles Haughey. They moved from Derry to Castlebar, then to Sutton and to a farm in Garretstown, Co. Meath before settling in Donnycarney in 1933.

Renowned soccer player, Tommy Eglinton (1923-2004) was born in Donnycarney. An outside left (the flying left winger of the 1950s) he played for Shamrock Rovers and in England, for Tranmere Rovers and Everton. He played internationally for Ireland on FAI and IFA teams. Many will remember him running a butcher shop on St Gabriel's Road, Clontarf after he retired from football. Tommy, beloved for his charismatic personality, has a street in Liverpool named in his honour.

Belton Park Road, Avenue, Gardens and Villas recall the Belton Family, who were involved in politics with the Fine Gael Party. The family also engaged in the building industry and were public house owners. Well known member of The Dubliners musical group, Barney McKenna (1939-2012) was born in Donnycarney, as was musician and composer, Paddy Moloney (1938-2021) founder and leader of The Chieftains, an Irish traditional music band.

A plaque at 9 Belton Park Road recalls Leo Rowsome, who lived there until his death in 1970. Leo was an ambassador for traditional Irish music. He was a skilled pipe maker and pipe player. He was a first-class broadcaster and a very successful recording artist. He was a founder member of Comhaltas Ceoltóirí Éireann. He taught generations of uilleann pipers including renowned piper, Liam Óg O'Flynn and the aforementioned Paddy Moloney.

The quaint but very famous little semi-circular street known as The Crescent (from the waxing moon), with its tall grandiose Georgian houses, joins the seafront ends of the Malahide and Howth Roads. Concave in design and fronted by the small Bram Stoker Park, the street has been referred to as Spite-Row or Ireland's most expensive hate-fence! The story goes that a Quaker, a painter-builder named 'Wild' John Folliott of Aungier Street (south Dublin City), built The Crescent houses in 1792, on land that he had obtained. He constructed them in that style and arrangement to extinguish the unobstructed view Lord Charlemont enjoyed from his Marino mansion. In those days — pre-Great Northern Railway embankment, Fairview Park, Presbyterian Church, Clontarf DART Station, etc — the view was indeed extensive right across Dublin Bay, with Howth Head to the north and the Dublin and Wicklow mountains to the south. Folliott' action was in revenge for a gambling bet between Charlemont and Folliott that went wrong and which, Charlemont apparently used to undermine Folliott's reputation. As well as destroying his view, 'the erratic' rear window arrangement of The Crescent houses affected the good Lord's sensitivities. Lord Charlemont objected to the development of The Crescent and the legal arguments ended in the House of Lords. Folliott was the winner in that the members of that august body voted that, in your residence, you are entitled to light but not a view.

Author Bram Stoker was born at 15 The Crescent. The well-known Republican and Fianna Fáil Boland family came to live at 15 in the years before 1916. Henry James (Harry) Boland (1887-1922) was president of the IRB in 1919-20. A brother of Gerard Boland (mentioned above) he was a TD from 1918-22. He was a close confidant of Éamon de Valera (1882-1922). He was fatally wounded in Skerries during the Civil War, in July 1922 and died on August 27. Jack Butler Yeats composed a well-known painting entitled *Funeral of Harry Boland*.

A famous story related that Boland went on a fundraising and propaganda trip to America, from June 1919 to December 1920, acting as private secretary to De Valera. While there, they met a (Russian) Bolshevik named Alexander Martins, whose own fundraising efforts were not very successful! Boland lent him 20,000 dollars and accepted some of the Russian Crown Jewels as security. (One would find it difficult to visualise De Valera being so 'flaithiúil' unless, of course, some Russian 'help' could be sent to Ireland at a later date – in the manner of Wolfe Tone and the French in 1798!). Boland arrived home with the said jewels and they were hidden behind a basement fireplace at 15 The Crescent for many years. The jewels were handed over to the Irish government when Fianna Fáil first assumed power in 1932. The original loan was finally retrieved and the jewels returned to the Russians in 1949.

Another story involving De Valera and Harry Boland concerns the key smuggled to De Valera to enable him to escape from Lincoln Jail in east England, in February 1919. De Valera promised to give the key to the man who made it, Alderman de Loughrey. After leaving prison he gave the key to Harry Boland, who gave it to his mother for safekeeping at 15 The Crescent. It remained there for 20 years. Sometime later, Harry's sister, Kathleen, returned it to de Loughrey. The key is now safely in the National Museum.

On Sunday 26 July 1914, about 1,000 Volunteers and some Fianna Éireann members marched to Howth from Fr Matthew Park, Fairview, to collect guns and ammunition to be landed that day in Howth by Erskine Childers (1870-1922) in his yacht the *Asgard*. Fianna Éireann was a nationalist youth body, founded by Countess Markievicz in August 1909. With the exception of a few officers, Volunteers and Fianna marching that morning had no idea of what was about to happen. Arthur Griffith was one who marched without any knowledge of the plan. Thomas McDonagh and Bulmer Hobson were in charge of all organisation and arrangements. Cathal Brugha was commander of the men who would receive the guns.

With the weaponry, they marched back towards Dublin City via Sutton, Raheny and Killester. However, as they approached the junction of the Howth Road with the Clontarf Road, their path was blocked by a phalanx of police and soldiers. The Volunteers turned right into The Crescent but were again confronted by the army and police at the Malahide Road. The Volunteer leaders outwitted the authorities by engaging them in long debate and argument while orders were issued back to the rank and file to disperse and melt away and, hide the guns and ammunition.

While a melee cum free for all took place between some Volunteers and soldiers, the main body disappeared through hedges and over walls with the arms, especially across the fields then surrounding St Mary's Christian Brothers' headquarters and the O'Brien Institute. The 'stash' was hidden, to be collected later variously in the then derelict Casino, in St Mary's sheds and outhouses in Father Matthew Park and, in many 'safe' houses.

The Howth Gun Running, as the event came to be called, was critical in the run up to the 1916 Rising and the declaration of the Irish Republic. With the Ulster Volunteers parading openly in arms and the British Conservatives nakedly supporting the Orangemen, it was clear that the battle for Home Rule and self-determination could only be achieved by physical force. The success of the landing of the guns and the march to Dublin, in broad daylight, gave the Volunteers new confidence and a fresh determination. It also gave new enthusiasm and courage to the people as well as a belief in the Volunteers.

Among those involved that day were most of the names that were to become household ones during and after the 1916 Rising. They included Éamonn Ceannt, Tom Clarke, Éamon de Valera, Darrel Figgis, Sean Heuston, Seán Mac Diarmada, The O'Rahilly and Pádraic Pearse. (The Howth Gun Running is further dealt with below, in our section dealing with Howth).

Before we leave the area, we will mention a few more interesting and well-known people associated with Fairview and Marino.

A somewhat forgotten figure born in Fairview is Michael Walker, whose Irish cycling team was given special permission to participate in the 1912 Stockholm Olympic Games under the Irish flag, despite the fact that we were under British Rule at the time. Four years later, Walker took part in the 1916 Rising, cycling around Dublin with dispatches in his trademark three-piece suit!

Scottish-born Margaret Skinnider (1893-1971) was a teacher and a revolutionary who lived at Waverly Avenue, Fairview. She was a member of Cumann na mBan and the Irish Citizen Army. She fought in 1916 as a sniper on the roof of the College of Surgeons in St Stephen's Green. Fellow revolutionary and trade union activist, Rosie Hackett (1893 – 1976) also lived in Fairview. She became a member of the Irish Citizen Army and was involved in the 1916 Rising. A bridge over the River Liffey was named in Rosie's memory in 2014. It is a road and tram bridge that connects Marlborough Street to Hawkins Street.

Executed 1916 leader, Thomas MacDonagh lived at 'Woodlands', Philipsburgh Avenue.

Revolutionaries Liam and Barry Mellows were reared at 10 Annadale Avenue. Liam (1892-1922) was a TD in 1921/22 and was executed by Free State forces in Mountjoy Prison in 1922.

Seán Óg Ó Ceallacháin, GAA broadcaster, author, journalist and actor grew up in Fairview, following his family's move to Dublin from Newcastle West in County Limerick and later lived on the Howth Road in Raheny. He played senior football and hurling for the Eoghan Ruadh GAA Club (having first played for St Vincent's) and for Dublin.

Actor Brendan Cauldwell (1912-2006) was born in Fairview.

Actress, singer and comedian, Maria Philomena (Maureen) Potter (1925-2004) lived at St Joseph's Avenue, Fairview and was educated at the local St Mary's National School. She learned to dance at the CYMS hall on Philipsburgh Avenue. She lived all her married life at Vernon Drive, Clontarf.

Actress, Maureen Toal (1930-2012) was born in Fairview. She is fondly remembered for her role as Teasy McDaid in the RTÉ rural soap opera *Glenroe*.

Radio DJ, Lorcan (Larry) Gogan (1934-2020) was born on Fairview Avenue, where his parents had a newsagent's shop.

Actor, Tom Jordan was born in Marino. He is mainly recalled for his portrayal of the much-loved character Charlie Kelly in the RTÉ television series, *Fair City*.

Fiddle player, John Sheehan (b.1939), an original member of the celebrated The Dubliners ballad group, was born in Marino. He will be long remembered for his beautiful composition *The Marino Waltz* and also for *The Marino Casino*, with fellow Dubliners' member, Eamonn Campbell.

The well-known Billy Barry school of dance operates from the CYMS Hall on Philipsburgh Avenue. Billy Barry (married name, O'Farrell) founded the famous school in 1964. She died in September 2014.

Fairview (main thoroughfare)

The Crescent

The Casino

Lord Charlemont

Peadar Kearney memorial, Dorset Street

Millennium Clock, Donnycarney

Clontarf Golf Clubhouse

O'Brien Institute

Fairview Flood 1954

Kevin Heffernan

St Joseph's School (Joeys)

Mount Temple School

John Sheehan

Maureen Potter

Paddy Moloney

Kevin Boland

Des Foley

Charles J Haughey

CHAPTER FIVE

Clontarf, Killester, Battle of Clontarf, O'Connell's Monster Meeting, Dollymount, St Anne's Park, North Bull Island

We now return to the seafront Clontarf Road to continue our trek towards Howth.

On the Clontarf Road, at its junction with the Howth Road, is a little plaque recalling the tragic death here of Eugene Maher, on 30 June 2015.

The name Clontarf is derived from the Irish, *Cluain Tarbh* – the Meadow of the Bull.

The Clontarf Road is Clontarf's longest roadway. It was once known as Strand Road or Strand Street and parts of it were known by various names – e.g. Whitehall Terrace, Cabra Villas, etc – until the umbrella Clontarf Road name was adopted in 1929. Commonly referred to as the 'seafront' 'coast' 'front' or even 'tram' road (it marks the old tramline from the city) the swirling road is flanked by a (reclaimed) wide decoratively grassy promenade with a cycle track, a concrete walk and a wall along the edge of the sea, begun in 1938. It escorts us through Clontarf's heartland, as far as Mount Prospect Avenue. The infill of the promenade (with city rubbish, sand, topsoil and seeded with green grass) was begun in the 1930s and finished in 1965.

The familiar landmark 'skew' embankment, 'stone arch' or 'twin/double arched' railway bridge at the start of the Clontarf Road was built by the Great Northern Railway Company in 1843, to facilitate a railway line from Dublin to Drogheda.

The railway line was totally surrounded by water as it crossed the open sea, as Fairview Park was not yet reclaimed – indeed, the railway embankment paved the way for that reclamation. Prior to any of the reclamation that gave us the areas now occupied by Clontarf DART Station, the Clontarf All-Weather playing fields, Westwood sports club and East Point Business Park (a modern business hive), this was a regular place of recreation for Dubliners, being a stretch of sand and shingle emanating from Fairview Strand towards Clontarf. It was commonly known as 'The Strand' and was also a place where lords and ladies promenaded in their stylish carriages, pulled by two, four or even six 'decorated' steeds! Regular citizens came to view and admire their grace and elegance and the general pageantry.

In equal measure, Dublin's wagging tongues caustically criticised the grandeur of the horses and carriages!

Just before the bridge is Clontarf Presbyterian or 'Howth Road' Primary School. It was first opened in 1890. On the opposite side of the road, just past the bridge, is Clontarf DART Station and alongside it, the Clontarf All-Weather football pitches, complete with a ball alley.

As we progress along the seafront, we have the sea with all its mysteries, moods and manifestations as our constant companion. Indeed, the promenade from Clontarf to Sutton, finally completed in 1965, acts as a barrier to incursions by the sea. As a warning however, that one day it could reclaim its own, the sea, when in the mood, sends its dashing briny waves over the sea wall, to flood the Clontarf Road and beyond.

We are now heading for the heartland of Clontarf, an area that, over the years, transformed from being a rural heartland with some residential hamlets, big houses, manors and villas to become a very desirable upper middle-class residential area.

On our right, at the junction of the Alfie Byrne Road with the Clontarf Road, is *The Sails*, a wind sculpture by Éamonn O'Doherty, erected in the Dublin millennium year of 1988. It represents the vibrancy of the North Bay expanse.

Further along the Alfie Byrne Road, on the right, is the Clasac Ceoltas Regional Resource Centre. Opened in 2008 with a 340-seat theatre it is operated by Comhaltas Ceoltóirí Éireann and promotes Irish culture. Just before the road joins the East Wall Road is the Count John McCormack (1884–1945) Bridge, complete with plaque. The bridge dates from 1983, the plaque from 2018.

The Alfie Byrne Road recalls Alfie Byrne (1882-1956), who was born at Lower Oriel Street and also lived at 63 North Strand Road. He has the distinction of serving as an MP with the old Irish Parliamentary Party at Westminster and as a TD in Dáil Éireann. He was also a senator for a time but, he is best remembered as a Dublin Corporation councillor, going about his business on a bicycle. He was elected Lord Mayor of Dublin a record ten times. He was known as 'the children's Lord Mayor' as he regularly distributed lollipops to children and constantly fought for children's rights. Over the years, he fought twenty-seven elections and lost only once. He represented various North Dublin constituencies as a TD. Alfie's son, Patrick Byrne, was TD for North East Dublin from 1956 to 1969.

On the Howth side of the Alfie Byrne Road the Hollybrook river enters the sea at a spot known as Brookside, from its source at Wad in Ballymun. It was originally known as the Wad or Wadda river. On the opposite side of the road is Strandville Avenue East, named after a villa at that spot. Strandville Avenue East was originally a laneway, running from Clontarf Railway Station on the Howth Road to the sea, just past the Alfie Byrne Road. It is at this spot that the Hollybrook river enters the sea.

Clontarf Royal Charter School once stood on the city side of Strandville Avenue. It was one of about forty such schools set up in Ireland by the Incorporated Society for Promoting Protestant schools in Ireland, which were unashamedly aimed at converting Catholic children to Protestantism. The school opened in 1749, accommodating one hundred boys and was finally suppressed and closed by the authorities in 1831, having failed in several ways. It was a landmark building in Clontarf, Palladian in style with a dome, colonnade and cupola. It became a bathing establishment called Kings Court House, which was shut down for being 'an outrage to public decency'! Later it, or a house on its site, came to be known as 'Informer's House' especially in Fenian times. The grounds of the charter school were used by Mountjoy School as playing fields up to 1948 – before Mountjoy became part of Mount Temple Comprehensive School. The site is now occupied by residential houses.

On the other side of Strandville Avenue is Clontarf Garda Station. Georgian in style, it opened in 1909, as stated earlier. It replaced barracks at Fairview Strand and on the Clontarf Road – today's Holy Faith Convent.

We pass Hollybrook Road (named after the Hollybrook river) and further along on the left, a building known as Anna Cottage, built in 1750, served as Clontarf Post Office from 1890–1963. The post office moved to number 64 Clontarf Road and finally closed down permanently in January 2017.

Next, on the left, is St Lawrence Road which recalls the family in Howth Castle of that name, who once had land here. At number 122 is a plaque to statesman, Arthur Griffith, who lived here from 1911 until his death in 1922.

After that is Seaview Avenue North and The Court just before Warrenpoint, a block of houses guarded by two sphinxes. Then comes Haddon Road with Haddon Court, which incorporates the old Presbyterian Manse House. The name Haddon recalls Haddon Hall in Derbyshire in England, an estate owned by the Vernons of Clontarf Castle.

Soon we reach Castle Avenue on our left. Named after Clontarf Castle and the oldest road in the vicinity, it joins the Clontarf Road with the Howth Road at Killester. Ascending Castle Avenue, we pass on the right, the Brian Boru Memorial Well, dating from 1850. This was a tourist gimmick at the time and it is certain that the acclaimed monarch never wet his lips from the water of the well that once existed at this spot!

Following that, we reach Clontarf Castle Hotel, on the left, where there has been a castle since 1172. The first castle was built by Adam De Phepoe, when he was granted the lands of Clontarf by the Norman lord of the then province of Mide (Meath), Hugh de Lacy (d.1186), which included Dublin. The castle was occupied, at various times, by the Knights Templars and the Knights Hospitallers. It came into the hands of the Vernon family during Cromwell's time in Ireland (1649-50) and they remained in the castle for over three hundred years. The present castle is a striking, noble construction built in a mixture of styles – Gothic, Norman and Tudor – to reflect its chequered history. Nowadays it is run as a luxury hotel by a board of directors.

Turning right after Clontarf Castle, we find ourselves on Seafield Road (West) named after the old Seafield House, which stood at the seafront end of that road. Soon after, on the right on Seafield Road, we have in one block, Belgrove National Schools and Clontarf GAA Club's clubhouse. Belgrove House was the original building on this site and the old Clontarf National Boys and Girls Schools moved to this building from Vernon Avenue in 1940. The schools became, officially, St John the Baptist Schools but, have always been colloquially known as Belgrove Schools.

When the schools moved to new premises each side of Belgrove House, Clontarf GAA Club acquired the building and opened their first clubhouse there (Áras Chluain Tarbh) in 1998. The club originated as the Brian Boru Hurling Club, founded at 23 North Strand Road in 1887. A then member, Pat Tobin, was general secretary of the GAA from 1891–1894. The club disbanded and reformed in Clontarf in 1919. The name changed to Clontarf GAA Club in the 1950–51 season.

Two men and six women club members have won senior All-Ireland football medals with Dublin. The men are Jim Ronayne and Jack McCaffrey and, the women are Sarah Fagan, Kate Fitzgibbon, Siobhan Killeen, Sarah McCaffrey, Katie Murray and Caoimhe O'Connor. The first director general of the GAA, Seán Ó Síocháin (1914-1997) was a club member and club president for many years.

Just past Belgrove Boys School is Vernon Court, where Cork-born Lieutenant Colonel Richard (Dick) Bunworth lived. He was the commanding officer of the 33rd infantry Brigade on United Nations peacekeeping duties in The Congo when nine of his unit were killed, following an ambush by Baluba tribesmen in November 1960 at Albertville in Katanga.

Further along (on Seafield Road East), on our left, is Seafield Avenue and here, on the right, in a private secluded setting, is the Church of Ireland-run Green Lanes Primary School. It was opened in 1952 and replaced the old school, which stood since 1854 on Seafield Road (West), opposite today's Belgrove Boys School.

Close by, on the left, was another Clontarf landmark, the Hibernian Marine School – "the nursery for the support, education and training of the orphans and children of marines". The school, a magnificent building, was opened in 1904 and became part of the social and cultural life of the Clontarf region. It eventually became part of Mount Temple Comprehensive School and the building was demolished in 1972. The Seacourt housing estate now stands on the site.

Returning now to Castle Avenue, just north of Clontarf Castle, is the premises shared by Clontarf Rugby and Cricket clubs, both of which were founded in 1876. The cricket club has been the venue for numerous international matches since 1964.

Further along, on the right, on Blackheath Grove is Clontarf Hospital, officially opened in June 2010. It was first established here in June 1941, as the Incorporated Orthopaedic Hospital of Ireland, which had three earlier homes. It was originally based at Usher's Island on the Quays from 1876, until it moved, in 1883, to bigger premises on Great Brunswick Street, now Pearse Street. It moved again, in 1902, to 22 Upper Merrion Street, from where it came to Clontarf. The original building (which has been incorporated into today's hospital) was the home of the Black family from whom the Blackheath name (Avenue, Court, Drive, Gardens, Grove and Park) are derived. The Irish Wheelchair Association has its home on Blackheath Drive since 1965.

Before we leave the Castle Avenue area, let us visit Killester, which lies at the northern end of that Avenue. Killester is a village area, mostly a residential suburb. It is bounded, in the main, by the Howth Road, the Malahide Road, Collins Avenue and Brookwood Avenue. Killester got its name either from the ancient *Quillastra* or *Cill Easra* – Easra's church or even, Lasera's church.

Prominent in Killester are the 289 cottaged, bungalow-type houses built by the Irish Sailors and Soldiers Land Trust in the 1920-23 period as a Garden Village under the Homes Fit for Heroes scheme. These were for returning Irish soldiers who served in World War I. The houses helped to transform Killester from being a rural village into a city suburb. In the main, the Garden Village consists of Abbey Field, Middle Third and the Demesne. A new railway station was opened in 1923 in Killester, just off today's Collins Avenue, to service the new community. In that year, 1923, a private omnibus company called Contemptible went into competition with the train service. The name was taken from 'The Old Contemptibles', the proud nickname of soldiers who had served since World War I began. The original railway station opened in October 1845 but closed two years later. Since 1984, Killester station is served by the DART system.

A landmark building in the Garden Village, Killester is the former British Legion Hall at Middle Third. It was built in 1932 and is now in private ownership. It replaced an ex-servicemen's hall that was destroyed in 1928.

Nearby, on Haddon Park, are the premises of Killester-Donnycarney Football Club. The club was formed in 2018 with the merger of Killester United and Donnycarney FC.

A very famous house in Killester is the 18th century Furry Park House on the right, on the Howth Road, just past Killester Village as you travel towards Raheny. It is now incorporated into the Furry Park Court residential scheme. The house was built in the 1730s, as a manor house in the early Georgian mode and was of considerable architectural style. The edifice gained an illustrious history as it became associated with notable people who were involved in the political and cultural fields of activity in Ireland. This was especially true in the 1920s, when Crompton and Moya Llewellyn occupied the house. One of these notable people was General Michael Collins, the bold and courageous freedom fighter and a central figure in Ireland's fight for independence. Moya, who often strolled in St Anne's Park in conversation with Collins, wrote articles under the pen name 'Delta'.

Collins had many connections with the area. We have already referenced his use of the tunnels beneath the Casino for gunfire practice. He regularly had consultations in the home of Thomas Gay on Haddon Road in Clontarf. There he met his detective spies in Dublin Castle, Ned Broy, Joe Kavanagh, David Nelligan and James McNamara and discussed with them the latest intelligence they supplied to him from inside British headquarters in Dublin Castle and, the IRA/Republican watching 'G' Division of the DMP at Brunswick Street (now Pearse Street) Police Station. In his little memoir, *Old Clontarf*, Haddon Road-born Canon FWR Knowles records, as a boy, Mr Gay's wife bringing him into the house, where he met Collins, Arthur Griffith and Éamon de Valera.

Furry Park House is recalled locally in Furry Park and Furry Park Road. Michael Collins is remembered by Collins Avenue, which joins the Howth Road (with extensions) to Glasnevin and Finglas and by a host of other street, road and place names in Dublin, including Collins Court, Collins Drive, Collins Green, Collins Park, Collins Place, Collins Row, Collinstown Crescent, Collinstown Grove and Collinswood. There is a bust of Collins in Merrion Square and a memorial plaque at Pearse Street Garda Station.

Collins Barracks on Benburb Street also recalls him – the barracks is now part of the National Museum of Ireland.

In his native County Cork, there are many Collins memorials. The Collins Barracks complex stands in Cork City and the Imperial Hotel in the city has a specially named Collins Suite, as well as a fine portrait of Collins. There is a Collins memorial monument outside Macroom while Clonakilty has the Collins Memorial Centre and a full-size Collins statue. And the site at Béal na Bláth where he lost his life has been turned into a 'shrine', with an annual commemoration ceremony.

The entrance to another famous house in Killester, Killester House, was just across the Howth Road from Furry Park House. It was the residence of Sir William Gleadowe Newcomen, a Royal Canal director and a member of the old Irish House of Parliament. In his time, Killester was often referred to as 'The seat of Lord Newcomen'. He voted for the Act of Union in December 1800. The house fell into a state of paltriness and was burned to total decimation in 1919. No trace of the building remains today. Its site and fifty acres of ground were built upon in the Homes Fit for Heroes scheme mentioned above.

Two notable road names in Killester are Dunluce and Dunseverick. Dunluce Road is named after the 14th century Dunluce Castle, near Bushmills in County Antrim. The castle is mainly associated with the McDonnell clan. Dunseverick Road recalls Dunseverick Castle near Ballycastle, County Antrim. The castle has a lengthy history, including a visit there (or to the original stone fort on the site) by Saint Patrick in the fifth century.

Killester (St Brigid's) Boys National School is situated on the Howth Road at its junction with Sybil Hill Road. It was opened in 1974. St Brigid's Girls National School is on Saint Brigid's Road since 1928. Opposite it is an old Holy Faith convent. St Mary's Girls Secondary School, which opened in 1967 is located nearby on Brookwood Meadows. Both schools are run under the auspices of the Holy Faith sisters, who have been involved in education here since 1928. Killester Post Office, once located on Collins Avenue, now operates within the local Supervalu complex on the Howth Road.

Now we return to the Clontarf Road and immediately on our left is Scoil Uí Chonaill GAA Club. O'Connell schools leased playing fields at this spot from 1931. In 1950, they bought land here and formally established the club (intimately known as 'Scoil'). The club have won the Dublin senior football championship on two occasions – 1983 and 1986. Robbie Kelleher, the stylish cornerback on Kevin Heffernan's very successful Dublin team of the 1970s is the only club member holding all-Ireland senior football medals.

Across the road, at number 123, is The Baths at Clontarf, open-sea swimming pool and restaurant opened in March 2018. This is on the site of the old Clontarf Baths, originally built in 1880 and beloved of many people, especially swimmers. The design of the baths was based on that of sea baths constructed at Leamington Spa in Warwickshire in England, in 1833. It was first known as Clontarf Baths and Assembly Rooms and it served the locality as a unique amenity until closing in 1996.

The baths facilities were used by many swimming clubs over the years but was especially associated with Clontarf Swimming Club, founded in 1884, whose members set records in Irish swimming and water polo that may never be matched. The club produced a string of international water polo players, including a number of Irish team captains. Two club players, JS Brady and S Barrett, were on the first Irish water polo team to take part in an Olympic Games – in Paris in 1924. Michael Kelly became Ireland's first ever representative in the European Swimming Championships in Budapest, in 1956. The famous annual and much-loved Liffey Swim Race was the brainchild of Bernard Fagan, a member of Clontarf Swimming Club and it first took place on 22 July 1919. The club's star of stars was RN (Richie) Case. In one year, 1936, he won all of the Irish freestyle men's championships. At his peak, he had no serious rival in Irish swimming and at one time or another, he held every Irish men's swimming record.

Next, on the left, is Oulten Road, called after the Oultens, the last family to live in Clontarf Castle. It was first called Beechfield Laneway. Clontarf Lawn Tennis Club has its home here since 1931 but has existed elsewhere in the locality since 1887.

Off Oulten Road, on Kincora Park, we find the Irish Embassy of the Republic of Cuba.

Just before we reach Vernon Avenue, on the left, is the Holy Faith Convent, founded in 1890. From 1846 until 1888, this was a Royal Irish Constabulary (RIC) police barracks. Behind the convent is the Holy Faith Convent Secondary School, opened by the Holy Faith sisters in 1890 as the Convent of Our Lady, Star of the Sea (*Réalt na Mara*). For many years, it had a junior boys and girls school attached. Four well-known figures attended that Junior School – TV personality and PR/communications guru, Bunny Carr, Superquinn 'tycoon' Fergal Quinn, later a senator and we already mentioned FX Martin and George Colley.

The site on which the school stands was originally occupied by a settlement of fishermen, in The Sheds village of popular and romantic memory. The Sheds contained wooden fabrics, often referred to as 'penthouses' or 'stages', erected by the fishermen as residences and, for the curing of fish.

Despite having an appealing and picturesque appearance, the habitations were dilapidated as well as appallingly unsanitary and unhygienic. The Sheds village was directly on the shoreline – there was no Clontarf Road or promenade then – mainly between today's Belgrove Road (named from Belgrove House) and Vernon Avenue.

Most of The Sheds inhabitants were moved slightly inland, to make way for the St John the Baptist church building. The new site, just off Vernon Avenue, was known as Snugboro or 'The Burrow', today's St Joseph's Square. Snugboro itself was described as having 'rookeries' as residences, which were 'almost reprehensible in their sanitary arrangements'. With Clontarf Castle literally a stone's throw away, we can see that back then the upstairs/downstairs socio-economic mix in society was well established.

Today's Clontarf Village stands at the junction of Vernon Avenue with the Clontarf Road. Vernon comes from the Vernon family, who owned Clontarf Castle and lands and, effectively 'ruled' the Clontarf area for so long.

Deceptively long, Vernon Avenue winds its way northwards, taking a major kink to the left when it meets Sybil Hill Road, to meet Castle Avenue, close to the Howth Road. At its seafront end, the brothers William Joseph and Arthur Shields lived at number twelve. Both attended the local Green Lanes Church of Ireland Primary School and became actors in the Abbey Theatre. Will (1888–1961), better known as Barry Fitzgerald, won an Oscar for his role in the film *Going my Way* in 1945, which starred Bing Crosby. Arthur (1896-1970) joined the Irish Volunteers and saw action in the GPO during the 1916 Rising. At that time, he had an address at 3 Seafield Road, Clontarf. Like his brother he too had considerable success as an actor on TV, stage and cinema. The two brothers are buried together in Deansgrange Cemetery, Deansgrange, Co. Dublin.

At the Castle Avenue end of Vernon Avenue, we find the Central Remedial Clinic (CRC). It was first founded in Pembroke Street, in the city centre, in 1951 by Lady Valerie Goulding and Miss Kathleen O'Rourke. It came into being as an after-care service for victims crippled by poliomyelitis after the great polio epidemic, which struck Ireland in the 1940s and 1950s. Today's specially designed clinic was officially opened by the then President of Ireland, Éamon de Valera, in October 1968. Over the years the clinic has achieved international recognition for its work in medical rehabilitation and the uniqueness of its integrated services.

Many people will also recall Verville Retreat, a private psychiatric hospital that stood close to the CRC. It operated as a hospital from 1857 until it was incorporated into the Verville Court apartments. Despite a cold and severe appearance from the outside, it was a very homely and relaxed residence for its patients. Its windows had the Queen Anne style of architecture.

Sybil Hill Road, off Vernon Avenue, recalls the name of a house and lands in the area, which eventually became part of St Anne's Park. On our right on Sybil Hill Road, close to the Howth Road, is St Paul's College, which was first founded in 1950 in Sybil Hill House (an elegant, late-Georgian building still standing) by the Vincentian order of priests. Today's school was opened in 1952 and has had extensions over the years. For many years, it had a preparatory school attached. From 1973 it had a swimming pool, which was used and very much appreciated by the local community. The site of the pool is now occupied by the Ardilaun Court complex of apartments.

The Grove teenage disco holds memories dear to the hearts of many Clontarf folk and Dubliners generally. The Grove originated in Belgrove FC clubhouse off Mount Prospect Avenue (hence the name), when the club set up there in 1958. A fire, in 1975, caused the Grove to move to St Paul's College. The Grove will always be associated with DJ Cecil Nolan, who spun the discs there for 30 years. The Grove closed in 1997 but reunions are held annually. Cecil died in November 2020, at the age of eighty-one. The Belgrove Park complex of apartments now stand on the site of Belgrove FC and the original Grove.

Across from St Paul's College is the Sacred Heart Nursing Home. It was opened in 1971 and is run by the Little Sisters of the Poor.

Now we return to the seafront and Clontarf Road and, on our right, among the familiar seaside shelters along the Clontarf promenade and close to the 'green lump' that is the pumping station opposite The Sheds public house, is a giant Maoi sculpture, which puzzles many. The sculpture was actually presented to the city of Dublin in 2004, by the government of Chile as a thank you for the major part played by Irishman, Ambrosio Higgins (1720-1801) and later his son, Bernardo O'Higgins (1778–1842) in Chile's gaining of independence from Spain in 1817/18. Ambrosio became Viceroy of Peru in 1795 and Bernardo became virtual dictator of Peru from 1817-1823. The Maoi sculpture comes from Easter Island, which lies 6,000 miles west of Chile. The concrete shelters themselves were put in place in the 1950s to facilitate swimmers.

On our left are Vernon Court and Fortview Avenue (named after the Pigeon House Fort) and soon we come to Clontarf bus garage. This was Clontarf's old tramshed or stable – it was given a modern brick frontage in the 1970s. Beside the bus garage is Clontarf's oldest club, Clontarf Yacht and Boat club. It has proudly flown the red-and-blue flag of Clontarf on its Belvedere headquarters since 1 March 1875.

Next, we come to the very historic Conquer Hill area, which many claim to be the true heart of Clontarf. The name 'conquer' may be derived from *coinicéar* (a rabbit warren) or *ceanncor* (the heron's head). The old Conquer Hill village, which survived into the 1950s, comprised of cabins erected in meandering rows with carefree orientation, which were locally named 'The Puzzle' and locals rejoiced in the name, Puzzlers!

Conquer Hill covers an area once known as Danespark. It is often erroneously stated that Conquer Hill acquired that name from the final routing or conquest of the Danes at this spot at the epic 1014 Battle of Clontarf. However, this is not true as, despite the name, it is almost certain that none of the battle action took place in the area we know as Clontarf today! However, we must remember that the whole area, from the present Clontarf down to the Tolka river, was then all known as Clontarf.

The Battle of Clontarf is one of the most famous battles – events, even – ever in Irish history. It was fought on 23 April 1014 and, in the main, pitched the forces of the Irish warrior king, Brian Boru against the Vikings. However, there were Irishmen and Vikings fighting on both sides, most notably Mailmora, the King of Leinster, who aligned his forces with the Vikings against Brian Boru. Most of the battle was fought between the Liffey and Tolka rivers, in the area between today's Phibsborough/Glasnevin/Drumcondra and the then tiny city of Dublin. Brian's forces won a decisive victory and terminated the last attempt by the Vikings to conquer Ireland. It was a battle that really mattered and indeed, changed the course of Irish history. If victory had gone the other way, we could ask, would the 1916 Easter Rising have occurred?

We have earlier stated that the name Clontarf is involved because final victory was gained at the River Tolka estuary, then known as the fishing weir of Clontarf. Many street and road names in the general locality recall this era. Danescourt and Danesfort in Clontarf recall the invaders. Brian Boru Avenue and Street in Clontarf and, Brian Road in Marino are named directly after the renowned king. All the Kincoras in Clontarf recall the monarch's headquarters at Killaloe in County Clare. Morrough Terrace in Marino recalls Brian's son, as Turlough Parade in Marino, along with Turlough Gardens off Phillipsburg Avenue in Fairview, commemorate his grandson, Turlough. Along the seafront, between the Alfie Byrne Road and the Bull Wall, are six information boards detailing all aspects of the 1014 battle and other items of local history and interest. They were put in place in 2014, to mark the thousandth anniversary of the Battle.

Daniel 'The Liberator' O'Connell (1775-1847) announced that 1843 was going to be Repeal Year – repeal of the 1800 Act of Union. His modus operandi was 'agitate, agitate, agitate' and achieve goals by constitutional means. His big weapon of persuasion was the holding of Monster Meetings. In the first nine weeks of 1843, he addressed thirty-eight of these meetings around the country. The largest and last was planned for a 9-acre site at Conquer Hill, at 2pm on Sunday, 8 October 1843.

Conquer Hill was chosen for historic reasons, as it was mistakenly (as already stated) believed to be the final place of conquest over the Vikings at the Battle of Clontarf in 1014. However, O'Connell's arch enemy, the British Prime Minister, Robert Peel banned the meeting. O'Connell, fearing bloodshed, called it off. The large platform and canvas pavilions erected at Conquer Hill were dismantled. The government put on a show of force all the way from the city to Clontarf, with soldiers-infantry and cavalry with ample artillery-and regular police 'buzzing everywhere'. It became the monster meeting that never was and the whole affair was a great disappointment to the half a million people expected to attend and indeed, to the Irish people generally. It came to be called O'Connell's bluff and it overshadowed his early achievement of gaining Catholic Emancipation. From then on O'Connell's power began to wane.

Between Seafield Road (East) and Mount Prospect Avenue (once called Black Bush Lane and also Heronstown Road) and bounded from the sea by part of the Clontarf Road is Dollymount. It is named after an old house of that name where Dollymount Avenue is today.

All of Dollymount is in the local area once known as Blackbush and also as Heronstown. Once a little village, some of its older cabins and houses were occupied until about 1950 but it has long been absorbed into the greater Clontarf area. The growth of the Bull Island gave Dollymount its extensive beach of smooth sands.

The Mount Prospect name is derived from that of a house that once stood on the site where Immaculate Conception House – the home, since 1873, of the Sisters of Charity of St Vincent de Paul – stands today.

Clontarf, which, in the not-too-distant past had four post offices now has just one. It is situated at Nolan's supermarket on Vernon Avenue. Two of the original four were on the Clontarf Road. One was close to the old St Anthony's Church, the other opposite Bull Bridge. There was a post office at the seafront end of Vernon Avenue and the fourth was on St Gabriel's Road.

At Mount Prospect Avenue, we reach St Anne's Park. Dublin City Council has about eighty parks under its administration but, because of its special appeal, its serene, placid presence, its suitability for so many activities, its abundance of wildlife and its follies, St Anne's is surely the showpiece. It is the 'Great Green Lung' of the north-eastern city and is a central ingredient to the very character of the Clontarf/Raheny area. It supplements the two other great natural amenities in the area: Bull Island and the sea itself. The seaward end of Mount Prospect Avenue is a lovely example of 'Rus in Urbe' – a country setting in the city with the sea and Bull Island thrown in as extras.

St Anne's was originally developed as a beautiful 19th-century estate, complete with luxury mansion. The money for the development of the estate came from that accumulated by the Guinness family and their famous St James's Gate brewery. Arthur Guinness first purchased the brewery in 1759. By 1810, it was Dublin's biggest brewery. By 1835 it was Ireland's biggest and by 1886, the biggest in the world. As a brand name, Guinness is one of the most successful in the world. It is recognised and appreciated around the globe, especially for its distinctive creamy head (due to its nitrogen mix) and available in just about every country.

Arthur Guinness can rightly claim the title of Ireland's most successful inventor and his invention is one of the most popular beverages available anywhere. The first of the Guinness' came to Clontarf in 1835 but the St Anne's estate, originally laid out by Benjamin Lee Guinness (1798-1868), became mainly associated with Lord and Lady Ardilaun.

Lord Ardilaun, Arthur Guinness the fourth (1840-1915), was actually born at St Anne's. He was to marry Lady Olivia White, the daughter of the Earl of Bantry and to represent Dublin as an MP at Westminster in 1868-69 and 1870-80. Then, as Lord Ardilaun, he had a seat in the House of Lords. By 1870, with the acquisition of local holdings, St Anne's expanded to 496 acres and Lord and Lady (they had no offspring) occupied the demesne and its Italianate, Palazzo-style mansion.

The name, St Anne's comes from St Ann's Well (no 'e' – it was added later) beside the pond at James Larkin Road and adopted as the estate's name by Benjamin Lee Guinness in 1837. We have little or no information about the well but, like most holy wells, it probably dates back to pre-Christian times and may have been associated with the Celtic goddess, Anu.

The bed of St Anne's Well is in a grotto setting, housed under a rustic cupola of stones and masonry. The well has been dry for over one hundred years and efforts to find the original source or spring from which the well received its waters have proved fruitless. However, we do know that the well was a place of pilgrimage up to the close of the 19th century and a 'pattern' day was held annually.

In 1938, the then Dublin Corporation (now Dublin City Council) acquired 450 acres of the domain and, in time, divided it into two parts. Close to half of the estate (220 acres) was allocated to serve as a public park – the largest municipal park in Dublin City. The rest of the estate provided playing fields, schools and housing. The housing gave us the St Anne's housing estate in Raheny, bounded by the Howth Road, All Saints Road and Watermill Road. During World War II, much of the park was turned into allotments, to grow crops. The park has been open to the public since 1975.

While utilising St Anne's Park and its treasured woodlands (including its sixteen acre Millennium Arboretum with a thousand species of trees), people can recall 'olden' times with the Red Stables (the horse's hotel!) and the follies. Lord Ardilaun commissioned the building of the Red Stables in 1885. The buildings are in Victorian Sussex style with a courtyard format. The stables, opened to the public in June 2006, are named after the Portmarnock red brick from which they are constructed.

The follies, which were the norm in such estates in the 18th and 19th centuries, were created for decorative purposes, commemorative reasons and indeed, 'show off' or 'vanity'! They include the artificial lake, the fake bridges, towers and tea houses or temples. The follies were put in place, over the years, by Benjamin Lee Guinness and his son, Lord Ardilaun and, there in the park too, to be admired is the Rose Garden, a living factory of colour and fragrance, a terraced bower of flowers with its masses of rose beds and pergolas. Begun in 1970, the Rose Garden was developed by Clontarf Horticultural Society, in conjunction with Dublin Corporation's Parks Department. It is one of the leading rose gardens in the world and international rose trials have taken place here since 1981.

A lovely attraction in the park is the magnificent tree sculpture, created by Tommy Creggs from the former, hugely imposing Monterey Cypress (*Macrocarpa*) tree that, for long years, marked the north-eastern boundary of the Guinness estate, at the meeting of James Larkin Road and Watermill Road. The 10-metre-tall woodcarving depicts, in wonderful, eye-catching detail, the wildlife and biodiversity in general of St Anne's Park and its close neighbours, the sea and Bull Island. It has become a local landmark in the area and is known as the *Tree of Life*. Notable, alongside it, is a weeping ash tree. Dublin City Council opened Dublin's first urban farm at St Anne's in 2019.

St Anne's Park has had many distinguished visitors over the years. One such was Queen Victoria of Britain, who paid a visit to the Ardilauns during her state visit to Ireland in April 1900. She entered St Anne's by way of an elaborate gate, a little past the seafront end of Mount Prospect Avenue, where Sea Lawn House now stands. This was actually the original entrance to St Anne's and the mansion first faced out over the sea. For the record, the good Queen left St Anne's via today's main avenue and her entourage took the Howth Road back into the city.

There is a bronze statue of Lord Ardilaun in St Stephen's Green (West). It is the work of Sir Thomas Farrell and dates from 1892. A statue of Lord Ardilaun's father, Sir Benjamin Lee Guinness by John Henry Foley, dating from 1875, stands at St Patrick's Cathedral, Patrick Street.

Clontarf may have mourned the loss of its 'offspring', Clontarf Island which, as we have already recorded, was washed away in the great storm of 9 October 1844 but, it had a ready-made replacement in the fast-accumulating sandbank that came to be known as the North Bull Island. The island, which is five kilometres long and one kilometres wide, is the most documented and written about of all the islands around our coast. First referred to as 'Sand Island' and 'Green Island', its lies on the right as we progress along the seafront: first the Clontarf Road, then the James Larkin Road (opened in 1949, recalling the great trade union leader) and finally the Dublin Road. Many refer to it as Dublin's 'Desert Isle'. It is uniquely situated seven kilometres from Dublin City Centre.

Strictly speaking, it is no longer an island, as it is connected to the mainland by two access routes. One is the familiar landmark wooden bridge, commonly known as Bull Bridge or the 'Woodener'. It is opposite the seafront end of Kincora Road and originally called Crab Lake Bridge, as it crosses the creek once named Crab Lake. The water area between the island and the mainland has also been known as Raheny Lake. It is now called the lagoon. Bull Bridge was first built, in the autumn of 1819, as a pedestrian bridge and to facilitate the building of the North Bull Wall. The bridge was rebuilt in 1906/1907.

The island can also be reached via the Causeway Road: essentially an extension of Watermill Road. It escorts us across the ever-diminishing lagoon separating Bull Island from the mainland. The road was built amid great controversy in 1964. Many believe – and still believe – that a bridge similar to Bull Bridge would have been a better option, as a safety valve to allow the tide to circulate freely around the entire island and avoid the silting that is now so obvious and ongoing. Since 2020, part of the Causeway Road has formed the Bull Island greenway facility.

In all, the island covers 1500 hectares (3700 acres) and is constantly growing by accretion. Essentially it is a low-lying sand spit running parallel to the shore from Bull Bridge to Sutton Strand. It has the renowned and extensive Dollymount Strand on its east (sea) side.

The growth of Bull Island began with the construction of the original South Bull Wall (known as 'The Piles') in 1715 and finished in 1730. Poolbeg Lighthouse, at the end of the South Wall, was in place in 1768 and today's wall completed in 1795. This, together with the building of the North Bull

Wall and the particular configuration of currents in Dublin Bay, led to the rapid growth of Bull Island as sedimentation (essentially sand and mud) accumulated on the northern side of the wall, leading to the ongoing development and growth of the island.

The South Wall, stretching from Ringsend to today's Poolbeg Lighthouse was the first real attempt to overcome the problem known as the bar of Dublin Port. This bar is essentially an underwater sandbank, stretching from Sandymount Strand, across the Liffey Estuary to Bull Island. Over many years, the bar caused much damage to and loss of ships entering and leaving Dublin Port. As ships began to be built bigger and heavier, they simply could not navigate Dublin Port unless it was dredged. It was hoped that the South Wall would create a greater depth in the harbour but, it only partially worked.

In 1776, an English engineer named William Chapman came up with the idea of building a sea wall from the Clontarf shore to the Spit Buoy – today's North Bull Lighthouse. The plan was to forcibly remove the bar by channelling as great a volume of water as possible in between the two walls, so that the ebbing tide would become a natural scour and literally wash away the bar. The Ballast Board members supported Chapman's idea but, it was 1804 before there was final agreement on the proposal.

Captain William Bligh (1754–1817) visited Dublin in 1800, as a captain of the Royal Navy at the request of the Admiralty. Bligh, of 'Mutiny on the Bounty' fame (which occurred in 1789), was a skilful marine surveyor and hydrographer and he was asked to survey the Liffey Estuary and Dublin Bay. He produced a very fine map of Dublin Bay, which he drew up in December 1800. On this map, he was the first to record the existence of Bull Island. He represents it as a small 'bump' of dry land just offshore from Manresa House. He made an alternative suggestion for a sea wall but his proposal was rejected.

In 1819, the building of what came to be known as the Great North Wall began and was finally finished in 1824, leading to the ongoing development and growth of the Bull Island. Built to improve and preserve the port of Dublin and to help keep the harbour silt free, the great dyke that is the North Bull Wall, with the familiar red, wrought-iron lighthouse at its seaward end, is built on a base about twenty-five metres wide. It is 2,750 metres long from shore to lighthouse. For 1,680 metres, it is some seven metres high and remains above water at all tidal stages. The rest of the wall (1070 metres) is known as the 'Half-tide Wall' and is covered by the sea at high tide. The lighthouse is controlled from the Poolbeg Lighthouse. At the seaward end of the 'supra-tidal' part of the wall, is a monument dedicated to Our Blessed Lady, entitled Our Lady of the Port of Dublin or

Realt na Mára. It consists of a tall tripod of solid concrete columns meeting at the top, surmounted by a globe to form a resting place for a bronze statue of the Blessed Virgin, sculpted by Cecil King protectively facing out over the docks area. The statue was unveiled in September 1972. It was originally commissioned by the Dockers Society.

Bull Island, being isolated from the beginning, naturally lent itself as a wildlife haven and habitat for many species of flora and fauna. It is a nature and wildlife reserve since 1976 and a bird sanctuary since 1931. In 1981, UNESCO declared it Ireland's first biosphere reserve – a place where people connect and interact with nature. All of Dublin Bay was awarded this status in 2015.

This island holds national, European and international designations for its habitat and wildlife, having many protected and endangered species. Its entire ecosystem is of tremendous international interest and importance. The island is a prime amenity area, an ornithologist's paradise and a ready-made educational and study area, with an interpretive centre opened in 1986. The centre was planned as an educational and information centre, aimed at conserving the island's natural resources.

A myriad of birds feed on the island's food rich mudflats, especially ducks, geese and waders. In all a staggering 180 species of birds have been recorded on the island. There can be some 40,000 birds feeding on the mudflats at low tide and they often roost on the salt marsh. Four species of geese travel, in large flocks, from the Arctic area to stay in Ireland for our winter months, namely barnacle geese, brent geese, Greenland white-fronted geese and greylag geese. The brent geese are probably the best known and about 4,000 of them travel annually to Dublin Bay. They can be observed on our route, all along North Dublin Bay and are especially fond of feeding on the Bull Island sloblands. Somewhat charismatic, they are surely the darlings of the Bull!

In the days of yore, when gentlemen sometimes settled their differences with duelling contests, the Bull Island was often the chosen venue – as the old Clontarf Island was previously.

A unique happening on the island was a rifle target shooting contest between Ireland and the USA, held on 29 June 1875.

On the outbreak of World War I, in September 1914, the British army commandeered the island, closed it to the public and practised bayonet trench welfare in the sandhills. Bullets can still be unearthed in the saltmarsh and even the odd piece of barbed wire.

The Bull Wall and indeed, the whole of Bull Island is a panoramic viewing area. Howth, Dublin Port, Dublin Bay, the Dublin and Wicklow Mountains and Clontarf's twin town of Dún Laoghaire can be seen. You can also observe the large ferry, cargo and cruise ships gliding in and out of the port.

Uses of the island and activities engaged in are many and varied. The beach is a facility for sunbathing and picnics as well as facilitating walking, jogging and running. Children can play, paddle and build sandcastles. The sea caters for swimming, bathing, fishing, and sailing. The dune part of the island is a public park but, by its natural character, it is very different from a regular urban park. The developing island, as a scientific working area and an educational workshop, is an invaluable asset and aid to students of many subjects at all levels.

Many enjoy the island simply as a haven of tranquillity and find solace and renewal in its peaceful atmosphere. Writers, poets and artists often retreat to the island and find inspiration in the 'away from everyday life' solitude it presents.

It is home to two golf clubs. The Royal Dublin golf club, originally founded in Grafton Street in 1885, has been on the Bull since 1889. The club has hosted all the major Irish golfing events numerous times over the years. Perhaps the club's most famous member was Christy O'Connor (senior) (1924-2016), who joined the club in 1959 as club professional. Christy, affectionately known as 'himself', lived with his family on Blackheath Park, Clontarf. He was one of Ireland's great sporting ambassadors and brought much acclaim and honour to himself, Royal Dublin Golf Club, Ireland and the game of golf itself. He played Ryder Cup golf on ten occasions

St Anne's golf club – loveliest of homely clubs – has had its home on the Bull Island since it was formed in 1921. Its original clubhouse stood on the site now occupied by the islands interpretive centre.

The island is just over two hundred years old and is still very much in the development phase. It is the only inhabited island in the North Bay, with the coastguard cottages on the left at the end of the Bull Bridge still inhabited.

Two rivers enter the sea close to Watermill Road. On the city side, the Naniken river enters Dublin Bay at the artificial pond in St Anne's Park at Naniken Bridge, on the James Larkin Road. It originates in Beaumont and the Naniken name is adopted from *Abhann na gCian*, which recalls the Cianacht sept or clan that ruled part of North Dublin in Celtic times. Some commentators incorrectly state that the river is named from the larger Nanny river, which flows from Kentstown into the Irish Sea at Laytown in County Meath. Actually, it was once known as the Ballyhoy stream. In fact, it flows under Ballyhoy Bridge on the Howth Road, close to All Saints Road just before it enters St Anne's Park.

On the Howth side of Watermill Road, the Santry river enters the sea under the James Larkin Road at Watermill Bridge. The name 'Santry' is derived from the Norse-Irish word *Skillinglas*. *Skil* or *Skyl* means a boundary and *glas*, a stream, although some sources suggest that it comes from *serstreibh* – the 'old tribe'. The name 'watermill' comes from an old water driven mill that once operated on the Santry river.

Many well-known names, from all walks of life, live in, have lived in or are associated with the Clontarf area. Clontarf always was and is a very desirable area in which to reside: its comfortable and relaxed setting by the sea and its proximity to city centre Dublin being two of its greatest attractions.

In the political field, the well-known republican Fianna Fáil Boland family, already referred to, have long associations with Clontarf. The family or branches of it lived at 15 Marino Crescent; at Lord Charlemont's old mansion in Marino; at Richmond Avenue, Fairview; at 5 Brian Road, Marino; at 102 Howth Road and at Castle Avenue. Kathleen Boland (sister of Gerald, Harry and Ned) lived at a house called St Michael's, opposite the Bull Wall at Dollymount, with her husband, Senator Sean O'Donovan.

The republican Fianna Fáil Colley family also have a long association with Clontarf. George Colley senior, a Fianna Fáil TD and minister set up home at Winstonville House, 62 Malahide Road. Later, the family moved to Mount Prospect Avenue. George (Junior) had two failed attempts to become leader of the Fianna Fáil party.

Arthur Griffith, who founded the Sinn Féin party in 1905, lived at 138 St Lawrence Road from 1911 until his death in 1922.

Thomas Ryder Johnson and his wife, Marie lived at a house they named 'Ralahine' at 49 Mount Prospect Avenue, from 1929 until their deaths. Johnson, the first leader of the Labour Party in Dáil Éireann, served as a TD and senator. A moment of high drama in Dáil Éireann came for Johnson in September 1927 when, had all members been present, he would have been elected President of the Executive Council (equivalent to the current office of An Taoiseach or Prime Minister) to replace WT Cosgrove but infamously and inexplicably, a certain alderman, John Jinks, a TD from Sligo, failed to show up for the Dáil vote and Cosgrave survived, on the casting vote of the chairman. And thus, we have the saying, 'there is a jinx (Jinks) on you!'

Kathleen Clarke, councillor, TD, senator and wife of 1916 leader, Tom Clarke lived for some time in Baymount House at the seafront end of Castle Avenue.

Many and varied are those who served and have served as TDs for the ofttimes rejigged constituency of Dublin North, Dublin North East, Dublin North Central and latterly, Dublin North Bay.

Dublin-born Oscar Trayor and Waterford-born Richard (Dick) Mulcahy both fought in the 1916 Rising, both served as TDs for the Clontarf area and became government ministers. Mulcahy became Commander-in-Chief of the Irish Republican Army and was Michael Collins' right-hand man. He also became leader of the Fine Gael party. Revolutionary Republican, Ernie O'Malley was elected as TD for North Dublin in August 1923. Hardly comrades-in-arms, O'Malley was somewhat bemused to be elected by Mulcahy's surplus votes. Traynor became President of the Football Association of Ireland (FAI) in 1948.

Others to serve the area as TDs included George Birmingham (later a court judge), Richard Bruton (a government minister and one-time challenger for the leadership of the Fine Gael party), Ivor Callely (also a senator for a time), Charles J Haughey (minister and Taoiseach), Sean Haughey (Lord Mayor of Dublin, 1989-90), Celia Lynch, Pat McCartan, Derek McDowell and Eugene Timmons (Lord Mayor of Dublin twice – 1965 to 1967).

A colourful figure on the political scene in Clontarf was Sean 'Dublin Bay' Loftus. A Dublin Corporation councillor for many years, he was a TD for a short period and Lord Mayor of Dublin from 1995-96. He is mostly remembered for his fight against pollution, his campaigning for proper planning permission for Dublin and especially, for leading the fight to prevent an oil refinery in Dublin Bay.

Mayo TD, minister and MEP, Sean Flanagan, who captained the All-Ireland senior football Mayo teams that won the Sam Maguire cup in 1950 and 1951, lived on St Lawrence Road in Clontarf. Wexford TD, Labour Party leader, minister and Tánaiste, Brendan Corish lived in Clontarf during Dáil terms. Fine Gael politicians, Nora Owen and Mary Banotti (sisters) were born in Clontarf. Their mother was a niece of Michael Collins. Nora Owen served as a TD and government minister while Mary Banotti became an MEP and a candidate for the Irish presidency in 1997.

Other Clontarf residents who served terms as Lord Mayor of Dublin were councillors Evelyn Byrne, Gerry Breen and Naoise Murray. And another resident was the illustrious government press secretary, PJ Mara, who served during the years that Charles Haughey was Taoiseach.

In the sporting world, we find many familiar names in Clontarf.

In his playing career, Senator Sean O'Donovan (mentioned above) played midfield on the Dublin hurling team that beat Cork in the 1920 All-Ireland Hurling Final. He is probably the only All-Ireland winning Dublin hurler to have lived in Clontarf – that is, with the exception of his brother-in-law, Harry Boland (also mentioned above), who won an All-Ireland hurling medal as a substitute, when Dublin beat Tipperary in the 1917 hurling final. While living in Clontarf, Harry was chairman of the Dublin County board for a number of years.

Other GAA administrators who lived in Clontarf include Clare-born Dr JJ Stewart, who was GAA president from 1958-61 and Seán Ó Síocháin, who lived on Oulton Road and was GAA General Secretary (a title later changed to Director-General) for 15 years – 1964-1979. Something of an Irish institution, Seán in his time was a footballer, a hurler, a ballad singer, a broadcaster as well as a GAA administrator.

Legendary Clare hurler Jimmy Smith lived in Clontarf and worked as an executive officer at Croke Park. Senior All-Ireland Gaelic football winners with Dublin, Tony Hanahoe, Gay O'Driscoll, Robbie Kellegher, Brian Mullins, Jim Ronayne and Noel and Jack McCaffery hail from Clontarf.

Long-time soccer administrator, Noel Kennelly resided in Clontarf. Soccer player, Paddy Ambrose (1928-2002) was born in and lived in Clontarf. An inside or centre forward, he played for Shamrock Rovers and was associated with the club for 25 years. He played five times for the Republic of Ireland soccer team. Donegal-born former Ireland senior soccer goalkeeper, Packie Bonner resides in Clontarf.

In the world of rugby football, fourteen Clontarf Rugby Club players have been capped for Ireland: CP Stuart, SE Polden, HST Cormac, GJ Morgan, DJ Longan, FG Moran, B Mullin, P Lawler, J Fortune, F Ennis, B Jackman, F Dunlea, J Downey and C Healy. And of course, Brian O'Driscoll, Irish captain for a record fifty caps, was born and reared in Clontarf. Brian's father, Frank O'Driscoll played for Ireland but was never awarded a 'full' international cap.

Clontarf Cycling Club, founded in 2012, operates from Clontarf GAA Club on Seafield Road West. The club advocates cycling for a more healthy lifestyle and has organised many fundraising cycling events for charitable causes. Clubman, Cathal Miller has represented Ireland at the Paralympic Games in Beijing, in 2008 and in London in 2012.

Well-known marathon runner, Michael Clohissey is a Clontarfite and so is Ellen Keane, Paralympics gold-medal swimming champion in Tokyo in

2021. Ellen was honoured by An Post, in March 2022, by featuring her on a postage stamp.

In the world of the arts, writer and film director Neil Jordan spent most of his young life living in Clontarf, although he was born in County Sligo. He was educated at Belgrove Boys National School and St Paul's College. Jordan, a rumpled figure with a deceptively easy-going manner, had a number of works featured on BBC radio and on RTÉ radio and television. He won an Oscar, in 1993, with the film, *The Crying Game*, for best original screenplay. His best-known film, *Michael Collins*, got mixed reviews. As a writer, he has won a Somerset Maugham Award, the Guardian Fiction Prize, the Rooney Prize for Irish Literature, the Irish Pen Award and the Henry Group Irish Fiction Award twice.

World renowned singer, mezzo soprano, Bernadette Greavy (1949-2008) was born in Clontarf and attended Holy Faith Convent, Clontarf. Singer, Geraldine Brannigan is Clontarf born. The Brannigans were a very popular family band and Geraldine came fifth in the 1975 Eurovision Song Contest in Stockholm, Sweden, singing a song called *Toi* for Luxembourg. She married Derry-born musician and songwriter, Phil Coulter in 1998.

Actress, May Ollis lived in Clontarf. She played many leading roles on stage, in films and in radio plays. She is best remembered for her role in the RTÉ series, *Tolka Row* and she also made a number of appearances in *Glenroe*.

There was and is, quite a Clontarf representation on our airwaves – mainly RTÉ radio and television. Newsreader of yesteryear, David Timlin was a Clontarfite. Gerry Ryan of RTÉ Radio 2 fame in particular and, his broadcasting daughter, Lottie, were born in Clontarf. Laois-born, RTÉ Gaelic Games correspondent, Mick Dunne resided in Clontarf and his newsreader daughter, Eileen Dunne was born in Clontarf. County Westmeath-born RTÉ newsreader and sports journalist, Colm Murray lived in Clontarf. RTÉ Radio 1 *Liveline* presenter, Joe Duffy lives in Clontarf. Damien O'Meara of the RTÉ sports department is Clontarf born and public relations/communications guru and journalist, Terry Prone hails from Clontarf, as does her radio and television presenter son, Anton Savage. Well-known radio and television presenter, Marty Whelan is also a Clontarf resident, as is journalist, Siobhan O'Connor.

In the business world, some famous names are associated with Clontarf.

For a few years in the 1850s, William Dargan lived in Maryville House (close to St Paul's College, Sybil Hill). He is remembered as Ireland's greatest railway engineer.

Kerry native, Denis Guiney, who owned the famous Clery's store on O'Connell Street, Dublin lived in Clontarf.

Lieutenant General Michael J Costello lived in Clontarf. Tipperary-born Costello, a freedom fighter and later 'regular' army leader, was a founding father of our state, who believed in the proper development of our natural resources. He became general manager of the Irish Sugar Company and played a major role in developing Erin Foods.

Supermarket tycoon, An Post chairman and senator, Fergal Quinn was born and reared on Vernon Avenue, Clontarf. It was there that he started his 'entrepreneurial' career, supplying home grown lettuce to Madden's shop on Vernon Avenue – now Nolan's Shopping Complex.

Lecturer, author, whiskey distiller and international mining magnate, John Teeling was born in and has lived all his life in Clontarf.

Donegal-born entrepreneur, Moya Doherty was reared in Clontarf and attended Belgrove Girls School. She is best known as producer and co-founder of *Riverdance*, the theatrical show of Irish music and dance and, for her time as chairperson of the RTÉ executive board.

Clontarf is and has been home to many writers.

Novelist, short-story writer, dramatist, children's author and fellow of the Royal Society of Literature, Roddy Doyle resides in Clontarf. Best known for his Barrytown trilogy of novels, all of which have been made into films (with *The Commitments* also adapted for stage) he won the Man Booker Prize in 1993 for his brilliant novel, *Paddy Clarke Ha Ha Ha*. He was also awarded the Irish Pen Award in 2009.

Professor Declan Kiberd, writer and scholar, is a leading authority on modern Irish literature in both the English and Irish languages and also on children's literature. Born and reared in Clontarf, Kiberd was taught in Belgrove Boys school by famous writer, John McGahern. Declan has lectured all over the world and produced a vast array of literary work, including articles, books and reviews.

Clontarf resident, Colm Lennon has written extensively on early modern Irish history, especially social, political and religious history. In the Dublin North Bay Area, he is best known for his publications concerning the Clontarf area.

Scottish-born John D Sheridan (1903-1980) lived in Clontarf. A novelist, poet, humourist he was principal teacher at the East Wall National School for many years. He edited the *Irish School Weekly* publication for 25 years. He became head of publications with the Educational Company of Ireland publishing company. He also wrote a regular humorous column for the *Irish Independent* newspaper.

Fiction writer and journalist, Sheila O'Flanagan is a Clontarf resident as is writer, playwright, poet and television presenter, Pat Ingoldsby.

Galway-born poet and scriptwriter, Kevin Faller (1920–1983) also lived in Clontarf and author, Catherine Dunne attended Holy Faith Convent, Clontarf.

One-time compiler of *Dubliner's Diary* – a pioneering social column in Dublin's once biggest selling evening newspaper, *The Evening Press* – Terry O'Sullivan (real name: Tomás O'Faolain) and his writer/journalist daughter, Nuala O'Faolain lived in Clontarf. Terry was originally a teacher and later, a lieutenant in the army and came to live in Clontarf in the mid-1950s.

The Westmeath-born disabled author and poet, Christopher Nolan came to live in Clontarf for some time, in order to be closer to the services offered by the Clontarf-based Central Remedial Clinic. He attended Mount Temple Comprehensive School.

A prolific writer who was on the staff of Belgrove Senior Boys School, Vincent O'Donovan, won the Listowel Writers' Week award four times, with two plays and three short stories. One of his award-winning stories, *A Light Upon the Water*, was adapted and presented on BBC radio as a play. He published two collections of poems: *Fantasia* and *Kittiwake*. His poems betray the keen eye of the acute observer. His writing has a touching, lyrical style with very perceptive, real, descriptive and beautiful images.

The Irish-language writer, Seosamh Mac Grianna, who was born in Rann na Feirste, County Donegal in January 1900 and was trained as a national school teacher, lived in Clontarf for some years in the 1950s. He lived in a little cottage in St Anne's Park called 'Lillyvale', close to the artificial pond, the city side of Watermill Road. Something of a nomad and a wayward character who became somewhat disturbed, Mac Grianna, who had opposed the Free State in the Civil War was, in August 1922, imprisoned for 15 months. In the late 1920s, he gave up teaching to concentrate full time on writing. In the Clontarf locality, he was affectionately known as 'the professor', as 'butts' and, for good measure, as 'Joe Feilini'! Without a regular income, he lived very frugally in Clontarf and was lucky to have some benevolent friends. He penned some of the best-known Irish books including, *Filí gan Iomrá, An Gradh agus an Ghruaim* and *Mo Bhealach*

Féin. He also did a considerable amount of translation work. His brother, Séamus Ó Grianna, was also a prolific novelist and short-story writer in the Irish language.

The outstanding Irish scholar and writer of the 1950s, Donncha Ó Céileachair MA, was on the staff of Belgrove Boys School in Clontarf. His best-known work is the famous book of Irish short stories, *Bullaí Mhártain*, which he compiled with his sister, Síle. From Cúl Aodh in west County Cork, Donnacha was an authority of the Irish dialect from that area. He was highly respected and often consulted by Irish scholars and writers of his era. Indeed, he collaborated with many writers in compiling their works. Notable in this area was his help in compiling De Bhaldraithe's famous *An Doinneanach*, the biography of the famous 'dictionary man', Patrick Dineen. Donnacha would surely have produced many more valuable contributions to Irish literature were he not to die in his early forties, in 1960.

Another Clontarf resident was Professor Niall Ó Dónaill, renowned for his massive Irish-English dictionary, which is generally accepted as the standard Irish-English dictionary.

Fluent Irish writer and speaker, Breandán Mac Raois was a Clontarf resident. He was born in Belfast and was taught Irish by the Christian Brothers. Many will recall his voice from his contributions to umpteen historical radio programmes.

A prolific Irish writer who lived in Clontarf and someone who was well acquainted with Seosamh Mac Grianna (see above) was Proinsias Mac an Bheatha, a fluent Irish speaker whose birthplace was Belfast but, who came to Dublin at a young age. A civil servant who lived in Clontarf for more than 30 years, he wrote eleven books, all in the Irish language. He is perhaps, best remembered for his biography of James Connolly (*Tart na Córa*) and for his once regular column in the (now defunct) *Evening Press* newspaper.

Kiltimagh, Co. Mayo-born Áine Cannon (1907-1999), who was, for many years, principal of Belgrove Girls Senior School in Clontarf, wrote the little primary book, *Dosean Scéal*. She compiled a work on the saints of Ireland as well as a book on the poet, Antoine Ó Raifteiri. She also edited a book of essays by various authors, about the famous 19th-century Archbishop of Tuam, Dr John McHale. She was the only female on the first RTÉ authority (then Teilifís Éireann), from 1960-1965.

In the educational field, Austrian-born (Vienna) Erwin Schrödinger, Nobel laureate and physicist was invited to Ireland by then Taoiseach, Éamon de Valera to establish the Dublin Institute of Advanced Studies. This was duly accomplished in 1940. A plaque on a house on Kincora Road marks Schrödinger' residence from 1939-1956.

Brian Boru

Daniel O'Connell

Lord Ardilaun

Arthur Griffith

Alfie Byrne

Denis Guiney

Michael Collins

Brian Mullins

Ellen Keane

Barry Fitzgerald

St Anne's Rose Garden

St Anne's Well

Sundial Clock,
Furry Park House

Old Tram sheds

Old Belgrove House

Sybil Hill House

The Sails sculpture

Ireland vs USA, Dollymount, 1875

Old Orthopaedic Hospital

CHAPTER SIX

Raheny, Kilbarrack, Bayside, Donaghmede, Sutton (1), Baldoyle

If we ascend Watermill Road, it will lead us to the village of Raheny, formerly Rathenny and in ancient times, Rathena. It owes its name to an ancient rath in the centre of the village, with the local stream (now the Santry river) as a moat. The rath came to be called Ráth Eanna or Eannaigh – Eanna's ringfort. It probably dates back to about 400 BC, when Eanna was a Celtic chieftain. The old graveyard in the middle of today's Raheny Village is on the site of that rath.

One charming aspect of Raheny Village is surely its distinctive, picturesque and quaint crescent of cottages on Station Road, beside the Manhattan public house, just across from the Millennium Clock in its position at the crossroads in the very centre of the village. The eight cottages are colloquially known as the 'Do, Re, Mi' (after the tonic solfa musical scale) or Alms Cottages. They were first built in 1790/91 by Samuel Dick, for workers and servants at his Violet Hill estate and house – later known as Edenmore House and estate on today's Springdale Road. The cottage nearest to The Manhattan pub was once the Raheny Village Post Office. Edenmore House was transformed into St Joseph's Hospital by the Sisters of St Joseph of Chambery, in 1958. It now operates as a rehabilitation hospital for patients of Beaumont Hospital.

Noticeable too, is the Marie Hayes Celtic cross, on a plinth since the year 2000 on the Howth Road beside the old graveyard. The cross was first erected in Raheny village in 1915. Marie Hayes was a young local doctor who died on missionary work in India.

Just past it is Raheny Library, opened in 1972 and built where once there were gardens. The busy library now has its own community garden.

Raheny has had a railway station (on Station Road) since the Great Northern railway line from Dublin to Drogheda was opened in 1844. The old station master's house still stands on the platform of today's DART station, opened in 1994. There is a memorial plaque to Richard Maunsell (1868-1944), distinguished railway engineer, at the station. Maunsell was born in Raheny. Another plaque put in place at the station, in 1994, records the 150th anniversary of the opening of the station and the Dublin-Drogheda railway line in May 1844, by the Lord Lieutenant Earl de Grey. There was a formal gathering for the attendance of Daniel O'Connell MP the previous night.

There are many schools in Raheny. Scoil Íde, Scoil Áine and Scoil Assam primary schools, all established in 1958 are located together on All Saints Drive, while Springdale Church of Ireland Primary School is on the corner of Springdale/Lough Derg Road. The old Church of Ireland school on Station Road is now a Montessori school.

Samuel Dick, in 1786, built a new parish school, which is now a restaurant on part of the graveyard site in the centre of Raheny Village. In 1820, the Sweetman family (of brewing fame) opened the first Catholic primary school in Raheny. Its site on Main Street was later occupied by Reynolds newsagents and now, by a firm of solicitors. The school was replaced, in 1875, by the former primary school hidden behind the old St Assam's Catholic Church, now Raheny Scout Den.

Ard Scoil La Salle, a co-educational secondary school, opened on Raheny Road (previously Grange Road) in 1968. It was built on the site of the old Kilbarrack House and is affectionately called 'the Bella'.

St Michael's House, a special school for people with disabilities, is on Grange Park Grove, with further premises on Station Road. Dick's old charity school built on part of the old graveyard is now a restaurant.

Probably the best known of the Raheny schools are Manor House Secondary School on Watermill Road and St Paul's Boys Secondary School on Sybil Hill Road. Manor House was founded by the Sisters of the Poor Servants of the Mother of God, in 1957. The original mansion on the site was built by the well-known St Lawrence family of Howth Castle.

We have already covered St Paul's College in Chapter Five.

Raheny Garda Station, on Watermill Drive, replaced the old Garda Station on Main Street, which operated from 1922 until the 1960s. This was, in fact, the barracks of the old RIC and itself had replaced an older building on Watermill Road.

Beside the Garda Station are the premises of two sports clubs. The first is Raheny GAA Clubhouse at 2 All Saints Drive. Founded in 1958, the club caters for all age groups, male and female. Six club members have won senior All-Ireland medals in Gaelic football: Alan Larkin, David Hickey, Pat Gogarty, Brian Fenton, Brian Howard and Sean McMahon.

The other premises is that of Raheny United Football Club. The club came into being in 1994, when Raheny Boys FC amalgamated with Dunseedy United. Raheny United's senior women's team won the Women's FAI Cup on three occasions and the national league twice. In 2015, the team merged with Shelbourne FC. 13 Raheny club members have played on the Republic of Ireland women's senior team.

One of Ireland's biggest athletics clubs, Raheny Shamrocks AC, was founded in 1958. Its clubhouse is the old, former, two-roomed primary school behind the old St Assam's Catholic Church. Two of the best-known members have been the brothers, Pat and Dick Hooper, both of whom represented Ireland at Olympic Games. Dick won the Dublin City Marathon on three occasions, including the inaugural race in 1980.

Of fond memory in Raheny is a pony-trotting track that existed straight opposite the entrance to Springdale Road. The pony meetings and events were very popular social occasions and usually held on Sunday afternoons and public holidays. St Vincent's GAA Club replaced the pony-trotting track with their playing fields in 1956 and when St Vincent's moved to their home base in Marino, in 1986, the vacant site was gobbled up by the Ashcroft housing estate.

Other buildings of note in Raheny are Raheny House Nursing Home, the Capuchins Friary, and Grange Woodbine Community Centre. The Raheny House Nursing Home on the Howth Road, opposite All Saints' Church, was once known as 'Ballyhoy' and, when the Barlow family came to live there in 1865, they named it 'The Cottage'. From the late 18th century, the house was occupied by the Seagrange family and later, the D'Arcy family, followed by the Barlows and then, Frank Gallagher. An Garda Síochána bought it in 1986 and transformed it into a nursing home.

Off Station Road at the locally named Capuchin Hill is a Capuchin friary, with St Francis Hospice beside it. They, together with the Belmont housing estate, occupy the site and land of Belmont House. On Station Road, almost directly opposite the entrance to Grange Park estate, is the Grange Woodbine community centre. Dating from 1970, it is a wonderful amenity for the community.

Two famous names from the world of entertainment resided in Raheny. One was the redoubtable comedian, Niall Tóibín (1929-2019) who lived at Avondale Park; the other, singer Joe Cuddy (1940-2020) who resided on Watermill Road. Among the well-known people who attended St Assam's was golfer, Harry Bradshaw.

The whole seafront or coast road northwards from the 'skew' railway bridge in Fairview, was first opened as a tramway and led only as far as Mount Prospect Avenue. Then the opening of the James Larkin Road, in 1949, joined the Clontarf Road with the (old) Howth Road, at a spot known as the 'Whip o'Water' at Blackbanks, where the culverted Blackbanks river enters the sea. The Whip o'Water is a name derived from the noise made by the meeting of the incoming northern and southern tides, until the building of the aforementioned Causeway Road blocked the path of the southern tide.

As the traveller proceeds along towards Howth, the road is called the Howth Road as far as its junction with the Kilbarrack Road. From this point, as far as Sutton Cross, it becomes the Dublin Road. Thence it is again known as the Howth Road until we reach Howth Village, where it becomes Harbour Road.

Now we return to the seafront and after Watermill Road and the Raheny area, we have Kilbarrack on our left. Kilbarrack gets its name from the Irish, *Cill Bearóg* or St Bearóg's church. Some suggest St Berreck (or Barroc) became Cill Beragh now Kilbarrack. Probably the best-known building in the area is Kilbarrack fire station, at the junction of Kilbarrack Road with Station Road. Kilbarrack Post Office is located in Kilbarrack Shopping Centre, on Grange Park View.

Further along is St Benedict's Primary School. Gaelscoil Míde and the North Bay Educate Together primary schools, are on Greendale Road, while Scoil Eoin Primary School is on Thornville Road. The North Bay (National School Project) National School is on Greendale Avenue. The former Greendale school site on Briarfield Villas is now occupied by a Coláiste Dhúlaigh campus and a St Michael's House special school. The clubhouse and grounds of Kilbarrack United FC, formed in 1970, are on Greendale Road while close by is Kilbarrack Health Centre at the Greendale Shopping Complex on Foxfield Crescent.

Kilbarrack DART Station stands at the junction of Briarfield Walk with Briarsfield Road.

Kilbarrack Sailing Club, founded in 1943, was located across from Baldoyle Road on the seafront. Later, it became a scout den but was burnt down and no longer exists.

Naomh Barróg GAA Club is located at Kilbarrack Parade. It was founded in 1974 inspired by Heffo's Dublin breakthrough team of 1974.

Locally born writer, Roddy Doyle, more than anybody else, put Kilbarrack on the map with his writings that are inspired by the area, especially the Barrytown Trilogy. The books are *The Commitments* (1987), *The Snapper* (1990), and *The Van* (1991). Barrytown is Kilbarrack in thin disguise and the trilogy is, in fact, excellent social history.

I often recall a Kilbarrack story related to me some years ago. During World War II, when public transport was only a fraction of normal service, a certain gentleman flew into a rage when he was not permitted to board the last bus leaving Dublin City Centre for Kilbarrack.

"I am one of the Glenns of Kilbarrack," he adamantly protested "and I am going home on this bus."

Rebuking him the bus conductor replied, "Sir, if you were one of the Glens of Antrim, I wouldn't be able to fit you aboard!"

The Kilbarrack Road separates Kilbarrack from Bayside, an area that takes its name from its scenic location along Dublin Bay. Bayside is a compact, residential area with a maze of streets webbing out from Bayside Square. Bayside Post Office is in the heart of Bayside Shopping Centre. Bayside DART station is on Bayside Park, while Bayside primary schools, Scoil Mhuire and Scoil Iosef, are positioned on Verbena Avenue. A hidden gem in Bayside is Bayside Community Orchard. Dating from 2009, it is situated on Bayside Square South. It is a walled garden in the Potager style, containing a variety of flowers, herbs, fruit and vegetables.

Among the well-known people who lived in Bayside are singer Ronan Keating (of Boyzone fame) and Steve Wickham, fiddle player with The Waterboys rock band. Also, snooker player, Fergal O'Brien and marathon runner, Pat Hooper, who was Dublin City Marathon referee for a time.

The part of Grange Road that escorts the traveller from Kilbarrack Road to Baldoyle divides the area known as Donaghmede into two just about equal parts. Donaghmede, which borders both Kilbarrack and Baldoyle, gets its name from *Domhnach Míde* – the church of Míde. It was traditionally an area of big houses (or gentlemen's seats) and farms.

The Donaghmede we are familiar with today began to come into being when the speculators and builders started building today's housing estates. The first of these was Grangemore, begun in 1970. Many more followed, including St Donagh's, the Donahies, Howth View Park, Millbrook, Grange Abbey, Newgrove and The Beeches, all built mainly between 1970 and 1974. Many years later, Clongriffin and Belmayne were added.

Some of these names were the names of big houses. Grange Abbey on Grange Road gave its name to the road itself. The Donahies was a big house of the Queen Anne style of architecture. Grangemore House, with its forty-five acres, stood on the site of Grange Road, where Holy Trinity Church is today and 370 houses. It was the home of former Taoiseach, CJ Haughey, since he moved there from his semi-detached property on the Howth Road in 1959, until he relocated to Abbeyville in Kinsealy, in 1969. The name 'Grange' is quite common in the entire locality, including Grange Abbey and Grange Park (Raheny).

Newgrove House, which stood at the end of the old Grange Road was noted for its ornate gates and public post box set in its boundary wall. Donaghmede House which stood behind Holy Trinity school and The

Beeches, were two other well-known big houses in the area. The Beeches, with the little Donagh stream running alongside, was for many years the home of hawker/businessman, Hector Grey. Scottish-born Grey's real name was Alexander Thomson Scott (1904-1985). The assumed name was that of a famous Australian jockey.

One of the strangest street names in the area – or in any area – is the Hole in the Wall Road, which connects Grange Road with Balgriffin (we will encounter the name again in connection with Burrow and Claremount beaches). A local tale relates that when a certain wealthy gentleman of this locality died, a hole had to be opened in a wall of his house to accommodate the removal of his coffin (thus the hole in the wall). This procedure was necessary because he had sworn never again to enter or leave the house by the front door, as his son had married a Catholic girl! Some suggest that the name actually came from an old tavern. Another theory is that in certain early Dublin property deeds, boundaries were defined from 'the hole in the wall' of one property to the hole in the wall of another property.

Donaghmede's primary schools are junior schools, Scoil Bhríde and St Kevin's and senior schools, Holy Trinity and Scoil Naomh Colmcille. They are all located together on Grange Road. St Francis of Assisi, Belmayne Educate Together primary schools on Belmayne Avenue were established to cater for children from the Belmayne general area.

There are four second-level schools in Donaghmede. Grange Community College and Reachrann (an Irish-speaking school founded in 2001) are on Grange Abbey Road, the Donahies Community College is on Streamville Road while Belmayne Educate Together Secondary School is on Belmayne Avenue.

Donaghmede has two public parks. Donaghmede Park lies in the Grange Abbey area while the larger Fr Collins Park is situated along the Hole in the Wall Road. Fr Collins Park was first established on original farmland and comprised of woodlands, hedgerows, open spaces and playing fields. Today's magnificently developed park was opened in May 2009. It is named after Fr Joe Collins, who was parish priest of the growing young parish area from 1975 to 1979. He was and he is held in the highest esteem for his general work in the Donaghmede community and, especially for his work with the youth and the role that he played in establishing Trinity Gaels GAA Club, whose homebase is at Fr Collins Park. The much-appreciated and much-used Trinity Leisure Centre, complete with swimming pool, is located adjacent to the park.

In Donaghmede Shopping Centre, opened in 1973, we find Donaghmede Post Office and Donaghmede Library. In matters concerning public transport, Donaghmede and Howth Junction DART station is just off the Kilbarrack Road at St Donagh's Road, while the trusty 29A (now the H1) bus service has served Donaghmede for many years.

Donaghmede has many people notable in the field of music. Among them are Keith Duffy and Shane Lynch, members of the former band, Boyzone. Shane's twin sisters, Edel and Keavy, formed part of the B*Witched girls singing group. Singer/songwriter, Damien Dempsey also hails from Donaghmede.

Sporting clubs in Donaghmede include GAA, soccer, athletics and boxing clubs. The area sports three Olympians – Bobby (Robert) O'Leary who competed in the 20 km walk at Barcelona in 1992. (His father, John O'Leary was a competitive international walker and represented Ireland many times in 20 km walks). Cycling brothers, Alan and Paul McCormack represented Ireland at the 1976 Montréal Olympics and in the 1988 Seoul Olympics respectively.

Trinity Gaels GAA star, Vinny Murphy played senior football for Dublin for ten years and won an All Star award in 1992 and an All-Ireland medal in 1995. Two other sports stars from Donaghmede are Pat Walsh, who was an all-Ireland boxing champion and Stephen Carr, who played soccer at senior level for Ireland.

Back to the seafront again and at Baldoyle Road, we enter Sutton and County Fingal. Fingal derives its name from the *Fine Gall*, the invading fair stranger or foreigners from Scandinavia. County Fingal was created in January 1994, when the old County Dublin was abolished and, for local government administrative purposes, divided into four units.

We pass Binn Eadair View on the left and, as we approach Sutton Cross, we have, again on the left, St Fintan's All-Boys High School. The school was originally founded in 1943, by the Christian Brothers, at the premises of a former school called Bellevue at Burrow Road. Then, the brothers opened a new junior school in 1966, on the site of the old Warren House on the Dublin Road and the today's St Fintan's High School was officially opened there in 1973. Modern apartments stand on the site of the old Bellevue school.

At Sutton Cross, four roads converge – Dublin Road, Station Road, Howth Road and Greenfield Road. Station Road is named after the old Sutton and Baldoyle Railway Station, first opened in 1846. Greenfield Road recalls an old house of that name, which stood where Santa Sabina school is today. Station Road, like Baldoyle Road before it, leads to the semi-rural village of

Baldoyle. The name Baldoyle is derived from *Baile an Dúill* – the town of the dark (Danish) invaders. It is sometimes translated as 'Baile Dubh Ghall', 'Dubhgall's' or 'Doyle's town' and the form 'Baile Dúill' is also used. It is actually in the heart of the larger Fingal, mentioned above.

The fine, biodiverse Baldoyle tidal estuary is a designated NATURA 2000 site. Two small rivers enter the sea here: the Mayne and the Sluice. As long as people have lived in Baldoyle, their lives have been inherently associated with the sea, in terms of food, travel, recreation, etc. The Vikings quickly realised its importance and had a base in Baldoyle since they first came to Ireland.

From 1831, two schools – one for boys the other for girls – stood each side of the St Peter and Paul's Church on Main Street. After a number of location changes over the years, what had become St Peter and Paul Boys Primary School and St Mary's Girls Primary School amalgamated in 2013, to become today's St Lawrence Primary School. The school operates from two campuses beside each other at Grange Road and Brookstone Road. At second level, the boys mainly feed into St Fintan's High School in Sutton. The girls generally go to St Mary's Girls Secondary School, which has a very prominent position bounded by Dublin Road (once called Slate Row), College Street (once Back Street) and Main Street (once Front Street).

The school was opened in 1967 by the Irish Sisters of Charity, who first came to Baldoyle in 1869. It operates from the present building since 1972. Their original convent and girls school, at the junction of Main Street with Willie Nolan Road, is now part of the huge St Michael's House complex, which borders on Main Street, Willie Nolan Road and College Street. St Michael's House took over the running of St Mary's Hospital (school) in 2008. It was first established by the Sisters of Charity in 1843, in response to the poliomyelitis disease epidemic in the area at the time and was replaced by a new hospital in 1956, which over time, came to cater for disabled and special needs children. It also developed a physiotherapy unit and some classrooms were added.

Willie Nolan Road recalls, since 1940, a very popular golfer called Willie Nolan (1896-1939), who was actually born in Bray, County Wicklow but lived locally at Burrowfield Road. He played his golf in Portmarnock and Howth golf clubs. He was Ireland's top professional golfer in the 1930s. The road was originally named New Road.

The Christian Brothers came to Baldoyle in 1885, acquiring a house called Park House on Dublin Street which they called St Mary's. Then they bought another house, Strand Lodge, on the opposite side of the street, which they called St Joseph's and this became their noviciate, for training their postulants, in 1886. Over the years, the Brothers established a very extensive estate in Baldoyle. St Joseph's was eventually sold to the Sisters of Charity and became St Mary's Girls Secondary School mentioned above. In 1966, the brothers opened a hospital at their Baldoyle premises. Nowadays, the premises of the Brothers on Dublin Road are covered by the modern Park House apartments and St Patrick's Nursing Home. Only the graveyard remains, on which we comment in Chapter Eight. A very popular secondary school in Baldoyle is St Nessen's (Scoil Neasáin), a co-educational community school on School Lane off Station Road. It was officially opened in 1983.

Baldoyle Post Office is located on Willie Nolan Road. Previously it was situated at The Mall, where today's public library stands. There was once an old RIC barracks at this site. The Baldoyle Health Centre is on Willie Nolan Road, while the old sorting office on College Street is now a singing/dancing/acting centre. The Baldoyle Community Hall on Coast Road has a plaque on its gable, commemorating all who served with the Irish Citizen Army from 1913-1923. As you travel from Baldoyle to Donaghmede, you cross Furnace's Bridge at Grange Road Bridge, which most accept as the boundary between the two areas. Many will remember a winding and much narrower road and bridge, now bypassed! On the left, a little before the bridge at Grange Rise, is Baldoyle Industrial Estate, which brings much business to Baldoyle.

Sudocrem – a little grey jar of which can be found in just about every household – has been made in a Baldoyle factory (TEVA) since 1931. Dublin pharmacist, Thomas Smith concocted the medical formula for the cream, which was first called 'Smith's Cream', then 'Soothing Cream' but, apparently, the Dublin accent turned it into Sudocrem! It is used in at least fifty countries worldwide. Sadly, TEVA moved the production of Sudocrem to Belgium in 2022.

Baldoyle has habitually been subjected to severe flooding from the sea and from the Moyne and Sluice rivers. The worst affected areas are usually around St Laurence O'Toole Church, the youth club building and much of Brookstone Road.

Baldoyle's two main sporting clubs are Na Dubh Gall GAA Club and Baldoyle United AFC. While there was a tradition of Gaelic games in Baldoyle, no team took real 'root' until the present club was formed in 2001. The club operates from its base at Baldoyle Racecourse Park. Like the GAA, there is a tradition of soccer in Baldoyle and the present Baldoyle United AFC dates from 1969. Affiliated to Shamrock Rovers, the club has its own premises at 18 Brookstone Road.

In terms of public transport, the denizens of Baldoyle are well served by the DART.

Depending on your place of residence, you can use Howth Junction, Donaghmede Station, Bayside Station, Sutton Station or Clongriffin Station. There was an original Baldoyle Railway Station with two railway cottages on the left, after crossing the bridge coming from Baldoyle. It was closed in 1846. The two cottages were knocked down to make way for the new bridge in 1998. Baldoyle has a magnificent, extensive and well-manicured public park. It is Baldoyle Racecourse Park and lies along Red Arches Road.

No account of Baldoyle would be complete without some mention of its once famous racecourse, which is situated along the Coast Road that leads to Portmarnock. The blocked-up, red brick archway in that somewhat forbidding grey wall on the left was the main entrance to the racecourse complex. The origins of the racecourse in Baldoyle can be traced back to a racecourse organised by Thomas Tristram (1802-1874), the third Earl of Howth, at Deer Park, Howth. The Earl put a herd of deer on part of the Howth Castle estate and it came to be called Deer Park.

The Earl, who had an overpowering love of horses, began races here in 1829 but even before that, there was horseracing in the area. A report from 1730 records a race at Warren House near Howth. Warren House was an inn on the site occupied by today's Elphin public house on Baldoyle Road. (This was Old Warren House, not to be confused with the Warren House that stood from 1748 until it was replaced by St Fintan's High School, already mentioned.). In 1851, a new racecourse was opened by the Earl on a course close to the townland of Stapolin in Baldoyle, which was to become Ireland's top racing course, as it pre-dated both Leopardstown and the Phoenix Park courses. The earl's most successful horse in this era was Peep o' Day Boy, named after the sectarian, Protestant Peep o' Day Boys gang that operated in County Armagh in the second half of the 18th century.

Over the years, Baldoyle racecourse proved to be a wonderful sporting and social success. For a long time, it was Ireland's premier racecourse. It brought a 'neigh' of high spirits, joviality and a sparkle of vitality to Baldoyle. The racing elite, the social elite, the celebrities and the regular punters were prominent in Baldoyle on race days. To steal a line from that wonderful ballad, *Spancil Hill*, you could say 'the young, the old, the brave and the bold' came to Baldoyle racecourse!

In colonial times, it was customary for the Lord Lieutenant to be present – with accompanying, virtually monarchical pomp! In Free State days, the President of the Executive Council, WT Cosgrave was known to present prizes at Baldoyle. Sports commentator, Michael O'Hehir was there regularly as were actor, Noel Purcell (1900-1985) and his friend, businessman Hector Grey. Princess Grace (1928-1982) of Monaco visited the place and well-known husband-and-wife actors, John Franklin and Pamela Hart (who lived locally at Newgrove House, Donaghmede Road) were frequent visitors.

The two big races annually at Baldoyle, were the Baldoyle Derby and the Baldoyle Steeplechase. The clockwise course always attracted quality horses, including Orby, winner of the Baldoyle Plate in 1907. The horse then went on to win the Epsom Derby and the Irish Derby. The horse's owner was the colourful Richard 'The Boss' Croker (1843–1922) of New York's Tammany Hall/Democratic Party fame. An Irish lady greeted Croker with the words "Thank God and you, sir, that we have lived to see a Catholic horse win The Derby!" (Orby was the first Irish-trained horse to win 'The Derby').

Orby won further victories at Baldoyle and at the Curragh and Croker received the Freedom of Dublin City. He contributed very generously to the Irish struggle for freedom and died in April 1922, four months after the signing of the Anglo-Irish Treaty in December 1921.

Prince Regent, in the 1940s, was the darling horse of Baldoyle. A horse fondly remembered from that same era is Caughoo, a gelding that won the Aintree Grand National in 1947. The horse was owned by the McDowell family, who lived on the seafront in Sutton.

The immortal Irish thoroughbred horse, Arkle (1957-1970) is generally accepted to be the best steeplechaser ever. At his peak, with jockey, Pat Taaffe (1930-1992), he practiced on the course's quality fences before big races.

Many top jockeys from abroad decorated the course with their prowess. On one occasion, a jockey who identified himself as Lester Piggott (1935-2022) was obliged to produce identification and 'sign in' as the elderly, somewhat dotty gentleman on the gate failed to recognise, arguably, the world's greatest-ever flat jockey!

Over the years, the Royal Irish Constabulary, the Dublin Metropolitan Police and An Garda Síochána have operated at Baldoyle Racecourse. Some days were very special at the course and none more so than 17 March – St Patrick's Day – when the course was always thronged to capacity. No one doubts the quality of the horses and the racing generally but, many people became devout, even fanatical racing enthusiasts on that day. And it is only human to wonder, if the fact that Baldoyle Racecourse was one of only two venues in Dublin allowed to sell alcoholic beverages on our National

Feast Day had something to do with the massive crowds in attendance – where they punters or imbibers!? Incidentally the second place where alcohol could be purchased and consumed on that day was the Dog Show at Ballsbridge, where there tended to be an inordinate interest in dogs for one day! If you were not at one of these venues, you went 'dry'. This situation lasted for many, many years.

BALDOYLE RACES

NEXT FRIDAY AND SATURDAY MARCH 16th AND 17th

FIRST RACE, FIRST DAY, 2.15

FIRST RACE, SECOND DAY, 2.0

Varied Programme, including the St. Patrick's Steeplechase of 200 sovs. On First Day; the Maiden Hurdle Race of 200 sovs; Metropolitan Steeplechase of 150 sovs, and the Juvenile Plate – the first two-year-old Race of the season – on Second Day.

Usual Prices of Admission – Grand Stand, 10/-; Ladies. 5/-. Motors – Reserved Enclosure, 5/-; Public Enclosure, 2/6.

Luncheons – Reserved Enclosure. 5/-; Grand Stand, 3/6

Teas – Both Enclosures, 1/6

Train Arrangements – Trains leave Amiens Street on FRIDAY for Sutton at 1.0, 1.30, and 2.30 pm. On SATURDAY at 12:30, 1.0, 1.15, 1.30, 1.45 and 2.30 pm.

Return Fares – First Class, 1/3; Third Class 10d.

Special Tram Service from City to Baldoyle Road. Return Fare, 7d.

RACE CARDS 6d. EACH

From *Irish Press*, 10 March 1934

The Central Remedial Clinic in Clontarf used the racecourse for big, open-air concerts on a number of occasions, as a culmination to very well organised and supported sponsored walks in the 1960s and 70s. Orchestrated by Lady Valerie Goulding and often times involving the British TV personality, Jimmy Savile. The fundraising walks began in Abbey Street, in the city centre and proceeded through Clontarf to Baldoyle.

In 1968, the death knell was sounded for Baldoyle Racecourse when the insurers reported problems in renewing cover for the grandstand buildings,

**Marie Hayes Cross
(Raheny Village)**

**Doh, Ray, Me charity
cottages (Raheny Village)**

Raheny GAA clubhouse

St. Fintan's High School

Kilbarrack Fire Station

**Manor House
Secondary School**

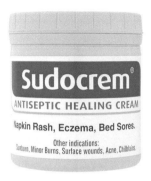

Sudocrem

**Hector Grey plaque at
Liffey Street**

Brian Fenton (footballer)

Michael O'Hehir (broadcaster)

Roddy Doyle

Ronan Keating

Noel Purcell

Joe Carr

Sutton Golf Club

Lester Piggott

Arkle

first erected in 1920 and finally demolished in 1985. On Saturday, 26 August 1972, the very last race took place on the course and a greatly loved institution passed into history.

Baldoyle Racecourse was to make world headlines for the last time on 31 October 1973. The Provisional IRA, in a coup masterminded by senior IRA man, Brendan Hughes, daringly and sensationally lifted three prisoners (IRA Volunteers) in a hijacked Alouette II helicopter from the exercise yard at Mountjoy Prison on the North Circular Road. Three leading IRA figures – Kevin Mallon, JB O'Hagan and Seamus Twomey – were landed at Baldoyle Racecourse, where a getaway car awaited them. This event inspired the very catchy *Helicopter Song* by The Wolfe Tones singing group, with the opening lyric, "Up like a bird and high over the city"!

Off Station Road and by way of Lauder's Lane, we reach Burrow Road, which becomes Claremont Road before joining the Howth Road. Alongside are Burrow Beach and Claremont Strand – colloquially jointly called the 'Hole in the Wall' beach with Sutton Golf Club, founded in 1890, at its southern end. The club's clubhouse is on the edge of Cush (or Cash) Point, a narrow sand dune jutting into the sea. The name 'Cush' is most likely a derogative of the Irish word *cois*, meaning near.

Golfers will recall that this was the home club of Joe Carr (1922-2004), one of Ireland's best ever amateur golfers. Joe won the Irish amateur golf championship six times, the British amateur three times and played in the Walker Cup a record ten times.

This was an area where golf has been enjoyed since 1880, first in a club called the Dublin Golf Club and later, in the Dublin Scottish Golf Club. The club was subsumed by and into the Sutton Yacht and Boat Club, founded in 1896 and based where Sutton Dinghy Club is today, on the Strand Road, Sutton. Scottish-born Edmund Lauder was its first commodore. He is recalled by Lauder's Lane, mentioned above. However golfing interests proved strongest and Sutton Golf Club became the permanent name. The present clubhouse was opened in 1967, replacing the old corrugated-iron one.

CHAPTER SEVEN

Sutton (2), Howth, Ireland's Eye

Now we return to Sutton Cross. Some associate the name Sutton with a certain John de Sutton, a 13th Century kinsman of the Lords of Howth. However, the name is more likely a corruption of 'South Town' or the anglicisation of *Suidhe Fhiontan* – the seat or hill of (St) Fintan.

Sutton mainly comprises of the familiar isthmus of Sutton and the western side of Howth Hill. The isthmus is a connecting neck, about half a kilometre wide, which joins the Howth Peninsula – once an island – to Dublin proper.

The landmark Marine Hotel at Sutton Cross backs onto (and originally fronted onto!) Sutton Strand. It was first established in 1897, as the Strand Hotel. It was later named the Golfers' Hotel. After a serious fire in 1932, it was rebuilt and opened as the Marine Hotel.

The Cross site has businesses and shops on both sides of the Howth Road. Sutton Post Office is on the left, across from the old Sutton Cinema building, which became part of Feargal Quinn's supermarket chain in 1968 and now operates as a Supervalu store.

Greenfield Road, on the right has, on our right, the *Luí na Gréine* monument on the seashore, as a memorial to the ancient people who first inhabited the area.

On the left is Santa Sabina Dominican Convent Secondary School for girls. In 1912 a kindergarten school named Santa Sabina opened in a house called 'Seafield' (later known as Greenfield) on today's Greenfield Road, under the auspices of the Dominican order of nuns. (Santa Sabina was an early Roman Christian martyr). The school grew and expanded rapidly and became St Dominic's High School in 1937. The Dominican sisters are still the schools' trustees, although they have had no presence in Sutton since 1992.

While traversing this area, we recall the prominent Dublin surgeon, Richard Carmichael, who was drowned in 1849 while riding his horse from Bull Island to his country residence at Sutton, having been given advice that it was a safe route.

Soon we reach Carrickbrack Road where, on the right, we have St Fintan's Co-educational Primary School, first opened in 1977.

A little further on, on the left, is Howth Golf Club. Founded in 1916, it has a splendid view over Howth Harbour.

Not far away to the right, is St Fintan's Road, where Sutton Park College is situated. It started life as Glenart School in Rathfarnham, on Dublin's southside. Later, it operated for two years from a premises at Balscadden Road in Howth. In 1957 the school changed to a Georgian premises called St Finton's, where it operates today as a co-educational, multi-denominational private school. It educates children mainly from north County Dublin but also, pupils from many countries around the world.

On Sheilmartin Road, off St Fintan's Road on the left, was the old Sutton Castle Hotel, formally Sutton House, which was built in the early 1800s, replacing an older Sutton House. Andrew Devonshire Jameson, whiskey distiller, acquired the house in 1894. He was a member of the Jameson whiskey distilling family from Alloa in Scotland, who founded the business and company in 1770. They first came to Ireland in 1780 and established the Jameson whiskey brand in Dublin. They were a wealthy Anglo-Irish protestant family, viewed as being southern Unionists.

They had a number of mansions in Dublin, mostly on the northside. These included the already mentioned Fox Hall (the Old Shieling Hotel) and Raheny Park House in Raheny. They also built Bettyglen House off Watermill Road in Raheny, the grounds of which are now occupied by the modern housing developments called The Village and the new Bettyglen, which includes one block called Jameson Court.

The Jamesons had a few residences in Howth, among them 'The Needles', 'The Pins' and 'Drumlech'. Andrew Jameson operated Sutton House very much in the 'big house' manner and tradition and lived the lifestyle of the gentry of the time. He became High Sheriff of County Dublin in 1902 and became chairman of John Jameson and Son in 1905. He became, somewhat surprisingly, a notable Home Ruler, becoming a senator when the Irish Free State was established in 1922. To this day, imbibers of their favourite Irish whiskey – Jameson – do not like to be reminded that the very 'Irish firm' and label is actually of Scottish origin!

A Mrs Van der Elst brought Sutton House in 1949 and some years later, a Belgian citizen Albert Loytax transformed it into the well-known, red brick Sutton House Hotel, later known as Sutton Castle Hotel. In 2003, the building was absorbed into a private apartments' development.

A coast guard station was opened on Strand Road in the 1850s, in an effort to prevent the illegal importation and smuggling of contraband – spirits, in particular. The station closed in 1905. Sutton Dinghy Club, as stated above, now operates on Strand Road.

Sutton has a Martello tower, situated at a somewhat bleak and desolate spot known as Red Rock, just off the Cliff Walk that takes you from the junction of Strand Road with Sheilmartin Road, around Howth Head. There were originally twenty-six of these towers dotted along Dublin's shoreline, north and south, from Balbriggan to Bray. There were about fifty in all around Ireland's coastline. The word 'tower' is somewhat misleading, as they are not really very tall – about forty feet. However, the walls are eight feet thick. They had flat roofs on which guns were mounted. They were built in 1804, as part of the strategy of the (grand old) Duke of York (1763-1827), in his defence plans to counter any attempt by Napoleon Bonaparte (1769-1821) to invade Ireland. However, it would surely have been a very brave or, even desperate Napoleon who would attempt to come ashore on this most inhospitable of coastal areas!

Ironically, the towers were named after the original one at Cape Mortella in Corsica, where Napoleon was born! We will meet two more on our travels: one in Howth Village, the other on Ireland's Eye. Most of the towers were built of granite but the Sutton tower is built from local red limestone – now plastered over.

Back on the main Howth Road, just before Church Road (once Saxe Lane) on the right is Sutton Lawn Tennis Club, at 176 Howth Road. It is in a triangular setting, bounded by Church, Greenfield and Howth Roads. It began as the Howth Lawn Tennis Club in 1882, with courts on Balkill Road, where Beann Éadair GAA grounds are now. In 1941, the club changed to today's site, then known as the 'Circus Field'. In 1958, the name Sutton Lawn Tennis Club was adopted and a clubhouse was built in 1974. Sutton Rugby Football Club was founded in 1899. In 1924, the name Suttonians was adopted and the club had playing fields on Church Road. Nowadays, Suttonians RFC is based at 13 Station Road – opposite Sutton DART station.

On the opposite side of the Howth Road, a little further on, is Burrow School, a Church of Ireland, co-educational national school. When the National School system came into being in 1831, the Church of Ireland community on the Howth peninsula requested to be included. A school called Burrow School was set up in that year, for the education of non-Catholic children. Its home was a very pleasant stone-and-brick building at the Warren of Howth, which was a former name for the Burrow area. In 1968, a new school replaced the old one, which is now a community centre.

Very close, on the right, is the Offington housing estate, which stretches to Carrickbrack Road. The name comes from Offington Park House in Worthing, Sussex, England, the home of the Gaisford family (see below).

Soon, we reach the area known as Corrstown, on the right, containing the remains of Corr Castle. This is within the townland of Burrow, which lay between Baldoyle Road and Corr Castle. This entire area, including Cush Point, was once noted as an extensive rabbit warren: hence, the local names of Burrow and Warren. Corrstown (*Baile an Chorraigh*) refers to the 'town of the round hill'. The castle was probably once occupied by the Lords of Howth for a time. The name Corr may also have been derived from Cornwalsh (*Corr na Waleis*) or the 'hill of the Welshman', as a Welsh family of that name once resided in the castle. In disuse since 1842, the castle was used as a vantage point to watch the Baldoyle Races when they took place at Deer Park. The derelict remains of the castle are now an antiquity and a curiosity.

Since 1177, Howth has been linked to the Norman St Lawrence family, who always claimed to be descended from Sir Tristan, a knight of the sixth century King Arthur's Round Table at Camelot. The original Tristan to arrive in Howth was Sir Almeric (or Armoricus) Tristan, the first Lord of Howth, whose forces, in a raging furious battle in 1177, defeated the Danes. The Danes had inhabited Howth since 819 and their numbers increased after many took refuge there, following their defeat at the 1014 Battle of Clontarf. Sir Tristan's victory occurred at the Battle of Evora (or Ivora) Bridge, which straddled a stream since named the Bloody Stream (blood during the battle entered the water), which today flows into the sea beneath Howth DART Station. Sir Tristan thus took control of the Howth peninsula and, in thanksgiving, adopted the name St Lawrence (the martyr) on whose feast (10 August) the battle was won, although some sources suggest the name was adopted from the town of St Laurent in Normandy, in the northwest of France.

The lands of Howth were then actually granted to him by King Henry II (ruled 1154-1189). Later, King John (ruled 1199-1216) was to confirm this and formally assign the Howth lands to the family. The St Lawrence family remained Lords of Howth from 1177 to 1909, when the male line ceased on the death, in March 1908 of William, Viscount St Lawrence 31st Lord and 4th Earl of Howth. The estate passed to a female family member (the sister of the last Lord of Howth). In 1859, Emily, Lord Howth's oldest daughter married Thomas Gaisford of Offington. The Gaisfords were to eventually succeed to the Howth Castle estate and later adopted the family name, Gaisford St Lawrence.

The very first castle in Howth was situated on Tower Hill, where the Martello Tower is today. The present Howth Castle dates from 1564 and is probably the third castle on that site. It was originally surrounded by a moat. It was rebuilt in 1738, enlarged and refurbished in the first half of the 19th century and again renovated in 1911, under the direction of English architect, Sir Edward Lutyens. Thomas of the St Lawrence family was created Viscount St Lawrence in 1748, by King George II and first Earl of Howth in 1767, by King George III.

Essentially, the castle is something of an irregular battlement building with square towers. Only the northeast gate tower and the keep are left of the 16th century building. It was the seat of the St Lawrence family, later the Gaisford St Lawrence family, until they disposed of it and its 470-acre estate to Irish investment company, Tetrarch in 2019. The somewhat elaborate entrance gates to the castle (and a gate lodge no longer there) were built from funds provided by the winnings of the horse, Peep o' Day Boy in 1866 (the horse mentioned in Chapter Six above).

Howth Castle demesne is famous for its colourful gardens, especially its fuchsia, azaleas, gorse and its 2,000 varieties of rhododendrons, with their numerous shades of red and mauve. Some of the latter were planted as early as 1850 and, though the shrub is native to the Himalayas and China, it has always flourished here.

Part of the rhododendron walk in the grounds features ten-metre-high beech hedges, planted back in 1710. The megalithic or portal tomb or dolmen, known as Aideen's Grave or the Cromlech of Howth, stands close to the rhododendron gardens in the castle grounds. A legend informs us that Aideen, daughter of Aengus of Ben Edar, is buried here. She is believed to have died of grief on hearing of the death of her husband, Oscar – son of Oisín and grandson of Fionn MacCumhaill (leader of the Fianna) – at the Battle of Garra (or Gabhra), near Tara in county Meath in the year 248 AD. The portal tomb dates back at least 2,500 years and consists of a number of blocks of quartz stone and a capstone that has collapsed over the years. It may have been a sepulchral monument or an altar but, its original purpose and use is lost in the mists of time. Sir Samuel Ferguson (1810-1886) has long immortalised Aideen, Oscar and the dolmen in his lengthy poem, *Aideen's Grave*. The Fionn or Fianna cycle of Irish tales allege that Fionn MacCumhaill and his band of Fianna warriors loved to hunt around Howth Head. The tale goes that they had a military headquarters there with a watchtower on the lookout for any enemy approaching from the surrounding seas.

In 1972, much of the grounds of Howth Castle was converted into golf courses. Later, a picturesquely placed hotel was added. Both were very popular with the public.

One of the great treasures of the St Lawrence family is a great two-handed sword. For many years, it has been displayed in an honourable spot in the great hall of the castle. A tradition within the family holds that the sword was actually used by Almeric, the first Lord of Howth, at the famous 1177 Battle of Evora Bridge mentioned above. However, modern research suggests that the sword was most likely first used by Nicholas, the Lord of Howth at the Battle of Knockdoe in 1504.

Ireland's Transport Museum has been housed at Howth Castle since 1985. It exhibits an astonishing and representative collection of vehicles from over the years.

Famous visitors to the castle over the years include singer/actor Bing Crosby (1903-1977), who was there in 1966 while recording the television move, *Bing Crosby in Dublin*. Quite a few films have the castle as a location: e.g. *Dementia 13*, *The Man Who Invented Christmas* and *Love and Friendship*.

A much-heralded narrative associates pirate sea queen Grace O'Malley (c.1530-1603, aka Granuaile) with Howth Castle. She was chieftainess of Burrishoole at Newport Bay in County Mayo. In 1593, she sailed from Clare Island, off the Mayo Coast in Clew Bay (where she had a naval base) to visit Queen Elizabeth I at Greenwich Castle, then located downstream from London, on the River Thames. Returning home, she landed at Howth to shelter from a storm. Calling at Howth Castle, she was displeased to find the castle gates locked while the family enjoyed dinner inside. Noting this as a breach of Ireland's renowned hospitality, she abducted the St Lawrence family's young boy heir and took him in her galley ship to Mayo. She refused to return him to the bosom of his family until the St Lawrences promised, in a written pledge, to forever keep the castle gates open at dinner time. And it became a custom at Howth Castle to leave the gates open and have a vacant place at the table for a hungry passer-by.

Grace O'Malley Drive (with Grace O'Malley Park at 1-15) and Road in Howth Village commemorate her, as does a wishing well mentioned in Chapter Nine. A bronze statue of Grace stands in the grounds of the country house owned by her descendants, outside Westport in Co. Mayo.

Exiting Howth Castle grounds back on to the Howth Road, we head for Howth Village. On our left is Howth DART Station as we enter Harbour Road, which escorts us through Howth.

The peninsula of Howth is said to have been inhabited since 3250 BC. The name Howth comes from the Norse word *hoved*, meaning a head. However, the old Irish name is *Beann Éadair*, which translates as Eadar's (or Edar's) Peak, Hill or Headland. Some authorities suggest that Eadar was a chieftain of the Tuatha de Danann, who is buried on Howth Head. Other sources claim that Eadar was a monk who founded a monastic settlement in Howth. Separate sources refer to Howth as *Benn na nEadair*, which can be taken to signify the 'Hill of the Oaks'.

Howth is a bulbous rocky promontory. It rises to a height of five hundred feet above sea level and is joined to the mainland by a low spit of land that is actually a gravel beach – an isthmus of fairly recent formation. The second century Greek astronomer and cartographer, Ptolemy (c.100-170), on his map of western Europe, shows Howth as an island, which he calls *Edri Deserta* (the deserted place of Eadar). This indicates that the isthmus of Sutton is less than 2,000 years old. Pliny (c.23-79), the Roman scientist and historian, referred to Howth as *Andros*.

Howth is on the northern edge of Dublin Bay. Seventy miles across the bay is its southern counterpart, Sorrento Point, Dalkey. Howth has been part of the Dublin Bay Biosphere since 2015. Most of the promontory, including Ireland's Eye (dealt with below) is protected by SACs (Special Areas of Conservation), SPAs (Special Protection Areas) and an SAAO (Special Amenity Areas Order). Howth also enjoys NATURA 2000 protection. All are aimed at safeguarding Howth's natural environment and wildlife.

Howth Urban District Council was established in 1918 and the district became part of Dublin County Borough in 1942. In 1994, it was incorporated into the newly formed Fingal County Council.

Howth Village, fifteen kilometres from Dublin City with its extensive (21 hectare/52 acres) harbour lies of the north side of the promontory. The harbour (really an artificial harbour), guarded by its West and East piers, was built between 1807 and 1813 in response to Howth being chosen, in 1805, to be the most suitable location for a storm harbour and the major Irish Mail Packet Station for the London-Holyhead-Dublin packet boat or packet steamer (the postal service boat/ship). This was to replace the old Pigeon House Harbour Centre, where there were increasing delays in unloading boats due to its position in the silting mouth of the Liffey, near Ringsend.

The packet steamer actually reduced the time for travelling between Ireland and Britain (Howth to Holyhead) from fifteen hours to just six. The cost was also reduced. At that time, quite a substantial amount of mail was posted between Dublin and London. Much of it was official mail to and from Dublin Castle, from where the British administration in Ireland operated.

The City of Dublin Steam Package Company was awarded the Irish mail contract. The company had four ships named after Ireland's four provinces: Ulster, Munster, Leinster and Connaught. Each ship had a sorting office on board, with personnel from Dublin Post Office doing the sorting. In order to accommodate the mail coach and, to ensure a fast transfer of all mail between the harbour and the city, the Howth Road was built. Telfords, the giant British engineering company, with Thomas Telford (1757-1834) in charge, began the construction of the road in 1808. It was known as the Dublin-London Road, as it was regarded as a continuation of the route from London to Holyhead (a road that was actually built under the same contract). The completed road proved to be one to compare with the best at the time and, complete with granite and cast-iron milestones, many of which still stand along the road, it is the real legacy of that era.

Scottish-born Telford was dubbed with the title, the Colossus of Roads by contemporary poet, Robert Southey because of his outstanding record in building roads and bridges, especially in Scotland. To mark his 250th birthday, a wall plaque to his memory was put in place at the junction of Bayside Boulevard with the Dublin Road.

The service from Howth began on 1 August 1818 but, its life as a package station was not to last long. It was obvious from the beginning that due to local sea currents, silting was going to be a problem too big to resolve. After just a few years, it was clear that it would not be feasible to keep Howth Harbour dredged to accommodate steam packet ships, which were being built bigger. Thus, the decision was made to move the station to Dún Laoghaire on the other side of Dublin Bay. This became permanent in 1833 and the village relapsed into an ordinary fishing village.

And perhaps the greatest memory from Howth's era as the Irish packet station was the unexpected landing there of King George IV, on 12 August 1821. After the death of his wife, Princess Caroline, the newly crowned king docked in Howth on his 59th birthday, in a somewhat inebriated state! He travelled on a regular steam mail package boat, as his own boat had become becalmed at Holyhead. It is suggested he came to 'meet' Elizabeth Campbell of Slane Castle. A stonemason by the name of Robert Campbell cut a copy of his footprints, in stone, on the spot where the royal feet first touched Irish soil! The footprints can be viewed as something of a curiosity on the right, as you stroll towards the end of the West Pier.

Dunleary, as Dún Laoghaire was first known, was renamed Kingstown in 1821, as it was the point of the good king's departure from Ireland 18 days after his Howth landing. However, its years as Dublin's packet boat station did little to improve or develop Howth although, the arrival of the railway and resulting train service in 1846 did. During the 19th century, rapid development and expansion changed Howth dramatically. Today, it thrives as a fishing village, sailing centre, a tourist venue and holiday resort and, a charming residential area. In the shadow of the dominant, scenic cliff and moor land of Howth Hill overlooking it, Howth portrays a quaint aspect, picturesquely appealing and laden with a rich history.

From Harbour Road, we turn left onto the West Pier. On the corner, on our left, on a little green is the Ready Boat Pillar, a 13-foot-high stone pillar with fifteen panels, representing the four ages of Howth. Erected by sculptor Sean O'Dwyer, it was put in place in 1996. There had been no real alterations or improvements in the harbour area since the packet station days, except in 1859, when both West and East piers were widened and breakers created inside the harbour.

Howth has been well documented as a fishing port since the ninth century and soon, on our left, the inscription on a large rock informs us that the (modern) fishing harbour was officially opened in 1986. This was after major development and modernisation of the entire harbour. It is the second largest fishing port in Ireland, after Killybegs Harbour in Co. Donegal. The West Pier is the centre of Howth's fishing industry. This is evidenced by the abundance of fishing trawlers there. The fishermen ply their trade in the Irish Sea, the bulk of their catches being of cod, place, whiting, mackerel, herring and prawn.

Again, on our left, further on is the Mariner's Hall, built in the 1860s of Howth stone and with a Gothic look. The hall provided an oasis of peace and tranquillity for seafarers. It also served as a place of worship for both Methodist and Presbyterian congregations until their own respective churches opened locally.

Back on Harbour Road, we find the old courthouse on the right. It dates from the middle of the 19th century and is markedly Victorian in style, with distinctive cross motifs. It too served as a place of worship and as a rent collection office for Lord Howth but, for one hundred years (1870 to 1970) it was the local courthouse. It now houses the Howth and District Association of An Taisce and also acts as a meeting place for some community groups. Further along, three carved wooden sculptures – a mermaid, a Viking type dragon ship head and a fisherman – depict aspects of Howth's history and heritage over the years.

On our left, on the Middle Pier reclaimed area, is a very conspicuous cross and anchor monument, roughly halfway between the West and East piers. It was erected in 1994 by the Howth Fishermen's Association, in memory of all people-everywhere-lost at sea. It is also dedicated to "God in thanksgiving for his eternal love for all of us."

In this mid-harbour area, we find Howth Yacht Club with its emblem, a large anchor sculpture, on its lawn and an array of yachts and sailing boats in the surrounding marina. Howth Harbour is a fine yachting centre and

Howth Sailing Club, as it was first called, was founded in 1895 and had a clubhouse on the left, near the seafront end of the West Pier. In 1968 the sailing club amalgamated with Howth Motor Yacht Club, which had operated on the West Pier since 1935, to form Howth Yacht Club. The present clubhouse was opened in 1987. Howth Sailing and Boating Club operates from the East Pier.

Just seaward of Howth Yacht Club is the home of the Howth branch of the Royal National Lifeboat Institution (RNLI). Back in 1817, the very first lifeboat was placed at Howth by the Dublin Ballast Board. Since 1824, the RNLI has been operating and providing a reserve service around the coastlines of Ireland and Britain. This vital and wonderful service is provided almost entirely by volunteers.

Back to Harbour Road and on our right, close to its junction with Abbey Street, is Howth House, one of the oldest in the village, built between 1807 and 1817. It was erected for Captain George Taylor (although an engineer called John Rennie was to replace him), the engineer who oversaw the construction of Howth Harbour as the Irish steam packet station. The garden area of this large edifice was once the village green.

It became known as Olympic House in January 2005, when the Olympic Federation of Ireland, an all-Ireland body, set up its headquarters there. Outside the building was a bust of Lord Killanin (1914-1999), the Galway native whose real name was Michael Morris, a journalist and author. He was president of the Olympic Council of Ireland from 1950 until 1973. He became the sixth president of the International Olympic Committee and served from 1972-1980.

Also outside the building was a commemorative representation of the Olympic flame. This recalls a visit to the house of the 2012 London Olympics flame. The visit took place on 6 July 2012 and the commemoration was put in place in May 2013.

The building also had an Olympic museum and memorabilia concerning Ireland's efforts at the various games. Howth residents were a little sad to see these emblems disappear when the council moved headquarters to the National Sports Campus, in the western suburb of Abbottstown in 2021.

At the seafront end of the East Pier is the landmark Howth Lighthouse, in a glorious setting with glorious views. It was built in 1818 and the adjacent lightkeeper's lodge was added in 1821. Electricity was installed in 1955 and its oil lamps were replaced by a 250 watt bulb. A matching lighthouse was built at Holyhead, at the same time.

On a wall beside the lighthouse is a plaque recalling the 1914 Howth gun running episode. It was at this spot on the East Pier that Erskine Childers, in his white yacht, *Asgard* landed the rifles and ammunition that led to the confrontation at the Crescent/Howth Road, Clontarf detailed earlier. Aboard the *Asgard* were Erskine Childers (father of Erskine 'Junior', who was to become Ireland's fourth president); his wife, Molly Childers; Mary Spring Rice, an Anglo-Irish aristocrat from County Limerick and a committed nationalist; Gordon Shepherd (a skilled sailor and a close friend of Childers) and two Donegal fishermen from Gola Island, Patrick McGinley and Charles Duggan. The *Asgard* is among the most famous of sea vessels in Irish history and certainly, the most iconic to ever enter Howth Harbour.

15,000 Mauser rifles (subsequently known as Howth rifles) and 49,000 rounds of ammunition were secretly purchased in Hamburg, Germany. The rifles were of the type used to rearm the German army after the 1870/71 Franco-Prussian war. A tugboat, called the *Gladiator*, had a rendezvous with the *Asgard* and the *Kelpie* at Ruytingen Lighthouse in the North Sea, off the Belgian coast and transferred the munitions. The *Kelpie* was owned by Conor O'Brien, a well-known nationalist and cousin of the aforementioned Mary Spring Rice. On the arrival of the *Asgard* in Howth at noon on that July Sunday in 1914, Éamon de Valera later recalled Bulmer Hobson (1883-1969. IRB member and Volunteer) remarking to him that this yacht was 'the harbinger of freedom'. It arrived after an arduous 23-day journey to and from the Belgian coast. A tugboat owned by Kerryman, John K Cotter pulled the *Asgard* into Howth harbour.

Nine hundred rifles and 26,000 rounds of ammunition were unloaded into the waiting hands of the Volunteers. The whole event was daringly and deliberately carried out in broad daylight to achieve the maximum publicity and arouse the people to the nationalist cause. *The Irish Times* newspaper – not known to be sympathetic to nationalism or republicanism – the next day described the event as one of the cleverest coups conceivable and by reason of its very audacity, outrivalled anything that has hitherto been attempted in the way of gun running. Meanwhile, the rest of the munitions were transferred to the *Chotah* and, after some trouble with the sails, was landed safely on the beach at Kilcoole, County Wicklow a week after the *Asgard* had delivered its cargo.

The Howth gun-running episode was a seminal moment in Irish history, pivotal in the momentum towards the 1916 Rising and Irish independence. British Military Intelligence failed to detect the gun running. Erskine Childers, with his extensive network of contacts within the British establishment, misled them into believing that munitions were heading for Ireland on Irish trawlers. Consequently, the Royal Navy concentrated its search on trawlers and the *Asgard* and *Kelpie* went undetected. The *Asgard* has been designated a national monument and is now on view in the National Museum at Collins Barracks.

Turning right into Abbey Street, named after the local St Mary's Abbey on our right, is a somewhat mysterious T-shaped, two-storey building dating from the 16th Century. It is known as The Collegiate but researchers are baffled as to its original purpose. Perhaps it was for use by the clergy in the nearby St Mary's Abbey?

Straight across the street from the Collegiate, a little laneway leads up to Tower Hill and Howth's Martello Tower overlooking village and harbour. The building of this tower – like all Irish Martello towers – was supervised by a royal engineer named Benjamin Fisher. For many years it housed a radio museum, known as Ye Olde Hurdy Gurdy Museum of Vintage Radio. Here Guglielmo Marconi (1874-1937) and Lee de Forest (1873-1961), early pioneers of wireless telegraphy, carried out many experiments in the 1900s.

Next to the Collegiate is the welcoming Abbey Tavern, with all the charm of the 16th century establishment that it is. The venue is noted for its 'Irish culture'-type entertainment. The College Steps between these two buildings lead us to Church Street where, on the left, is the Harbour Bar (Cock Tavern), first opened in 1750. Beside it is the Gráinne Mhaol/Pirates' Wishing Well. Further along Church Street is Howth Garda Station, in an island setting surrounded by Church Street and three terraces – Howth, Evora and Dunbo.

Now back on Abbey Street and at its confluence with Church Street and Main Street is the Parochial Hall, built in 1814. The hall is now used for business concerns. Abbey Street ends at St Lawrence Road and we move on to Main Street. On the left is the site of the old Bailey Court Hotel. This was formerly the Royal Hotel and first built as the Stagecoach Hotel. It was later known as the Postillion Coach House in the 1830s and catered for passengers travelling between Dublin and London. It was at the centre of the then little port of Howth, which was, for many years, the main point of entry for visitors to Ireland. We must recall that one very unwelcome visitor came to Ireland, we believe, through Howth Harbour in August 1348. That visitor was the Black Death plague.

On the subject of hotels, it is notable that, apart from the Marine Hotel at Sutton Cross, the Howth and Sutton area has no hotel. This contrasts sharply with the days when the Asgard, Sutton Castle, Howth Lodge (formerly the Claremont), Deer Park, Saint Lawrence (with its Saints nightclub) and the

Bailey Court hotels were a central ingredient to the very character of the region.

Just past the Bailey Court site is Howth's stately public library. Opened as a library in 1936, it was once the local dance hall. Across the road, at 8-10 Main Street, is Howth Post Office. It was previously situated on Harbour Road.

At this point, there is a Y-junction in the road. If we follow Main Street to the right, on our right is Tuckett's Lane, where we find Scoil Mhuire, Howth Primary School. The school opened in 1956 to replace the old school on Balglass Road. If we follow Balglass Road, which becomes Balkill Road, we will reach Howth summit. The 'bal' in these names indicates a town or townland.

On our right off Balkill Road is Howth (Beann Éadair) GAA Club. Founded in 1885, it is one of Dublin's oldest GAA clubs and has a majestic setting, with a view out over Howth Harbour that Midas himself could not buy! An interesting little anecdote relates that many years ago, Fingallians GAA Club (in Swords) and Howth had a playoff match for the right to ownership of the name Fingallians! Having lost the match, Howth became Saint Laurence GAA Club before eventually becoming Beann Éadair.

If we return to the Y junction mentioned above and this time keep left, we reach Howth summit by way of Thormanby Road. The Thormanby name originated with a racehorse called Thormanby that won the Epsom Derby in 1860. North Thormanby Island, one of the Gulf Islands off British Columbia in Canada, was thus named by surveyor, George Richards in 1860. There is also a village called Thormanby in North Yorkshire in England.

Both routes converge at Bailey Green Road in the final ascent to the summit. Another route to Howth summit is via Balscadden Road, which takes us along Balscadden Bay. The Balscadden name is derived from the Irish *bal* (town) and *scadán* (herring). The old Howth baths were situated in Balscadden Bay and in Charles Lever's novel, *Tom Burke*, the place is called 'Bolskatin'.

Then on to the cliff walk beginning at Kilrock, we pass many landmark place names including the Nose of Howth, Casano Rock, Piper's Gut and Fox Hole en route. This majestic pathway was first opened by the great Northern Railway company, to entice visitors to explore the area. The Kish Bank Lighthouse can be observed to the left far out to sea. It is a telescopic structure of reinforced concrete with its base sitting on the seabed. It was put in place in 1965. Nowadays, the cliff walk is but one of the many designated walks on the Howth Peninsula.

Howth Head is a place of salubrious, scenic, wild and rugged grandeur. Novelist HG Wells (1866-1946) called the view from Howth Head 'the most beautiful in the world'. It is a truly kaleidoscopic view. From its high cliffs above the Irish Sea the spectacularly invigorating views include Dublin City and Dublin Bay across to Dún Laoghaire and the Wicklow Mountains. Also (in clear weather) you can see, on the horizon, the Mourne Mountains in County Down, Slieve Gullian in County Armagh and even the Cambrian mountains in north Wales, including the 3,560 feet high Snowdon.

At the very summit are high points Sheilmartin, Dun Hill (an island promontory fort) with the very highest point on the Howth peninsula being Black Linn – 563 feet (170 m) above sea level. On Shielmartin is a cairn, which is thought to cover the grave of Crimthann (or Criffon), a one-time king of Howth whose death occurred about the year 90 AD. He is said to have sailed across the sea to Britain, returning with slaves and other bounty. His wife was Nar of Brugh but the cairn is much older than this and, most likely, covers other Neolithic or early Bronze Age burials.

The Bailey Lighthouse at Dun Griffin, designed by George Halpin, on the Bailey promontory (a low narrow headland jutting out to sea) dates from 1814. The name Bailey or Bally is derived from the Irish word *baile*, meaning a home, a place or a town. It replaced an older lighthouse further inland, which had been first built in 1667 by Sir Robert Reading, in the reign of King Charles II. The lighthouse was first lit by oil and, from 1865, by gas. It went automatic in 1972, when it was first powered by electricity. In 1997, it became totally automated.

The terrain of Howth Head demonstrates nature at its best, with an abundance of plants and shrubs including heather, gorse, bracken, brambles and ferns, while a diverse array of wildflowers abounds. The area is an ornithologist's paradise and its vast numbers of waders and sea birds include curlews, dunlins, auks, shags, razorbills, ravens and cormorants. The whole area is very rich in insect life. Mammals to be observed in the environment include foxes, rabbits, stoats, pygmy shrews, field mice and bats. And surely adding to the allure of the area is the re-introduction of goats. Indigenous goats freely grazed on Howth Head until the 1940s. In September 2021, a trip of twenty-five 'old Irish' goats were transferred from the National Herd Sanctuary of Mulranney, County Mayo to settle and live on the Hill of Howth. The goats were put there to control the rapid growth of furze on Howth Head, thus reducing the risk of fire and to enhance the biodiversity of the area.

Howth Head, in its wild splendour, is a place of inspiration for artists and musicians as well as writers and poets.

Something of a curiosity but also a national artefact on the East Mountain is the *Eire 6* sign, a large World War II aerial recognition marker signalling Ireland's neutrality during the Second World War. Historically, it reminds us of an uncertain era in the area's, indeed Ireland's history. It recalls the volunteers of the Coast Watching Service (CWS) who manned the early CWS lookout post from 1939 to 1945. It was they who installed the *Eire 6* sign in 1943, with twelve metres high letters of whitewashed local quartz stone. It was Outpost 6 of 83, put in place around the Irish coastline at the time. These volunteers played their part in maintaining Irish neutrality during the course of World War II.

Irish emigrants have taken the name Howth to Howth in Waller County, Texas and to Howth in the Australian island state of Tasmania.

Visible from Howth summit and also from Howth Harbour is Ireland's Eye, a wedge shaped, windswept, rugged and craggy island. Formed of quartz rock, its steep cliffs rise perpendicularly from the sea. It is picturesquely beautiful and lies a mile and a half offshore, northeast of Howth Harbour, for which it forms in natural breakwater. It was once known as Inis Mhic Neasáin (Inismacnessan), the 'island of the sons of Neasáin' who was a descendant of a Leinster royal family. The sons were Dichull, Munissa and Neslug, pious and reclusive who liked the remoteness of the island. Ireland's eye was later known as Inis Erean (also Ereann or Eria). *Erean* came to mean Ireland (or Erin). The Vikings changed *Inis* for *Ey*, which is the Norse for island, so it became Erin's Eye, today Ireland's Eye.

The island's Martello tower has mostly just local birds for company. These include gulls, kestrels, fulmars, gannets and kittiwakes. These birds love soaring cliffs and fortress islands, so Ireland's Eye is tailor-made for them to make their sanctuary on its cliffs, sharp ledges and shelves – where they can also shelter from the prevalent and often fierce north-easterly gales. At the north-eastern side of the island is a large and extensive craggy rock, known as 'The Stack'. This conspicuous rock is a favourite of these birds as a refuge and breeding ground. They feel safe too, as the island is a bird sanctuary. Grey seals are very numerous in the surrounding waters.

A notorious murder took place on Ireland's Eye in 1852 and the ensuing trial was one of the most captivating ever witnessed in Ireland. In the end William Burke Kirwan was found guilty of murdering his wife, Maria Louisa, whose body was found at a spot on the island known as 'The Long Hole'. During the trial, it emerged that Kirwan had a mistress called Maria Teresa Kenny, with whom he had a number of children. He was sentenced to servitude for life and served 27 years in Spike Island prison in Cork Harbour. He was then sent to America, where it is believed that he joined his mistress. Nowadays cared for by An Taisce, Ireland's eye is a very popular venue for day trippers using local ferries. The landing bay on Ireland's Eye is on the western side at Carrigeen Bay.

The Baldoyle, Sutton and Howth area had and has many well-known residents.

Sportsmen who lived in the area include the aforementioned, affable Irish professional golfer, Willie Nolan (1896-1939. See Chapter Six above.), who lived on today's Willie Nolan Road in Baldoyle and is buried in Kilbarrack Cemetery. A leading Irish professional in the period between the two world wars, he won the Irish professional championship in 1934. He was only forty-two when he died.

Mick Fitzpatrick who earned 10 Irish Senior rugby caps in the 1980s lived in Strand Road, Baldoyle. The family home 'Cúl Coill', later became Sutton Nursing Home.

Irish senior international soccer player, Robbie Brady hails from the Meadowbank Estate in Baldoyle.

Showband singers, Sean Dunphy and Harry (Glen) Curtin lived in Baldoyle. Sean Dunphy (1937-2011) sang with the Hoedowners Band and came second singing for Ireland in Vienna, Austria at the 1967 Eurovision contest with a song called *If I could Choose*. He lived on Willie Nolan Road and later at Stapolin Lawns. Glen Curtin (1943-2009) lived for many years on Grange Road. He sang with the New Blues and Nevada showbands and had a number one hit with *Tears on the Telephone* in 1980. He then followed a solo career in America and in England.

Nicky Byrne, a member of the Westlife musical group and well known for radio and television work, was born at Seagrange, Baldoyle.

There are quite a few 'faces' from television and 'voices' from radio from the area. They include Doireann Ní Bhrian, a former pupil at Santa Sabina School. Sean Moncrieff lived on Station Road and Mark Cagney and Ian Dempsey are both Sutton residents. Broadcaster and film producer, Morgan O'Sullivan, though born in Clontarf, lived on the seafront at Kilbarrack. Poets, Pat Boran, Paula Meehan and Theo Dorgan all lived at Moyclare, Baldoyle. Boran and Dorgan were also familiar voices on the radio.

The Fenian leader James Stephens (1825-1901) lived, from 1891-1895, in a Gothic-style house called 'Berkeley Villa' on Station Road, Sutton. Stephens liked to be known as a COIR, the Central Organiser of the Irish Republic and also as the Head Centre of the IRB. Back in 1865, as he was planning an uprising against British rule in Ireland, he was arrested and imprisoned in the Richmond Bridewell Penitentiary (now Griffith College) on Dublin's South Circular Road. However, just two weeks into his detention, he was daringly sprung from the jail by a team of rescuers led by Baldoyle man,

John Flood, a leading Fenian. Later, he was smuggled out of Ireland by another Baldoyle man, Captain Nicholas Weldon (1836-1905) – a friend of John Flood since boyhood. The Weldons were wealthy merchants and boat owners who lived on today's Weldons Lane in Baldoyle, formerly Seafield Avenue. Captain Weldon, a nationalist sympathiser and a man with a buccaneering style and nature, got Stephens secretly aboard his brigantine, *Concord* under the noses of the British authorities at Batchelors Walk and escorted him to Scotland, from where Stephens escaped to France and later to America.

The famous American-born, British-based artist, James Abbot McNeill Whistler lived for a time in 1900, in a house at Sutton Cross called 'Craigne', situated at the junction of the Howth Road with Greenfield Road, the site of which is now occupied by a small shopping complex. He was friendly with Oscar Wilde and like Oscar, he was associated with a group who advocated 'Art for Art's Sake'. A very popular and much sought-after painter, Whistler is mostly remembered for his 1871 painting known as *Whistler's Mother*.

Artist, Jim Fitzpatrick (b. 1944) resided on Burrow Road for many years. His highly individual and imaginative Celtic artwork became extremely popular around the world. One image in particular – that of Argentinian revolutionary, Che Guevara (1928-1967) – an iconic red and black poster entitled, *Viva Che* from 1968 became very famous. In its time, it was a very powerful anti-Vietnam War symbol.

Disabled author and painter, Christy Brown lived in Shielmartin in Sutton for some time (see Chapter Twelve below).

Michael Hurley, surely the bard of the area due to his series of local history/ memorial books, lived at Abbey Park, Baldoyle.

Fianna Fáil politician, Patrick Hillery (1923-2008), sixth President of Ireland, served as President from December 1976 until December 1990. In retirement, he lived in Grasmere House at Greenfield Road, Sutton with his wife, Maeve until his death in 2008. He is buried in St Fintan's Graveyard, Sutton.

A well-known resident in Sutton – if only for his imposing physique and stentorian voice – was Irish Olympian David (Dave) Guiney (1921-2000). His home was named 'Duhallow'. As an athlete, his specialist discipline was the shot putt, in which he represented Ireland for twelve consecutive years – 1944-1956. He had a career as a sports journalist, author and historian.

Rockstar Phil Parris Lynott (1949-1986) lived with his wife, Caroline Crowther (m.1980-86) and two children at 'Glen Corr' on Claremont Road. In 1969 the Thin Lizzy rock band came together under Phil, who was the group's principal songwriter, lead vocalist and bassist. With hits such as *Whiskey in the Jar* and *The Boys are Back in Town*, the band left an indelible mark on rock music. His mother, Phyllis lived at a house called 'White Horses' on Strand Road, Sutton. The house was a shrine, a museum of memorabilia to the singer with a memorial plaque to him on the wall. At one stage, Phil bought the popular Asgard Hotel in Howth Village, for his mother but, it was destroyed in a fire in July 1982 and later replaced by the Asgard apartments. In 2005, a sculpture of Phil was put in place on Harry Street (off Grafton Street in Dublin City Centre). In 2019, the 50th anniversary of the band's formation, An Post issued a postage stamp in memory of the group. Phil and his mother are buried side by side in St Fintan's Graveyard. Phil in 1986 and Phyllis in 2019.

Another member of a rock band, Larry Mullen of U2, has a residence on Claremont Road.

The family of poet, WB Yeats (1865-1939) came to live in Balscadden House at Kilrock Road, Howth in 1880. Some months later, they moved to a house called 'Island View' on Harbour Road, where they remained until 1883. From here, for two years (October 1881- December 1883), the adolescent Yeats travelled by train to the Erasmus Smith High School in Harcourt Street. Howth was an exploration area for the young Yeats. He loved the sea, the mountains, the valleys, the dells, the streams and the woods as he reconnoitred the area. Already writing poetry, many critics argue that it was here that he began incubating the aesthetic theories that manifested themselves in his later poetry. Certainly, the special charms of the locality helped his poetic juices to grow and flow. Balscadden House has a plaque in Yeats' memory (see Chapter Twelve, below).

Philomena Lynott later lived at the house before moving to Strand Road Sutton.

One of Oscar Wilde's (1854-1900) professors at Trinity College was John Pentland Mahaffy, a Greek scholar who later became Trinity's Provost. Oscar spent the summer of 1874 at Mahaffy's house, 'Earlscliffe' in Howth, where he helped the professor with his book, *Social Life in Greece from Homer to Menador* (see Chapter Twelve, below).

In her time, Annie MP Smithson (1873-1948) was the top-selling Irish romantic novelist. Born in Sandymount in south Dublin, as a young girl her family often rented a house in Howth where, with her cousins, she loved to bathe in Balscadden Bay and generally ramble around the coastal area and cliff walks. In 1882, they rented Abbey House beside St Mary's Abbey and Graveyard. Two of her best-known novels are *The Walk of a Queen* and *Norah Connor*.

Prominent republican, IRA leader, author and broadcaster, Ernie O'Malley (1897-1957) spent the last fifteen months of his life living in Nashville Park, Howth, where he died in March 1957.

Conor Cruise O'Brien (1917-2008), a one-time local TD and Labour Party government minister and author lived in Howth with his wife, Máire Mhac and tSaoi (1922-2021). Máire, an Irish language scholar and a poet, was the daughter of Seán MacEntee (1889-1984), a former Fianna Fáil government minister and Tánaiste.

Gabriel (Gay) Byrne (1934-2019) television and radio presenter and best known for presenting RTÉ's *The Late Late Show* for 37 years between 1962 and 1999, lived in Howth with his wife, Kathleen Watkins. They first came to live in Howth in 1967. Kathleen, herself a very talented lady, is a broadcaster, an author and a harpist.

Three times winner of the Eurovision Song Contest – as singer, singer-composer and composer – Johnny Logan (real name Seán Sherrard who was born in Australia) came to live in Howth as a three-year-old and later moved to Drogheda. His father, Charles Sherrard, was a tenor. He performed under the stage name Patrick O'Hagan, singing mainly traditional Irish and Celtic songs.

Another well liked singer to live in Howth is the soulful jazz and blues performer, Mary Coughlan.

Film actor and director, Stuart Townsend was born (in 1972) and reared in Howth as was model and media personality, Vogue Williams, who maintains a residence there.

And the great muse of WB Yeats, Maud Gonne (1865-1953), lived in Howth for a while.

Politician (local councillor and TD) businessman and publican, Patrick (Paddy) Belton (1926-1987) lived in Howth. He was Lord Mayor of Dublin in 1978.

Others who live or have lived in the area include Senator and retail pioneer, Fergal Quinn; The Dubliners' band player, Barney McKenna; novelist and Booker Prize winner, John Banville; Dolores O'Riordan of The Cranberries musical group; Larry Mullen, drummer with the U2 band; Ombudsman, Emily O'Reilly; actors Brendan Gleeson and Saoirse Ronan and Peter Aiken of Aiken Promotions.

Éire 6 sign

The Asgard

Irish Goat

Sutton Cross

Marine Hotel

Howth Castle

Ireland's Eye

Grace O'Malley

Martello tower, Howth

Ready Boat Pillar

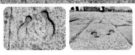

Footprints of King George IV

Erskine Childers (snr)

Asgard plaque, Howth

Bing Crosby

Telford plaque at Bayside

Lord Killanin

CHAPTER EIGHT

The Churches and Graveyards of the Dublin North Bay Area

Our churches have always been chief among the pillars of communities and society in general. The baptismal font in the local church is where most Christians were initiated into their parish communities. Churches have been the very fabric of the parish structure and at its very heart's core. That may have all changed now in the 21st century but, nobody can erase the central role of the church in the past. While the authority and dominance of some religions is now history, maybe we need to re-realise how much we need each other and a focus or focal point to achieve that new togetherness. We surely would be the better for that sense of meitheal – the band of workers or working party – which was once a major factor in Irish life. With an ever-changing world and environment, the old Irish *seanfhocail* (proverb) *Ar scáth a chéile a mhaireann na daoine* (We live in each other's shelter) was never so relevant. We need that parish spirit and sense of community as much, if not more, than we ever did. The church gave everyone a sense of belonging, stability, togetherness, solidarity and tenacity. The church provided close social support.

Churches are true public buildings for worship and prayer. They are public rather than private property. After all, the church is the people and the people paid for the church building. In Dublin (leaving aside Georgian Dublin and certain other individual buildings of note), its ecclesiastical edifices provide the city's most interesting architecture. Including all religious persuasions, at peak, there were about seven hundred places of worship in the greater Dublin area. For Catholics, especially, churches were a shelter and a refuge and presented hope.

Our North Bay area has an abundance of churches. The area also has many ruins of very early churches, especially in old cemeteries. Many of these are on religious sites of worship or sacred grounds that predate the coming of Christianity to Ireland, with St Patrick in the fifth century. Most of today's older churches date from post-Reformation times, especially the late 17th century and early 18th century. Many are of the classical or Gothic style. In the 19th century – especially after Catholic Emancipation in 1829 – a large number of Catholic churches were constructed. And after the creation of the Irish Free State, the building of Catholic churches continued. In Dublin, as the city began to grow large suburban areas from the period after World

War II, numerous basilica-style churches appeared in suburbia, to cater for the vast population of Catholics in the new parishes that were created.

As we look at the churches on our route from the Customs House to Howth, it is fair to say that every church has its own individual merit, history and even the most modest has some architectural feature(s) of note.

Trinity Church, Lower Gardiner Street

The former Trinity Church of Ireland – one of Dublin's largest – stands at 50 Lower Gardiner Street, close to its junction with Beresford Place. It was built in 1838. Over the years, as decline and decay hit the area, the church became redundant. It was deconsecrated in the 1930's. The Department of Social welfare acquired the building and converted it into a Labour Exchange and the building is called 'The Exchange'. It is doubtful if the many unemployed, collecting social welfare payments here, realise the history of the building of black calp, with its classical yellow brick facade. Part of the building is occupied by the Exchange Trinity Church.

Church of Our Lady of Lourdes, Seán McDermott Street (Catholic)

The Catholic Church of Our Lady of Lourdes on Lower Seán McDermott Street was built in 1954 and is neo-Romanesque in style. Cruciform in plan, it replaced a corrugated iron temporary church, known as the old tin church, which was on the site since 1915. It acted as a chapel of ease to the nearby St Mary's Metropolitan Church – the Pro-Cathedral on Marlborough Street – until it was constituted a full parish in 1970. It is a mensal parish, having the Archbishop of Dublin as its parish priest.

Of special interest in the church is the tomb of the ascetic Venerable Matt Talbot (1856-1925). His remains were enshrined in the church in 1972, in a granite mausoleum. Many pilgrims come to the church to pray at his tomb. The church and parish are now administered by clergy from the Salesian Society of Don Bosco, Ireland.

On his retirement as Archbishop of Dublin and parish priest of Our Lady of Lourdes parish at the end of December 2020, Dr Diarmuid Martin mentioned a rather special 'pilgrim'. "This is a vibrant parish with great people," he remarked, "indeed, courageous people who take real leadership in their community. The last time I brought a visitor to this parish it was Pope Francis (during the Pope's visit to Ireland in 2018). This is the only simple parish church in Ireland ever visited by a Pope."

Then he jokingly added to his successor, the former Bishop of Ossory, Bishop Dermot Farrell, "You have a lot to live up to!"

St Laurence O'Toole, Seville Place (Catholic)

St Laurence O'Toole Church is prominently situated on the corner where Sheriff Street meets Seville Place and, from where its commanding tower is a landmark for the whole docks area.

The church and the parish are named after St Laurence O'Toole (c.1130-1180) who became Dublin's first Irish-born archbishop in 1162 and is Dublin's patron saint. At the time of the Norman invasion of Ireland in 1170, he first organised resistance but, on realising the strength of the Norman forces, he parlayed for peace with Henry II and with Strongbow. He encouraged Strongbow to build Christ Church Cathedral, where the saint's heart is preserved. He died at Eu in Normandy, in France, in 1180. He was canonised a saint in 1225 and is one of only two Irish people to be canonised – the other being St Oliver Plunkett (1625-1681), who was canonised in 1975, almost 750 years later.

The site for the St Laurence O'Toole Church was donated to the then Archbishop of Dublin, Daniel Murray (1768-1852) by a Catholic businessman called Charles Kennedy. Work began on the building in 1844 and it was officially opened in 1850, as a chapel of ease within St Mary's Pro-Cathedral parish. It is built of limestone in the early English Gothic style, the designer being JB Keane. St Laurence O'Toole became an independent, full parish in 1852.

A relic (a plange bone) of the saint has been venerated in a shrine at the church since 1914. It was brought by Archbishop Brady from Eu in Normandy, in France, where the saint is buried. A noticeable feature in the church is its Carrera marble altar.

St Joseph's, Church Road, East Wall (Catholic)

This church is situated at 3 Church Road, where St Mary's Road meets Caledon Road in the very heart of the East Wall area. The original church here was a simple 'tin church' on Church Road opposite Seaview Avenue. Built of wood and iron in 1919, it was a chapel of ease to the St Laurence O'Toole parish church. It was needed due to the ongoing population increase in the area. In 1941, St Joseph's became a full parish in its own right. Today's St Joseph's Church was built in 1954 and formally opened in 1956. It is a large but pleasant building of brick in the Romanesque or Lombardy architectural style.

St Agatha's Church, North William Street (Catholic)

St Agatha's parish was originally part of the sprawling parish of St Mary's (the Pro-Cathedral). Its parishioners attended services in the chapel in the long-established convent on North William Street. In 1853, St Agatha's was constituted into a full parish and its first parish priest, Fr Frances Doran, decided to build a new and fitting church. However, he died in a boating accident in July 1877.

The next parish priest, Fr Matthew Collier, selected a site for the church at the junction of North William Street with Dunne Street and building began in 1878. Funds ran out however, at the string course and Fr Collier died in 1892.

Fr John O'Malley was then appointed parish priest and he was adamant that a 'backstreet' was not a suitable environment for a parish church. He had a site in mind – where a Georgian house stood on the North Circular Road facing North Great Charles Street. This house actually became the St Agatha Church presbytery for many years.

Then in 1902, a benevolent anonymous parishioner willed €8000 towards the building of the church, stating that it must be on the site at North William Street. And the Archbishop of Dublin, William Walsh insisted on sticking to what the will stipulated. In a most unusual move, Fr O'Malley then took a court case against the archbishop. The court proceedings were not completed when Fr O'Malley died suddenly, in 1904. The building of today's St Agatha's Church then carried on to completion – you could say that it had a hard birth!

It was officially opened and blessed in October 1908. It is a spacious building in the classical Roman Renaissance style, with Corinthian corner pilasters. Of particular note are three large paintings in the arches of the church's apse: The Agony in the Garden, The Supper at Emmaus and The Annunciation. The church also has statues of Christ, St Patrick and St Agatha. The fine ornate decorative work in the baptistery was completed by Harry Clarke. The church had its windows blown out in the 1941 North Strand bombing (referred to above).

St Agatha was a Sicilian virgin who lived in the third century. Her 'indomitable chastity' led to her canonisation.

North Strand Church (Church of Ireland)

The original North Strand (episcopal) Church was established in Spring Garden Street in 1786, as was the accompanying school. The makeshift church and school were situated at today's number 68 North Strand Road – on its junction with Spring Garden Street. The present church, which dates from 1836, with St Columba's school attached, stands on the North Strand Road between Waterloo Avenue and Nottingham Street. The church came to be known as the 'Ivy Church'.

In 1890 the church became the official North Strand Parish Church. It now forms one parish with Drumcondra and St Barnabas', East Wall in the Anglican Diocese of Dublin and Glendalough. A tablet on the north wall of the church was put in place in 1973, in memory of a well-remembered rector, Rev Canon Hall. The church also has a memorial to all parishioners killed or missing in world wars.

Fairview Gospel Hall

Fairview Hall at 13 Annesley Bridge Road is one of eight Gospel Halls in Dublin and dating from 1912, it is one of the oldest. It is of the same red brick, simple character of the houses around it and thus is not as prominent in its setting as many churches and religious institutions tend to be. It is situated at the junction of North Strand Road with Addison Road. It forms part of the Gospel Hall Brethren local assembly.

The Free Church, North Great Charles Street

The Church of Ireland Free Church stands in railed grounds on North Great Charles Street, which runs between Mountjoy Square and the North Circular Road. Mountjoy Square was completed in 1818 and railed off for residents, until Dublin Corporation took it over in 1938. The building is at the head of Sean O'Casey Avenue (formerly Upper Rutland Street), which joins North Great Charles Street with Summerhill.

The Jesuits had chosen this as a Jesuit church site in 1823 but, the owner of the plot refused to sell it for the agreed €2000 when he realised it was to accommodate what he termed a 'masshouse'. The Methodist community acquired the site and built the church as the street itself was being built from 1795. It is a classical building with a plain granite facade. They opened the spireless building in 1800. Then, the Methodists built a Central Mission Church in Lower Abbey Street and no longer needed the Charles Street Church. The Church of Ireland purchased the property and the inscription over the front doorway reads:

Free church consecrated IV May 1828

'Free' refers to the fact that no pew rents were paid and the incumbent cleric depended on voluntary subscriptions from the congregation. This was in accordance with the spirit of evangelism at the time. The last service was held there in 1988.

Bought by a charity, the information board on its lawn today reads –

Pavee Point Traveller and Roma Centre

A little historical research tells us that 21 North Great Charles Street was the ordnance survey office where poet, James Clarence Mangan began working in 1833. It was here that he composed one of his better-known poems, *The Woman of Three Cows*. He is mostly remembered for his lyrical, patriotic poem, *Dark Rosaleen*.

The first Governor General of the Irish Free State, Timothy Michael Healy, and CS Parnell's bitter enemy during the Kitty O'Shea divorce scandal, lived at 50 North Great Charles Street and at 1 Mountjoy Square.

Holy Cross Church, Clonliffe Road (Catholic)

Holy Cross College on Clonliffe Road was founded in 1859 by one of Dublin's most prominent Catholic Church leaders, Cardinal Paul Cullen (1803-1878) and formally opened in 1863. It was built as the Dublin Diocesan Seminary on the site of Jones' 'Red House'. The college incorporates a church erected in the classical style with a granite facade. Its interior is in the style of a Roman basilica. This was due to the cardinal's close links with Rome and the Vatican and with Pope Gregory XVI. The north and south altars in the church were presented to Dr Cullen by a later pope, Pius IX. There are statues of Cardinal Cullen and Pope Pius IX in the church and the cardinal is buried in the crypt of the church under the apse. Cullen is credited with creating the prototype traditional Irish Catholic that defined Irish Catholicism between the Synod of Thurles in 1850 and the Second Vatican Council 1962-65 (Vatican II).

All Hallows College, Grace Park Road (Catholic)

The industrial revolution, which went on in Britain until the middle of the 19th century, changed the face of British society and created large cities, especially in the midlands while also producing serious social and economic problems. Thousands of poor Irish Catholics flocked to these new cities seeking work. Many ended up living in terrible squalor in the filthy slums that grew up in these cities.

Their situation greatly concerned the Irish clergy and a priest named Father Hand established the missionary college of All Hallows in 1842, to provide clergy to minister to the faithful in these desolate areas of industrial England. The college was founded at Drumcondra House, on the grounds of the old monastery of All Hallows (on today's Grace Park Road) and soon had to expand to provide missionary priests when the Great Famine (1845-1848) forced millions of Irish people to emigrate, especially to America and Australia. Fifty years after its foundation, the Vincentian Fathers took over the administration of All Hallows. Since its foundation, the college has sent thousands of priests to preach the gospel in every corner of the English-speaking world.

The original college chapel, opened in 1850, was built for eighty clerical students. In 1895, there were 170 students. Plans were afoot to replace the church when it was completely burned down in a fire. A truly noble chapel was built to replace it – its style being early Gothic. Notable is the way the broad sanctuary is slightly elevated above the body of the church, to provide ample space for its many solemn ceremonies of ordinations. A little further along Grace Park Road is the now unused, little Carmelite convent church, on the original Hampton site – now a housing estate. And across the road from All Hallows is the lovely Rosminian St Joseph's Church. It is a chapel of ease serving the Marino Parish.

Church of the Visitation of the Blessed Virgin Mary, Fairview (Catholic)

A pious merchant named James Young, working with the Carmelite order, organised a chapel at Fairview, which was blessed and officially opened by Dr Troy, Archbishop of Dublin in 1819. This was to be Fairview's church until the new Church of Our Lady of the Visitation was opened on Fairview Strand in 1855. Mr Young willed the place to his niece, Mrs Brophy to whom rent was paid. So, the chapel came to be called 'Brophy's Chapel'. It was also known as 'The Monastery Chapel'. Part of it was on the site of the old cinema in Fairview.

A Father Kennedy, a curate in the parish of Clontarf (Fairview was then part of the Clontarf parish) decided, in 1847, that the time had come to provide Fairview with a church suitable for the growing population of the area. The building process was slow, especially due to the shortage of the necessary finance and it was eight long years before the church was opened for public worship. That opening took place on 5 January 1855.

Built on a site then facing the Tolka river, at the junction of today's Fairview Strand with Philipsburgh Avenue, it had and has a commanding position. Its architectural style is that of pointed Gothic of the Plantagenet period. Cruciform in design, it is built of black limestone with the facings of the doors and windows of Wicklow marble. Of particular note is the grand stone cross of medieval design at the apex of the front of the church, with the little oval window underneath. The entrance to the church from Fairview Strand was constructed from the stones of a turnpike gate, which existed until the close of the 19th century at the end of Fairview Avenue. Fairview became a full parish in 1942.

Famous Galway-born writer Walter Macken (1915-1967) and Peggy Kenny eloped and were married in this church in February 1937.

St Vincent de Paul, Marino (Catholic)

The population of the Marino area expanded rapidly in the 1920s when most of its roadways were built. The 'spine' of the locality, Griffith Avenue, was constructed between 1924 and 1928. As a church and schools were needed, the Christian Brothers, well established here by now, donated part of their lands on the north side of Griffith Avenue, where a classic group of three buildings were opened in 1928.

In a prominent position on high ground, the centrepiece is the architectural gem that is the distinctive St Vincent de Paul Church. It is flanked, to the west, by Scoil Mhuire Boys National School and, to the east by Scoil Uinseann De Pól Girls National School. All three buildings are of a continental architectural style, as are many local houses. The church first opened as a chapel of ease to the Church of the Visitation in Fairview. Marino became a full parish in 1942. The high altar within the church was donated by the government in honour of Arthur Griffith.

St Mary's Christian Brothers establishment (today's Marino Institute of Education) beside St Vincent de Paul Church had its own inbuilt chapel from the beginning. As previously stated, St Joseph's Church on Grace Park Road is a chapel of ease in the parish.

Clontarf Presbyterian Church, Howth Road, Clontarf

Officially called the Clontarf and Scots Church, the Clontarf Presbyterian Church stands in a very prominent position at the junction of the Howth Road with the Clontarf Road. This particular congregation, after operating in South Dublin City, became established at the Ebenezer Chapel on D'Olier Street, in the city centre.

In 1845 they moved to what became known as 'The Scots Church' on Lower Gloucester Street (now Seán McDermott Street). This Doric building with the Greek inscription on its facade is still standing, albeit in a ruinous condition.

A very 'larger than life' figure, Rev JL Morrow, took over as minister in 1884. He decided to move their base to Clontarf and today's church was opened in 1890. The distinctive tower – which is unusual for a Presbyterian church – was added in 1897-98. The outstanding feature of the church, built of granite stone, is the fantastic 1914-18 Great War memorial stained-glass window, which was designed and made by Harry Clarke RHA in 1918-19.

Our Lady of Consolation, Donnycarney (Catholic)

It is reputed that St Patrick founded a little church in today's Donnycarney. It was dedicated to St Cearnach (who was originally from Cornwall, a disciple of St Patrick) or to St Carnach, who lived in county Louth in the sixth century. No trace of the old church remains but, the present Church of Our Lady of Consolation may be on the same site – where a 'tin church' served the parish for many years.

Today's church, prominently positioned opposite the Millennium Clock at the junction of Collins Avenue with the Malahide Road, was opened in May 1969. Collins Avenue was constructed in the late 1920s but the houses in the vicinity of the church mainly date from the 1940s. The church is large and cruciform in design. Notable are its full-length windows of abstract stained glass and its doors of hand-beaten copper, depicting New Testament scenes. The parish was part of Marino until it was constituted as a full parish in 1952.

St Brigid's Church, Killester (Catholic)

The ruin of an old convent or abbey, which predates the Norman invasion, with a little church and round tower lie on Killester Avenue. Tradition holds that this foundation was dedicated to St Brigid (c.453 - c.524) after she performed a few miracles while visiting the place. There are only the vaguest of remains of the establishment in the old churchyard.

The modern Church of St Brigid was opened on the Howth Road in September 1926. Its architecture is of the Florentine style, with its distinctive circular windows. It houses a relic of St Brigid. That relic is a jawbone preserved in a reliquary in the church. It was brought from Portugal on behalf of the parish priest, Fr Traynor and enshrined in the church on 27 January 1929 by Most Rev Dr Byrne, Archbishop of Dublin. The skull of St Brigid was originally taken to Portugal, in 1283, by Irish knights for their protection during a crusade against the Moslems. These knights lost their lives in the Moorish wars and the skull was given to the parish church of Lumiaer in Lisbon, by Queen Dinez.

The church was lengthened in 1952 and in 1955, it became the parish church for Killester and Raheny. In 1966 Killester and Raheny became two separate independent parishes. A resource centre overlooking a Peace Garden was added in 2004.

Clontarf, Clonliffe and Sutton Methodist Churches

John Wesley, the father of Methodism, preached his first sermon in Dublin in 1749 in St Mary's Church, Mary Street. The Methodist City Mission

Church was founded at Lower Abbey Street in 1820. As Dublin's population grew rapidly in the second half of the 19th century, Methodism in the city also grew and churches were erected in suburban areas, including Clonliffe and Clontarf, effectively born of the City Mission congregation.

Clontarf's first Methodist church – affectionately known as 'The Wesley Church' – was built in 1867 at the seafront end of St Laurence Road. It was replaced by another church in 1891. Today's church – on the same prominent site – was constructed in 1906. The handsome granite church, adorned with the familiar clock in the gable end, has been a landmark on the Clontarf seafront for successive generations of passers-by.

The Methodist community built a church in Clonliffe, on Jones' Road close to its junction with Clonliffe Road, in 1882. It was on the Methodist Circuit with City Mission on Lower Abbey Street but transferred to the Clontarf Circuit in 1940. However, with ever dwindling numbers, it closed in 1949 and the church building no longer exists.

The Sutton Methodist Church, situated at the junction of Church Road with the Howth Road, dates from 1903. A lecture hall was added in 1927 and a manse in 1933.

Church Road is aptly named with a church at each end. It was originally called Sack Lane and later Saxe Lane. Today, Clontarf, Sutton and Skerries form the one Methodist Circuit.

St John the Baptist Clontarf, Seafield Road West (Church of Ireland)

The old church ruins in Clontarf Cemetery on Castle Avenue are those of the first Protestant church built in the area, in 1609 – itself, most likely erected on the site of St Comgall's little church of 550.

A new church on Seafield Road (West) replaced this church. It was built on a site donated by John E Vernon of Clontarf Castle and officially opened on 14 May 1866. Built from granite stone, it is a comfortable, neat and elegant church with Gothic windows. It is a cruciform building and two features in particular stand out. The first is its 150-foot-high spire – a local landmark, conspicuous from far out in Dublin Bay. The tower actually forms the porched entrance. The second is the east window behind the altar. Its stained-glass representation of the twelve apostles is acknowledged as an outstanding work of art and unusual in that Mattias replaces Judas as the twelfth apostle.

In the churchyard is a war memorial honouring all parishioners who served and died during the First World War. Bram Stoker (author of *Dracula*) and his four brothers and two sisters were baptised here and playwright, Sean O'Casey was confirmed in the church.

In 2007, the select vestry of the parish decided to centralise the parish community, so they disposed of the old parish hall and the sexton's house, which stood further along Seafield Road opposite Belgrove Boys Schools. The old Glebe House beside the church, which was first built in 1878, had been disposed of some years previously and a new rector's residence built. In 2007, a new hall and parish centre were provided.

The old St Brigid's Church of Ireland Killester parish was merged with the St John the Baptist parish in 1686.

Clontarf's Three Catholic Churches

After the Reformation, the old Catholic parish system was destroyed and all churches confiscated. A new era, with a Catholic fight back began, with the Church Synod of Leinster, held in Kilkenny in 1614. A sprawling parish of Clontarf was established to include eight of the old parishes that made up the Fingal area. The eight were Clontarf itself, Raheny, Coolock, Drumcondra (or Clonturk), Santry, Glasnevin, Killester and Artane. It was really a union or district of parishes and was to last unbroken until 1879. After that, slowly, over the years, redivision happened to give us the parishes that we have come to know in modern times.

1. Church of St John the Baptist, Clontarf Road

In 1824, the parish priest of Clontarf, Dr Paul Long, had 'a plain rectangular edifice' erected on a strip of ground running west to east, behind a modern terrace of houses adjoining the residence known as 'Summerville', a site now occupied by Holy Faith Secondary School, Belgrove Road. This Church of St John the Baptist was Clontarf's first Catholic church since St Comgall's foundation, in Clontarf Cemetery and it actually predated Catholic Emancipation, which came in 1829. In 1838, the present Church of St John the Baptist on the Clontarf Road, close to Vernon Avenue, was opened. Thus, it is Clontarf's oldest church.

A famous 'religious name' associated with the church is that of Matt Talbot, 'The Servant of God'. His parents, Charles Talbot and Elizabeth Bagnall were married in St John the Baptist Church on 16 September 1853. They lived at nearby number 2 Rutland Street, now part of Clontarf Park. Later, they moved to 13 Aldborough Court in the north inner city.

2. Church of St Anthony of Padua, Clontarf Road

Up to the year 1900, Clontarf was a separate township from the City of Dublin, with its own town hall, built in 1894, on that part of the Clontarf

Road then known as Strandville – close to St Lawrence Road. However, when the boundaries act of 1900 incorporated Clontarf into Dublin City proper, the hall was no longer needed as a 'town centre'. It was bought by Canon Dempsey, parish priest of Clontarf, who extended the building, added the familiar cut-stone frontage and, skilfully and happily transformed it into a chapel of ease, to serve the western end of his now bulging parish.

It was blessed, officially opened and dedicated to St Anthony of Padua in August 1927. It became a full parish church in July 1966, when St Anthony's parish was constituted from that of St John the Baptist. In 1975, a modest, modern and comfortable new Church of St Anthony was built to replace the old church, just landward of it.

A traditional story in the area goes that, in the days of old and badly lit roads, Clontarf folk travelling from Dublin City felt home and safe when they came to that familiar cut-stone frontage of St Anthony's Church. The old building is one of Dublin's most historic edifices.

The hall became a secret meeting place for the Supreme, Executive and Military councils of the IRB, made possible by Michael McGinn, the caretaker of the hall. Himself a member of the IRB, McGinn was a friend of Tom Clarke since their days of living in Co. Tyrone. At a vital meeting held in Clontarf Town Hall on 16 January 1916, the IRB decided to 'in fact' go ahead with an uprising. This was the crossing-the-Rubicon moment and made the Easter Rising of 1916 inevitable. Another decision made at that meeting was to meet with James Connolly and blend his and the Citizen's Army path with that of the IRB. This duly happened a few days later, with the so called 'January Agreement'.

3. Church of St Gabriel the Archangel, St Gabriel's Road

As development and building (of houses) in Clontarf and Dollymount continued in the late decades of the 19th century and early decades of the 20th century, Dollymount ceased to be separate village and merged with Clontarf. As a large population settled into the new housing estates, it became obvious that the Dollymount area needed its own church. The local Sisters of Charity of St Vincent de Paul in Immaculate Conception House donated a site and, the new Church of St Gabriel was built there and opened in October 1956. Built on St Gabriel's Road it served as Clontarf Parish's second chapel of ease until, like St Anthony's, it was constituted a full parish church in July 1966.

It is an imposing building of concrete in the Hiberno-Romanesque style of architecture. The interior is adorned with artworks in two mediums: mosaic and stained glass. The stations of the cross are beautifully executed in Italian mosaic frieze. The figure of St Gabriel, in a large, stained-glass window, is very eye-catching.

A distinguished visitor to St Gabriel's Church on one occasion was the Italian, Cardinal Montini. He visited the building in 1962, accompanied by Dublin's Archbishop McQuaid. The next year, 1963, he became Pope Paul VI, on the death of Pope John XXIII.

Today, Clontarf's three Catholic parishes have been reunited or clustered under a moderator parish priest.

Manresa House, Clontarf Road

Dollymount is home to Manresa House, which is situated on private grounds just off the Clontarf Road, between Dollymount Avenue and Mount Prospect Avenue. Dating from at least 1835, it was originally part of the Vernon (Clontarf Castle) estate and was, at various times, known as Granby Hall, Baymont House and Baymont Castle. Overlooking Dublin Bay, it is a castellated building of a unique architectural design. It served many purposes over the years.

The founder of the Irish Loreto nuns organised a school there in 1845. Lord Ardilaun acquired the property in 1898 and it became a preparatory school for boys, which closed in 1946. The Jesuits (Society of Jesus order of priests) acquired the property in 1948, renaming it Manresa, after the Spanish cave of that name where the founder of the Jesuits, Ignatius Loyola, composed his famous 'spiritual exercises'. For many years – up to 1991 – students studying to become Jesuit priests spent the first two years of their noviceship at Manresa. Then it blossomed into a vibrant centre of spirituality, which nowadays offers guidance in prayer and spirituality and Christian living through retreats and workshops. It has its own little church.

Manresa also commemorates Fr William Doyle (1873-1917), the Irish Jesuit Chaplain of World War I, who was killed during the Battle of Ypres on 16 August 1917.

Raheny Churches

Raheny, Ráth Eanna, got its name from Eanna's Fort. It was a defence fort and the remains of it is the high mound in the centre of Raheny Village. Here stood a medieval chapel dating from the 12th century. It was replaced, in 1609, by the Church of Ireland Church of St Assam (some sources say 'Assan'), which itself was rebuilt in 1712 and its ruins lie in the middle of the graveyard on the mound.

Patrick Grattan, grandfather of the later politician, Henry Grattan was a rector here from 1680 to 1703. When St Assam's became unsuitable for further use, Lord Ardilaun, the Thane of St Anne's Park, presented the site and built the beautiful All Saints' Church. This became the new Protestant church of the Raheny parish and was opened in 1889.

The church, in its lovely setting in the groves of St Anne's Park, is built of Wicklow granite and limestone, with Caen stone used inside. Its style is a very elaborate Victorian Gothic type with the tower and steeple modelled on the famous Salisbury Cathedral in Wiltshire, England. The church is cruciform in structure and the elegant octagonal spire is 110 feet (34 metres) high. However, the outstanding feature of the interior is the exquisite font of marble and alabaster.

Lord and Lady Ardilaun are buried in the mortuary chapel of the church, in sepulchral tombs where, in 1987, the parish set up a columbarium, in which parishioners may leave the ashes of deceased family members in their own niche.

Bono (Paul Hewson) of U2 and Alison Stewart were married in All Saints' Church on 21 August 1982.

The old St Assam's Catholic Church stands on the corner of Main Street with the Howth Road. Built in 1864, it had a simple nave and chancel. However, it soon proved too small for a very fast-growing area and now has community uses. Its replacement church, straight across the road – the Church of Our Lady Mother of Divine Grace – was opened in 1962 to replace St Assam's as the Catholic parish church of Raheny.

The large church dominates the whole village of Raheny, from its position at the junction of Station Road with the Howth Road. The building displays a style of modern Celtic architecture. The church's triangular main entrance, facade and door motif is based on the 12th century, Irish-Romanesque west door of Clonfert Cathedral in County Galway. Very notable in the church are its numerous, finely handcrafted, wooden statues.

Raheny became a fully independent parish in 1966.

Raheny Capuchin Friary, off Station Road on the Belmont housing estate, was opened as a residential house or hostel of studies in 1946. It was here that many student friars studied before being ordained. Complete with church, the centre also served as a centre of worship for the people of Raheny. The present friary and public church were built in 1948-49. In 1957, a retreat house became part of the establishment. In 1989, the Capuchin friars donated some of their grounds where, in temporary buildings, St Francis Hospice was founded. The friars donated more land and the full hospice that we know today was opened.

Kilbarrack Churches

1. Kilbarrack Church Ruins

The ruins of Kilbarrack Church lie in the old Kilbarrack Cemetery on the Dublin Road, halfway between the Kilbarrack and Baldoyle roads. The ruins date from the 12th/13th centuries but, it is likely that a church has existed here since the sixth century. The church was still in use down to 1615. It is here (most likely) that St Berach had a small Christian foundation in the sixth century. Kilbarrack is named after the saint – Cill Bharróg, the church of Berach.

St Berach's Holy Well was just north of the church ruin. It was reputed to have curative powers, especially for those with eyesight problems. Often referred to as the Mariners Church, local legend suggests that it was built at this seaside spot to be near to and, available for shipwrecked sailors and general seafarers. It certainly was the votive church of mariners who came ashore there and went inside to pray for comrades lost at sea and to give thanks for their own survival.

The church was also known as the Chapel of Mone, which some sources suggest links it with Anglesey Island, off the north Wales Coast, which was once called Mone. Yet another theory is that Mone is derived from the Irish word móna, meaning turf, indicating that the church was built in a bog or marshy place.

2. St Benedict's Church, Grange Park View (Catholic)

The small, homely little Church of St Benedict on Grange Park View was constituted as a full parish church in 1971. It served as a parish church for Donaghmede in the years before the Church of the Holy Trinity was opened.

3. Church of St John the Evangelist, Greendale Road (Catholic)

The Church of St John the Evangelist, serving the Foxfield St John area was established in 1982, in a very prominent corner setting at Greendale Road/ Foxfield St John/Foxfield Crescent.

In 1988, the lovely St John's Walk was put in place in the church grounds. Ideal for a contemplative walk, it has twenty-one depictions concerning the life of Our Lord from the Gospel of St John. St John the Evangelist (John the Apostle) is traditionally regarded as the author of the Gospel of John. He is the patron saint of love and authors.

Grange Abbey, Grange Abbey Drive

The old ruins of Grange Abbey lie on Grange Abbey Drive, Donaghmede beside the Donaghmede roundabout. It is the oldest building in the area and the first recorded Christian structure in the entire locality. The earliest reference to a church here was in 1472, when it was termed 'The church at the Little Grange'. For a long time – before modern Donaghmede developed – this was listed as part of Baldoyle.

The Abbey was founded in the 12th century by the Canons of the Order of Arosia. There were works carried out on the abbey in the 15th and 19th centuries. However, excavations have indicated that, in all probability, a pre-Norman structure existed here. And the fact that there was a Holy Well nearby, likely involving traditional rituals and pattern days, would suggest that the entire site is a religious one, with connections stretching back to the early Christian period in Ireland. By the year 1630, it ceased to function as a church.

A notable story concerning Grange Abbey recalls that the Lord Deputy, Sir William de Windson, convened a parliament in this small church in 1369 – the so called 'Hungry Parliament'. Apparently, the Lord Deputy deliberately picked this place for its inconvenience and to make members as uncomfortable as possible, as there were few facilities, or provisions, or food and no lodgings. In this way, he hoped to compel all members to agree to his proposals to raise funds by increasing taxes and levying subsidies. It was also the middle of winter, so the members acquiesced pretty quickly to get away from the place and its 'cramped quarters'. However, King Edward III later rescinded the decisions made during this 'Hungry Parliament'.

In the 1980s, the Office of Public Works (OPW) took charge of the old ruins and 'tidied up' the entire site, placing modern stone carvings on each side of the main gate. Grange Abbey is now a national monument.

Holy Trinity Church, Grange Road (Catholic)

Holy Trinity Church, Grange Road, Donaghmede serves the areas of Donaghmede, Clongriffin and Balgriffin. The parish of the Holy Trinity was first constituted in 1974 and the church was officially opened in 1978.

While awaiting a church, the school hall of the Holy Trinity Primary School, just across the road, was used for Mass celebrations, as was St Benedict's Church, mentioned above. The first parish priest of the new parish was Fr Dermot O'Mahony, who later became an auxiliary bishop for the archdiocese of Dublin. Fr Joe Collins was parish priest (1975-79) at the time that the church opened and, he is fondly remembered for his great work in 'settling the new sprawling parish'.

Religious orders have always played a major role in the Holy Trinity Parish, including the Franciscan Missionary Mary order of nuns, the Holy Rosary Sisters, The Sisters of Mercy and the Columban Fathers.

Baldoyle Churches (Catholic)

St Peter and Paul's Catholic Church has a beautiful setting, overlooking the harbour on Main Street Baldoyle. It stands serenely on the seafront, just past the junction of Main Street with Strand Road. It was built in 1831, on the site of an older thatched 'Mass house' that dated back to 1662. The Parochial House and Parish stand on the site of the old boys school. The present church was totally refurbished in the 1990s.

Baldoyle's second Catholic church, the more modern St Laurence O'Toole Church, is at 91 Grange Road and dates from 1982. Close to this church, in Marian Park, a poignant little wall plaque recalls all the deceased residents of Marian Park between 1953 and 2003. Baldoyle also enjoyed the small Sisters of Charity chapel at St Mary's convent and, close to it, the Christian Brothers little church.

Church of the Resurrection, Bayside (Catholic)

The Catholic Church of the Resurrection at Bayside Square North was opened in 1971 and celebrated its golden jubilee in 2021. The main feature of this comfortable church is its stained-glass window of *The Resurrection*.

St Fintan's, Greenfield Road (Catholic)

The ruins of the old St Fintan's Church lie on Carrickbrack Road in Sutton. There were many Saint Fintans but, the one concerned here was born in County Laois and lived circa 520-603. In later life, he was noted for the austerity and severity of the rules for monks serving under him.

The old church is in ruins since the 16th century and it occupies the site of two earlier churches. It displays architectural features that range from the ninth century onwards. It is very likely that there has been a 'Holy Site' at the spot since very early Christian times.

St Fintan's Well, which is located close to the old church ruins, has a reputation of being healative, particularly for eye and stomach complaints.

In 1912, what became known as the 'Tin Church', built of corrugated iron and wood, was put in place at the junction of Greenfield Road with Church Road. It was replaced in 1973 by the new St Fintan's Church, which is somewhat unusual in aspect and 'differently' attractive. The whole church site is fan shaped and displays a copper roof and walls of ribbed concrete. It is very suitable and fitting to a seafaring location with a seafaring tradition.

The entire site consists of spacious buildings with the church itself as its heart's core. In individuality the church tower stands in the atrium, the pavement of which is of Liscannor stone. In the church grounds is a sculptured rock dedicated to peace. Beside the church is a memorial plaque to Fr James Gaffney, a curate in the Clontarf parish, who was killed in an accident nearby in 1876. He died tragically when his horse shied and reared and threw him on to some rocks.

Howth Churches

1. Howth Presbyterian Church, Howth Road

Howth's small Presbyterian Church, at 103 Howth Road, is situated a short distance before the entrance to Howth Castle and almost directly across the road from Howth Lodge apartments, which stand on the site of the Old Howth Lodge Hotel.

The church was built in 1898, followed by its manse in 1899. Both church and manse are Gothic in style. The church sports a red-tiled roof and has a square, battlemented tower built of grey limestone.

2. St Mary's, Howth Road (Church of Ireland)

St Mary's Parish Church of Ireland is on a lovely, elevated site on the Howth Road, at the entrance to Howth Castle demesne. It was constructed in 1866 of granite stone and has a school attached. Its style is 13th century English, with the spire being its most attractive feature.

The church has a two-light window, *St Peter; The Calling of St Andrew* by Evie Hone, dating from 1943. It also has three lights, *Faith, Hope and Charity*, from 1905 by Sarah Purser.

Lord Howth built a primitive church on this site in 1700, which was replaced by another church in 1816.

3. St Mary's Abbey, Church Street

The beautifully kept ruins of St Mary's Abbey lie on Church Street, Howth. Commonly known as the Old Abbey, its site precipitously overlooks Howth Harbour, with breath-taking views way out around and beyond Ireland's Eye and Lambay islands. The ruins are of the Collegiate Parish Church of the Blessed Virgin Mary and the entire site is a national monument.

St Mary's was still in use as an Anglican church in the early 18th century. The site, in its time, was the very heart of Howth Village and is the spot where Sitric, the then Norse King of Dublin, built a church in 1042. A new church replaced Sitric's church in 1235, most likely on the instructions of

Luke, the Archbishop of Dublin at the time. The present ruins date from the 14th and 15th centuries.

4. Church of the Assumption of Our Lady, Thormanby Road (Catholic)

At the Y junction of Howth's Main Street with Thormanby Road, in an island setting, stands the Catholic Church of the Assumption of Our Lady. It first opened in 1899. Before that, the Parochial Hall – built in 1814 and standing at the confluence of Abbey Street with Church Street – was, for many years, the place of worship for Catholics in the Howth/Baldoyle area. This building had, in turn, replaced an old, thatched edifice, which acted as a Catholic church. The present Church of the Assumption dominates the whole area, both physically and architecturally. Its proposed spire was never added.

Ireland's Eye

Ireland's Eye has the ruins of the *cill* or church of St Nessáin/Nessan (Cill Mac Nessan from the early Christian period) with a small round tower. The church was obviously named after Neasáin and his sons. It served as Howth's parish church until it was replaced by St Mary's Abbey in 1235. The abbey became more prominent and more convenient in Howth Village. It is difficult to date the ruins but, the church was probably 10th century built on the site of a seventh century foundation. The island church has not been used since the 13th century.

The church was raided by the Vikings. It is believed that the illuminated manuscript containing the four gospels, known as the *Garland of Howth*, dating from the eighth century, was taken from the little church. It is now in the library in Trinity College Dublin.

Graveyards

The word cemetery means a place to sleep or a dormitory. The subject of cemeteries or graveyards or burial grounds or necropolises can be doleful and melancholic – even depressing. However, all human life is there – the famous as well as the ordinary folk. In his chilling poem, James Shirley rightly stated:

Scepter and Crown
Must tumble down
And in the dust be equal made
With the poor crooked scythe and spade

We like to organise a dignified 'send off' for our loved ones – a wake and funeral, the doing of which, the Irish have no equal. Then, we have the place of calm that is the graveyard for burial. There is a completion when the body is laid in the grave. And there is a togetherness about family graves or plots.

Our graveyards are a very important part of our heritage – sadly, often overgrown and neglected. They are a great resource for historical and social research. The inscriptions and epitaphs on monuments and tombstones/headstones can be short biographies. A researcher can spend endless hours in large necropolises, 'lost in the past'! Yew trees are often found in graveyards. They give a sense of serenity and lucidity. They are chosen for longevity, which represents the immortality of the soul.

We often joke that Glasnevin is the 'dead' centre of Dublin and that we are all 'dying' to go there! The truth is that just about every village and town in Ireland has its own 'dead' centre and many of the villages that make up Dublin had a local graveyard before the bigger ones, like Glasnevin and Deansgrange were established. And while cremation is quite popular, burial in a regular grave is the choice of most.

Let us take a look at some of the graveyards, in our historical trail from the Customs House to Howth. Some are well documented; of others, we have scant information.

St Vincent's, North William Street

On our trail from the Customs House to Howth, the first burial ground we pass is at the premises of the Daughters of Charity of St Vincent de Paul in North William Street. Originally, an orphanage was established here by the Trinitarian order of nuns. Then, Mother Mary Aikenhead opened the first convent of the Irish Sisters of Charity on the site in 1815. The Carmelite Sisters took over the establishment in 1830 and in 1857, they were succeeded by the French Filles de Charity or the Daughters of St Vincent de Paul – commonly known as the Vincentian Sisters. They organised St Vincent's School for girls and in 1893, added a boys school. Brendan Behan was one of their more famous students.

In the little graveyard lie the bodies of many nuns, who dedicated their lives to ensuring the whole foundation ran smoothly.

Suicide Graveyard, Ballybough Road

At the junction of Clonliffe Road with Ballybough Road, there is, we believe, the site of an unconsecrated suicide graveyard. These burial places were once fairly common in Ireland and the corpses of people who took their own lives were buried in them, as they were not allowed to be interred in regular consecrated cemeteries. Here, too, the bodies of unbaptised infants were buried.

Suicide victims were buried in the time-honoured fashion, transfixed with stakes through their hearts, which supposedly prevented their unhappy spirits from wandering around. In fact, suicide victims were supposed to become vampires unless they were given the 'stake' treatment. We believe that Bram Stoker, creator of *Dracula*, was partly inspired for his creation by this graveyard. He lived in two houses not far from the graveyard – 15 The Crescent, Clontarf and 17 Upper Buckingham Street. As a youngster, he played regularly in the graveyard and with his vivid imagination, one can see how he could have visualised those buried without the stake through the heart, resurrecting at night to suck the blood of the living. (See section on Bram Stoker in Chapter Twelve).

The site is now a small, landscaped garden with seats.

St Vincent's Hospital Graveyard, Convent Avenue, Fairview

On Convent Avenue off Richmond Avenue in Fairview, the Presentation Sisters founded a convent in 1867. The sisters later moved to Terenure and the well-known institution that is St Vincent's Hospital now stands on that site. A graveyard with burials from 1867 is on part of the grounds. A wall plaque in the hospital has a list of those buried there.

Ascending Richmond Road towards Drumcondra and taking a right turn on to Grace Park Road, we find three cemeteries, all on the left-hand side.

All Hallows, Grace Park Road

The first is All Hallows Graveyard that is part of the grounds of the once famous All Hallows training seminary for missionary priests. Much of the buildings are now a campus of Dublin City University.

All Hallows originally opened in 1842, sending its priests all over the world. It was run by the Vincentian Fathers until it closed in 2016. The graveyard there opened in 1846 and is in the care of the Vincentians.

Carmelite Graveyard, Grace Park Road

The second cemetery on Grace Park Road is the burial ground at the site of the Carmelite Sisters' convent – the Monastery of the Incarnation. The original site was known as Hampton and much of it is now covered by the Hampton housing estate. The graveyard here was first opened in 1858. The sisters chose to come here from their convent in North William Street, as they felt that area had become too congested.

High Park Graveyard, Grace Park Road

The third is further along Grace Park Road, close to its junction with Collins Avenue, is the graveyard at High Park Convent, where members of the order of the Sisters of Our Lady of Charity of Refuge have been buried since 1861. They first came here in 1853, to manage the institution called the Mary Magdalen Asylum, which dated back to 1831. They later opened St Mary's Refuge on the site with a commercial laundry, which closed in 1991.

Drumcondra Graveyard, Church Road

Drumcondra Church of Ireland Graveyard at Church Road adjoins All Hallows College grounds. It has been in use since medieval times and is colloquially known as 'God's Little Acre'.

Among many well-known people buried there are members of the Jameson whiskey distilling family. The famous architect, James Gandon, who designed the Customs House was laid to rest here. Patrick Heeney, who composed the music for Peadar Kearney's *The Soldier's Song*, which became our national anthem, is also buried here. A wall plaque close to the entrance gate of the cemetery commemorates him.

Jewish Cemetery, Fairview Strand

On Fairview Strand there is one standout building – number 67 – a somewhat quaintly shaped edifice, which is contrastingly different from its neighbouring houses and is now a listed building. It has the Jewish year 5618 inscribed over the front door. This is the equivalent of 1857 AD (or the Common Era) – the year that the house was built. The building was totally refurbished in 2022 but still bears the date plaque.

Behind the house is the first Jewish cemetery to be opened in Ireland. Christopher Philips of Drumcondra, a well-off landlord and MP for Askeaton, County Limerick made a plot of land available to the Jewish community at this spot and the cemetery was opened in 1718. The house was later provided as a residence for the cemetery caretaker. It probably served as a mortuary for some time also. It replaced a smaller building which dated from 1798.

There was a Jewish community, formed in the early 1700s, of about one hundred near the house, at a place called Annadale, which has long since been absorbed into Philipsburgh Avenue. Annadale was connected to Fairview by Ellis Lane, which also has been absorbed into Philipsburgh Avenue.

There are 148 tombstones in the cemetery, inscribed in Hebrew and English. The oldest of these is on the grave of Joseph Wills, a jeweller, dated 1777. The last internment there was in 1958. Sometimes known as Fairview Strand Cemetery or Ballybough Cemetery, it is in the care of the Dublin Jewish Board of Guardians.

Priests Buried in Church Grounds

As we move along the 'graveyard route', we find that some priests chose to be interred in the grounds of the church in which they ministered. The first of these we come across is at St Anthony's Church, Clontarf Road, where former parish priest from 1971 to 1984, Fr John Gunning is buried close to the church building.

Further along the Clontarf Road, we find Rev James Callinan (parish priest – 1829-46) buried beside St John the Baptist Church. Other priests buried in church grounds include Rt Rev Monsignor Fitzpatrick (parish priest, 1952-72), Very Rev Joseph O'Hare (parish priest, 1972-82) and Very Rev Canon John MacHale (parish priest, 1982-86) all buried beside Our Lady of Divine Grace Church in Raheny.

The Very Rev Joseph Collins (parish priest, 1975-79) is buried beside Holy Trinity Church, Donaghmede and Very Rev Bernard Dennan, who was parish priest of Baldoyle from 1881 to 1889, lies in his grave on the right, as you face Saints Peter and Paul's Church, Baldoyle.

Clontarf Cemetery, Castle Avenue

The wall plaque at the entrance to the old cemetery on Castle Avenue names it as St John the Baptist Cemetery. However, my own research finds that it has always been simply called Clontarf Cemetery. It adjoins the grounds of Clontarf Castle and is under the care of Dublin City Council Environmental Health Department.

In the middle of the graveyard are the ruins of an old Protestant church, dating from 1609. This is most likely the site of the very first church in Clontarf, founded by St Congall, Clontarf's original patron saint in 550. That original church was built of 'clay and wattles' when Christianity first drew breath in the area. The graveyard is not officially closed but, no new graves are available. Notable graves there include the Vernon family vault and the Oulton family grave. Both these families resided in Clontarf Castle. Also buried there are Thomas Johnson, first leader of the Labour Party in Dáil Éireann and the entertainer, Maureen Potter.

Grave robbers, resurrectionists or 'sack-'em-ups' regularly robbed corpses from graves around Dublin in the early nineteenth century. There was great demand for bodies from the medical profession and good money to be earned. Families used various ploys to stop the body robbers, including placing heavy stone slabs over graves and installing mort safes or cages around graves. Examples of these can be seen in Clontarf Cemetery.

Killester Cemetery, Killester Avenue

One of our more forgotten graveyards is on Killester Avenue. The medieval little church that stood on the site was dedicated to St Brigid and most likely fell into ruin around 1536. A small, engraved stone outside the graveyard wall recalls Michael Neville who, in 1922 during the Civil War, was executed in the cemetery. The site is under the care of Dublin City Council Environmental Section.

Saint Assam's, Howth Road, Raheny

St Assam's Graveyard and old church ruins are located, in an island setting, beside the Howth Road in the centre of Raheny Village. The church, dating from 1609 and built on the site of a previous church, dating back to at least the 12th century, was a simple structure.

Services continued in the church until it fell into a 'dangerous' condition and was replaced by All Saints' Church, built in St Anne's Park in 1889. The oval shaped graveyard is close to two metres above the Howth Road, as it sits on a mound. There are thirty-nine gravestones on the site and the graveyard was closed in 1924. The earliest gravestone dates from 1738.

In the very beautiful All Saints' Church of Ireland, there is a columbarium, where parishioners can leave the ashes of deceased family members in their own niche. Lord Ardilaun, who was the proprietor of St Anne's estate, is buried in the Mortuary Chapel in the church, with his wife Olivia. In the crypt, two members of the Guinness family are buried: Benjamin Lee Guinness, brother of Lord Ardilaun and Olive Guinness, daughter of Edward Cecil Guinness. Outside the east windows of the church is a lone grave containing the bodies of Bishop Plunkett, the last owner of St Annes, his wife, Dorothea and her brother, Thomas Butler.

Kilbarrack Cemetery, Dublin Road, Sutton

This old, three-acre graveyard is not closed, as some families still have burial rights there. There are about one thousand gravestones in the graveyard. The earliest dates from 1654 but, this does not mean that burials only began then.

One of the most obnoxious characters in Irish history, Francis "Sham Squire" Higgins (1746-1802) is buried here. A Catholic, he went over to Protestantism and became a government informer, betraying United Irishmen leader, Lord Edward Fitzgerald (1763-1798) and the Shears brothers, Henry (1753-1798) and John (1766-1798). When this became public knowledge, sixty-four years after Higgin's death, a group of irate and indignant Dubliners marched to Kilbarrack Cemetery and defaced his grave.

Martin Joyce, the only Joyce family member to survive the infamous Maamtrasna murders of August 1882, is buried in Kilbarrack Cemetery. He came to live in the Kilbarrack area sometime after five members of his family were murdered in that tragedy.

The MacNeill brothers, Eoin and John, are interred here. Eoin (1867-1945) was a founder member of the Gaelic League and commander-in-chief of the Irish Volunteers. However, his place in Irish history is unsure due to his countermanding order to the Volunteers, which prevented the 1916 Rising going ahead on Easter Sunday 1916 and his disastrous role with the Boundary Commission of 1924/25. James (1869-1938) was Ireland's second Governor General in the 1928-32 period.

Several IRA members are commemorated in Kilbarrack Cemetery, among them, Dan Head of Seville Place and Sean Doyle of Amiens Street, who were both killed in the course of the IRA attack on the Customs House in May 1921.

Frank Flood, a nineteen-year-old IRA member from Summerhill Parade was executed in Mountjoy Prison, in March 1921 and is buried in Mountjoy. He and his brother, John Joseph Flood, also an IRA member who died in 1929, had a memorial stone erected in Kilbarrack Cemetery by their parents.

Another IRA member, John William of Upper Rutland Street, who was killed at his home in June 1922, is also commemorated in the graveyard, as are Charles Lyons (d 1919), his brother John Edward Lyons (d 1933) and Michael Kiernan (d 1922).

Thomas Wall who was killed in the Four Courts during the Civil War is also buried in Kilbarrack Graveyard.

Although a story called *The Dead*, concerning the activities of the 19th century 'sack-'em-up' boys (or body snatchers) is set in Kilbarrack Cemetery, the graveyard was not popular with graverobbers because of its exposed position along the coast.

The Irish Sisters of Charity have their own beautifully landscaped burial plot within Kilbarrack Cemetery.

Grange Abbey Graveyard, Grange Abbey Drive, Donaghmede

The old graveyard at the ruins of Grange Abbey, beside the Donaghmede roundabout, dates back to the foundation of the abbey in the 12th century.

Burials took place here up to the 18th century. Two old gravestones survive: one dated 1737; the other, 1756.

Christian Brothers Graveyards

Two Christian Brothers community graveyards feature in our Dublin North Bay area. The first is at the present Marino Institute of Education on Griffith Avenue, the former St Mary's Christian Brothers 'Mother House'. Over 160 brothers are interred here, each grave marked in the same way, with simple limestone plinths. Some of the brothers laid to rest here had known and worked with the order's founder, Edmund Rice.

The second Christian Brothers graveyard was opened at their St Joseph's premise and church on today's Dublin Street in Baldoyle, in 1916. Nearly seven hundred brothers are buried there.

On 29 May 1994, a crowd numbering over one thousand people were present at an open-air Mass to mark the beatification of Blessed Edmund Rice (Brother Ignatius). The Mass was celebrated by Bishop John Kavanagh. As a memorial to Brother Ignatius, the graveyard was renamed after him.

St Fintan's Cemetery, Carrickbrack Road, Sutton

St Fintan's Cemetery is located on sloping ground overlooking Dublin Bay and Dublin City. There have been burials here since 1850.

The layout of the cemetery is in four distinct sections. The original old graveyard, where the old church ruins stand, is known as the 1889 section. The second section is called the 1907 section and is really an expansion of the old. The third is referred to as the 1954 section, indicating the year in which it was opened. The fourth section is named the Lawn and was opened in 1972. All of the monuments and memorials in St Vincent's are laid horizontally on the ground. This certainly makes lawnmowing and general maintenance an easier task!

A bronze statue of St Fintan stands in the cemetery. St Fintan's Cemetery marks the final resting place of some well-known people.

Longford-born Padraic Colum (1881-1972), writer and playwright and a major player in the Irish Literary Revival is buried here beside his Sligo-born wife, writer and teacher, Mary (née Maguire, 1884-1957). They lived for some time in a cottage in Howth after they married in 1912, before emigrating to America in 1914.

London-born actor, painter, writer and poet, Micheál Mac Liammóir (1899-1978), whose real name was Alfred Willmore, is buried in St Fintan's beside his companion, actor and producer, Hilton Edwards (1903-1982). An Post issued a stamp in 1999 to mark the centenary of Mac Liammóir's birth.

**St Peter and Paul's
Church, Baldoyle**

**Church of the
Assumption, Howth**

Fairview Gospel Hall

**Clontarf Presbyterian
Church**

**St John the Baptist Church
of Ireland, Clontarf**

All Saints' Church, Raheny

Sutton Methodist Church

**Our Lady of Consolation,
Donnycarney**

St Vincent de Paul Church, Marino

Old St Anthony's Church, Clontarf

Old St Assam's, Raheny

St Fintan's Graveyard, Sutton

Graves at Jewish Cemetery, Fairview

Kilbarrack Graveyard

Clontarf Cemetery

Railed grave at Clontarf Cemetery

Rockstar Phil Lynott (1949-1986) of Thin Lizzy rock band fame is interred in St Fintan's. In June 2019, his mother, Phyllis was buried beside him.

Former Taoiseach Charles Haughey (1925-2006) is buried in St Fintan's, as is broadcaster, Gay Byrne (1934-2019) and former President of Ireland, Dr Patrick Hillery (1923-2008).

Howth Graveyards

St Mary's Abbey Cemetery is a well-known and much visited place on Church Street in Howth. Burials here go back many centuries but all burials in the cemetery ceased on 31 May 1973. A medieval tomb in the chancel of St Mary's Abbey, on the site, is the final resting place of Christopher St Lawrence, the 14th Baron of Howth, who died in 1462. A relatively unknown graveyard in Howth, also called St Mary's, is located behind the Parochial Hall at the junction of Church Street with Main Street. It has been in use since 1813 and is 'manicured' to perfection in its secluded position!

CHAPTER NINE
Public Houses

Pubs have been part of our culture for centuries. Shebeens were the first pubs. These were essentially premises selling alcoholic beverages without a licence to do so.

In 1650, when Dublin's population numbered about 4,000 families, there were 1,189 drinking establishments! When Arthur Guinness bought St James's Gate brewery on 31 December 1759, competition in the drinks trade was extremely intense, with thirty-five other breweries in the then very small city of Dublin. The Guinness brewery was only one of seven brewing beer at James Street.

Dublin has always been noted for its myriad of pubs and its chequered, effusive, exuberant pub life and the pub has traditionally been at the heart's core of social life in Dublin. The pub culture in the city, its traditions, customs, atmosphere and characters has given Dublin itself a unique, even distinctive, make-up, reputation and standing, even an individual spirit and ethos! Most of the pubs were and are wonderful establishments, often a home from home – social venues for very sociable Dubliners! There can be no doubt that the pub has played a huge role in the social history of the city, as a place where you encounter Dublin wit, banter and wisdom, and a place where information and gossip are exchanged.

Pubs are also very historical, helping to record our history. Names of pubs often recall significant events and famous people while, inside many pubs, we find the walls 'wallpapered' with pictures and prose concerning numerous prominent and momentous episodes in local and national history.

And the pub is expected to serve only excellent alcoholic beverages! In the pub you will meet the world and its mother! Social divisions are 'blacked out', if only for the duration of a session! In the pub all are on a level footing. Indeed, the pub can be seen as a meeting place for two sides of Irish life, business and leisure. The pub ambiance beckons everyone. Brendan Behan declared that he was a drinker with a writing problem... Maybe many of us, in various trades and professions, might utter the same sentiment, at least at times!

Dr Samuel Johnson (1709-1784), the witty English lexicographer, author and critic declared that "There is nothing which has yet been contrived by man, by which so much happiness is produced as by a good tavern or inn."

This is still true despite all the changes over the years. These changes have included the serving of food in pubs and the arrival of the gastro pub. Music became common in pubs and the 'singing lounge' came to us. The smoking ban changed the very 'feel' of pubs and the more stringent application of the breathalyser laws certainly stopped many driving to the pub. The Covid-19 pandemic did untold damage to the public house trade (a total of 33 pubs closed in Dublin between 2019 and 2021) and the ever-increasing price of alcoholic drinks in the pub turned many towards the off licence.

At its peak – maybe in the latter half of the 20th century – Dublin city and county had close to 1,000 pubs. That number dropped to 752 in 2021 but the punter still has plenty of choice … and the freedom to change watering hole if barred or if the local pub 'character' is boring you towards more drink! We have early houses, hotel bars, cafe bars and club bars in GAA, soccer, rugby and golf clubs, as well as community (centre) bars.

For those who have overindulged in the 'demon drink', we have some choice synonyms including: being drunk, inebriated, intoxicated, under the influence, rubber, three sheets to the wind, fluthered, maggoty, scuppered, scuttled, locked, canned, paralytic, well-oiled, jarred, stomached, under the weather, plastered, mickey monk, pissed, stocious, blotto and, surely the daddy of all Dublin terms, transmogrified! We also refer to people as being a martyr to the drink, on the batter, on a binge and on or off the wagon!

Dublin's oldest licensed pub is the Brazen Head (Lower Bridge Street) dating from 1613. It is the third oldest on the island of Ireland after Sean's Bar in Athlone, dating from 1600 and Grace O'Neill's in Donaghdee, County Down, licensed since 1611.

As we take you along on a tour of the Dublin North Bay alehouses, it is necessary to point out – especially as a result of the Covid 19 pandemic – that some may have ceased to trade.

On our trail from the Customs House to Howth, we first escorted you along Gardiner Street, which connects the Customs House area with the old route to the sea at Parnell Street and from there, to Fairview via Summerhill and Ballybough.

The first pub that we encounter along here is O'Shea's at 19 Talbot Street but, actually on the corner with Lower Gardiner Street. It doubles as a hotel and was previously known as Moran's Hotel. A venue noted for music, such luminaries as Phil Lynott, Bono and The Edge and Bob Geldof performed here at various times.

Across the street is Ned Keenan's Bar at the Maple Hotel, 74 Lower Gardiner Street.

Further along, at 28 Middle Gardiner Street, is the drinking establishment called Hill 16. It was originally opened in 1800. Much later, after Hill 16 was built in Croke Park, (from rubble taken there in the aftermath of the 1916 Rising), the pub was named after the viewing area so beloved of Dublin GAA followers. Hill 16 is very representative of the archetypal Dublin pub and, very much a place of pilgrimage for Dublin GAA fans. The late Jack Charlton, of Irish senior soccer team management fame, was a patron of the place.

Coming north through Summerhill Parade is the Little Tree public house. For many years it was known as Sunset House. Further along, at number six, is the Bridge Tavern. Locally it is often referred to as 'Bernos', as it was once called Berminghams.

We find Lowry's at 16 Summerhill Parade, which previously traded under the names Belton's and O'Neill's.

Moving along, still on our right is Marley's at 66 Summerhill Parade, sometimes only operating as an off licence. It previously traded as Cleary's.

We find Cú Chulainn's at 69 Summerhill Parade. This establishment first opened in 1908 and has had a variety of names – The Barrel Inn, The Castle Inn, The Millennium and Whelan's. Nowadays, it tends to trade only when big events are staged at nearby Croke Park.

Before we move on to the drinking establishments in Ballybough, we will nip up the North Circular Road where, on our left at number 512, is the Hogan Stand or Phil Ryan's pub. It is named after the Hogan Stand in Croke park, a short distance away at Jones' Road.

Almost directly opposite The Hogan Stand on the North Circular Road (NCR) is Gill's Corner House. It is at 555 NCR on the corner with Russell Street. It is a very famous and landmark pub dating from 1920. It mainly opens on big match days at Croke Park.

Croke Park stadium has its own Sideline Bar in the Croke Park Hotel, across Jones' Road from the stadium.

We now return to Ballybough and we find the Ref Pub at 70 Ballybough Road. This pub has operated at various times as Tom Clarke's, Collins', The Blind Ref and Molly's.

On our right, at the railway bridge in Courtney Place, Ballybough stood Roches Pub. Older locals recall the actor, Christopher Lee recording a film scene at the pub. I wonder if he knew then, just how deep into Bram Stoker and Dracula country he was, with the Suicide Graveyard just across the road!

At 44 Ballybough Road, at its junction with Poplar Row, is Clonliffe House, previously known as Noctor and McCann's. It was also once named The Fluther Good, after a local street character who features in Sean O'Casey's famous play, *The Plough and the Stars*. Fluther Good (1865-1940), in Dublin lingo, might be referred to as a bit of a 'bowsie'!

At 283 Richmond Road, at its confluence with Fairview Strand, is Meagher's pub, once popularly known as The Log Cabin. On the front of the building is a plaque to honour the memory of all from the area who took part in the 1916 Rising.

On our left, at 47 Fairview Strand, we pass the Fairview Inn, once a very popular pub venue but no longer in operation. There has been an inn here for three hundred years. In previous times, it was known as Paddy Ready Penny's Inn (or ale house) and as Murphy's. It last traded as The Player's Lounge.

Now we return to the Customs House and follow the pubs along the new (North Strand) route to Fairview. The first licenced premises we meet, on our left, dating from 1840, is The Brew Dock gastro pub at 1 Amiens Street. This was originally the Dock Tavern, named after the Old Dock, which stood where Memorial Road is now. It later operated as the Master Mariner.

At 21 Store Street, opposite Bus Áras, is the Beresford Hotel with Dudley's Bar. The hotel once traded under the rather unusual name 'The Good Bits' and the bar was variously known as The Isaac Butt, the Le Monde Café Bar, Radio City Café Bar and the Cavern Bar.

A spacious Ryan's Bar trades on Store Street where it is joined by Frenchman's Lane.

Then we come to the familiar building at 17 Amiens Street that houses the pub known as Grainger's, on the corner with Talbot Street. Grainger's is a familiar name in the Dublin pub scene. This Grainger's was first opened in 1928.

We divert up Talbot Street and, on the right at number 37, is the Ripley Court Hotel with its Ulysses Bar, which was previously called Austin Kelly's Bar, the Dark House Bar and the Theatre Bar.

Further along Talbot Street, on the left at number 59, is Molloy's pub. It is at the Talbot Street/Talbot Place corner and was first opened in 1966.

On Talbot Place, we find Ryan's Lounge, smaller than the above-mentioned Ryan's Bar, as well as the extensive Jacob's Inn.

On the Talbot Street junction with Store Street is the James Joyce public house. A small pub, it was once owned by Thomas Cormac and was later known as Mother Kelly's.

At the Mabbot Street (now James Joyce Street) corner with Foley Street was the famous but no longer existing Shanahan's public house. A plaque records the pub's location. Phil Shanahan, the proprietor, fought in the 1916 Rising and was interned in Frongach internment camp. He later became a TD. He was a facilitator for republicans and the pub was a hive of republican and nationalist activity, particularly during the War of Independence. It was a key meeting place for General Michael Collins and his fellow freedom fighters.

Montgomery Court, at 1-15 Foley Street, contains the small Cleary's bar.

Back to Amiens Street and the familiar North Star Hotel, on our left is now known as The Address, Connolly. The hotel, directly across the road from Connolly mainline railway station, is in business since 1900. Its McCoy's bar no longer operates. The hotel has long associations with Irish revolutionary movements and features in Neil Jordan's film, *Michael Collins*. The premises is owned by the McGettigan family.

Next, all on the left, are four pubs in close proximity on Amiens Street. They are Cleary's at number 36, Mullet's at 45, Lloyd's at 46 and Burke's at 47-48.

Directly under the Amiens Street Railway Bridge, JM Cleary's pub, a listed building, was named the Signal House in 1846. A Thomas Hayden owned the premises in 1904 and later, Jim Cleary became the owner. It was yet another Michael Collins' haunt and it too features in the *Michael Collins* film, as it does in *The Commitments* film.

Mullett's bar, adjoining Montgomery Street (now Foley Street) dates from 1860 and was named Dooleys. It sometimes operates only as an off-licence. It began life as a hotel and tavern. A Timothy O'Neill ran the premises for some time. Patrick Mullet became its proprietor in 1876 and it has borne the Mullett name ever since. A very traditional Dublin pub, it features in Joyce's *Ulysses*, in a scene where Stephen and Bloom go 'bevelling around Mullets'.

Lloyd's pub dates from 1893 and was owned by Thomas Hayden and then, Daniel Bergin. Tim 'Bass' Lloyd purchased the pub about 1935. Like many of the pubs in the area, it benefits from a mixed clientele of dockers, railway workers, people from the local tenements and travellers from Connolly Station.

Burke's, on its corner site with Buckingham Street, is no longer trading. A Victorian-style establishment, it was once named Timlin's. It was owned for a time by Tim 'Bass' Lloyd.

And in the main concourse of Connolly Station is Madigan's bar, part of the long-lived Madigan chain of public houses.

Another pub close by at 3 North Strand Road, the Five Lamps or Humphreys has also ceased to trade.

Further along on our right is The Strand House at 172 North Strand Road. It was previously named Grainger's. A feature of the pub and of all pubs in the locality is that much of the clientele represent the character of the people in the Amiens Street/North Strand area – the people who make up local society.

As we move along, Cusack's Bar is on our right at 145 North Strand Road. Historically themed, especially seafaring history, it is alleged that the Venerable Matt Talbot had his last drink here before turning to a new way of life.

Cusack's once had an unexpected visit from a famous celebrity couple. They were actors, Richard Burton and Elizabeth Taylor, when Burton was making the film *The Spy Who Came in from the Cold*, in north county Dublin in 1965. The visit to Cusack's occurred on an occasion when they were returning to their city centre hotel from a filming session. Elizabeth was apparently short taken by a call of nature. While she was powdering her nose in the gentlemen's toilet (there was no ladies) a few locals chivalrously did sentry duty on the door and everyone on the premises were treated to a round of drinks by Burton.

Next, on the left, at the junction of North Strand Road with Annesley Place, we pass Annesley House at 7 North Strand Road, which is named after the nearby Annesley Bridge. It previously traded under the names Chaser's and Grainger's. The building displays a plaque to the memory of all the people of the area who partook in the 1916 Rising.

If we stray slightly from our path and take a right turn down the East Wall Road, we soon reach Seabank House or Dillon's on the right, at 123 East Wall Road. This was once known as The Wharf Tavern.

Now, we come to Edge's Corner, Fairview, where the old and new routes from the city become one.

Gaffney's pub is on our left, as 5-6 Fairview. In the early 1700s, it was known as The Big Gun Inn and was renowned for seafood. Around 1840, there were two pubs on the site: one run by James Sweetman; the other, by Bridget Halpin. About the middle of the 1850s, Thomas O'Mara bought both and amalgamated them into one. O'Mara was succeeded as landlord in the mid-1860s by Thomas Carroll, who named the premises The Emerald Isle Tavern. Later owners included John Carey and John Keogh, who sold it to Cavan-born Thomas Gaffney, circa 1914. The pub is now in the hands of a third generation of Gaffney's. Before the reclamation of Fairview Park, the sea was a mere twenty yards from its front door. The present pub is late Victorian in style. Gaffney's is a famous 'pit stop' for followers of the Dublin senior Gaelic football team, better known as 'The Dubs'.

Further along from Gaffney's is Bru House, at 12 Fairview. In the years after it first opened in 1800, it was colloquially called 'Shellfish Tavern' and middle-class Dubliners came to the area on horseback or in carriages to indulge in the shelled seafood served on the premises, particularly mussels and oysters. Most people will remember it as Coles although, before that, it was The Grafton House. It traded as Smyth's before it became Bru House.

The pubs along the route that we have traversed so far, especially the Ballybough/Fairview locality, benefit greatly from the dominating presence of the GAA's Croke Park stadium. For big matches, concerts and other events, the stadium can accommodate 80,000 patrons. Since the great Kevin Heffernan revived the fortunes of Dublin's senior inter-county team back in the 1970s, Dubliners converge on Croke Park in their thousands for Dublin matches. Before and after matches, they certainly keep the bar staff in the entire area busy and their tills ringing. Very conspicuous in the Ballybough/North Strand area are the very fine wall murals depicting Dublin players, especially those of the Heffernan era. My own favourite is the one on the gable wall of Clonliffe House, showing Heffernan (or 'Heffo') himself; the much-loved team free taker, Jimmy Keaveney and, the late Anton O'Toole, the Blue Panther.

We now turn left up the Malahide Road and on our right is Kavanagh's Marino House at 16 Malahide Road. This is a traditional family run pub. It was once called J Maguires and sported a swinging sign outside, bearing the legend *J Maguire, late of Stag's Head*.

A little further along, at 74 Malahide Road, is the 1884 public house. With GAA symbols on its logo, it obviously takes its name from the year (1884) that the GAA was founded in Hayes Hotel, Thurles, County Tipperary. The deceptively large premises was first known as Miss Cocoman's Charlemont Stores, until it became a licenced premises in 1945 and was operated by the Gallagher family. It was later named The White House and Hugh Grainger ran the premises as 'Grainger's' for many years before it became the 1884.

As we travel along the Malahide Road, we pass, on the left, the site almost opposite Donnycarney Church, where Parnell Park public house once stood. At different times, it bore the names 'The Donnycarney House',

'Millers' and 'The Refuge'. The latter name allegedly originated from referees 'taking refuge' there from irate GAA fans at nearby Parnell Park GAA grounds!

If we take a right turn onto Collins Avenue, very soon, on the left at 145 Killester Avenue, we come to the Ramble Inn. In a lovely 'Village Green' setting, it is a warm, cosy local pub.

Back on the Malahide Road, again, we soon arrive at the Goblet pub, situated just past the Kilmore Road junction with the Malahide Road in Artane. The premises has been owned and run by Jim McGovern since 1970, when he took over from Bill Costello.

We now return to the seafront and take the next left, which is the Howth Road and to the right, just off it at Hollybrook Park, we find The Hollybrook. The original Hollybrook House building here can be dated back to 1812 but, the edifice mainly associated with this spot is the Hollybrook Hotel, which for many years was the only residential hotel in Clontarf. The comfortable quiet hotel within a short bus ride of Dublin City Centre was owned by the Bresnan family. The hotel was a very popular choice of venue for wedding receptions and a host of other social functions. The bar, lounge and restaurant later traded under the name 'Gilbert and Wright' before reverting to the Hollybrook name. The main bar has variously been called Brooks Bay, Captain Weldon's and the Parlour Bar.

Back on the Howth Road, shortly on the right at 107, we arrive at Harry Byrne's public house. A coaching inn has existed here since 1809 (some sources say 1798) and it became one of two official coach dispatch depots when the Holyhead-Howth-Dublin mail service formally began, in 1814. It had livery stables, a forge, and its own well. The well is now encased within the pub.

The first licensee was David Helliseyard about 1845. Thomas Carolan leased the premises from Lord Howth and the place was known as Carolan's on the Hill, when that part of the Howth Road was open country. It was also known as 'Biddy Carolan's'. The premises, also operating as a grocery shop, opened at 6am to cater for country carmen making their journey from country outposts to Dublin City markets. In 1906, James J Corbett (whose benefactor was John Deneefe) became its owner and in 1947, one of his barmen, Harry Byrne, acquired the premises for €22,000. Since then, it has been known as Harry Byrne's although its official name is Hollybrook House and, it is still run by the Byrne family. Bram Stoker, Oscar Wilde and William Carleton are known to have imbibed there. The building itself is red bricked with wood panelling and its large snug is a real gem. The premises also provides a stylish and popular beer garden.

Further along the Howth Road, we come to Killester Village with The Beachcomber pub on our right, at 179 Howth Road in the centre of the village. The pub was established by Jack Duignan and remains in the Duignan family name. The Howth fishmonger family, Doran's on the Pier, run a seafood restaurant at the Beachcomber.

Off the Howth Road, at 44 Brookwood Rise, Harmonstown is the traditional pub called the Horse and Hound. It was earlier known as the Brookwood Inn.

Now we follow the Howth Road into Raheny Village. On our right at 413 Howth Road is the Watermill public house. It has a popular restaurant (steakhouse) upstairs. For many years, it traded as the Green Dolphin.

From its prominent position on Station Road, at its junction with the Howth Road, in the centre of the village and, its distinctive Tudor-style exterior, The Manhattan is Raheny's best known pub and restaurant. Manhattan may recall the well-known cocktail or, the borough in New York City. In 1843, Felix McGowan built the first pub here and named it The Manhattan. Since then, it has had many proprietors including those named Delaney, Dwyer, Spillane, Whelan, Maguire and Farrelly. In 1991, after total refurbishment, it was named The Station House. Later, it was called The Cock and Bull but, in 2019, it became the Manhattan again. To the rear of the main bar is a very inviting, cosy and well landscaped beer garden.

The Raheny Inn on Main Street started life in 1898 as O'Connor's. Between 1898 and 1962, three members of the O'Hanlon family owned the premises. One of them was Mrs O'Connor, whose maiden name was O'Hanlon. In 1962, the building was demolished and today's premises built in its stead. This was named The Inn, later renamed The Raheny Inn.

Tucked away in a quiet relaxing spot on our left, off the Howth Road on St Assam Road, is the Cedar Pub. It is a traditional local pub and features in the film *The Snapper*.

Also featuring in *The Snapper* is The Old Shieling (later The Shieling Hotel and, originally, Fox Hall), which stood on our right on the Howth Road, close to its junction with Orchard Road. It closed in 2006 and its site is now occupied by Shieling Square apartments, built in 2010. Renowned for its musical nights, the Old Shieling was a landmark in the area and central to the culture and life of the area for many years. The last owners were the McGettigan family. The original structure was built in 1726 and was known as Fox House, later Fox Hall.

Now we return to the Clontarf Road and, on our left at number 73, at its junction with St Laurence Road is The Yacht. This was once the grocery shop and public house of Thomas Carolan (owner of Harry Byrne's, mentioned above), who acquired it in 1861. In 1937, the McAuley family became proprietors who, in turn, sold it to Michael Tobin in 1947. The Tobin family operated the business until 2003, when they disposed of it to Eamon O'Malley. It was the McAuley's who first named the premises The Yacht, which traditionally had a Tiller Room. This was really a snug albeit, a large one!

After The Yacht, we take a left turn up Castle Avenue where, on the left, we reach Clontarf Castle Hotel. A castle has stood on this site since 1172 but it was first officially opened as a licensed premises, named The North Dublin Hostelry, by the acting Lord Mayor of Dublin, Alderman Lorcan Bourke on 10 May 1957. The first licensee was Mrs Egan, who sold it to the Regan family in the 1960s. They developed it to cater for weddings. The castle was acquired by the Houlihan family in 1972 and it became one of Ireland's best and biggest cabaret venues until that ceased in 1997. Then, under a board of directors, it opened as a luxurious, four-star hotel and in 2007, it was further upgraded to the magnificent standards enjoyed by patrons today. It exudes a superb baronial atmosphere and, with its castellated exterior, it has been transformed into a new world of luxury in an old-world setting. Fittingly, the proprietors have preserved, wherever possible, the characteristics of the 1835 mansion. The grey and historic turrets of the building still dominate western Clontarf, just as the castle once dominated the old medieval village of Clontarf. It is a premises with a sense of occasion and every room is beautifully and comfortably furnished and splendidly maintained. Carved oak canopies, black marble, panelled walls and period-style, decorative features are to be found throughout the edifice. The Knight's Bar is the main bar but, the Castle also sports The Indigo Lounge. While imbibing in either (and there is a stone snug too!) you will feel and sense echoes of its military and ecclesiastical days of yore. The architecture of Clontarf Castle Hotel is neo-Gothic but overall, it reflects its Norman, Tudor and Gothic history.

Again, we return to the Clontarf Road and, at number 198, we find the long-established Sheds public house. Records from 1719 suggest that a property in the old Sheds fishing village, called The Sign of the Ship, may have been an alehouse, later known as The Sign of the Star and Garter. Today's premises, named after that colloquial and most romantic of places, 'The Sheds' village, was first opened as a pub and a hotel by James Gerard Mooney in 1845. He went on to establish the large chain of 'Mooney' pubs. John Clinton acquired the premises in 1882, now a pub with a grocery shop. A Patrick Powell is listed as running the pub in 1915 and later, the Collen family from whom Peter Connolly purchased the premises in 1927. Since then, it has been run by the Connolly family. The famous author,

James Joyce, who loved to stroll along the seafront and the Bull Wall, is known to have enjoyed a tipple or two on the premises.

As we traverse along the Clontarf Road, on the left at 18 Conquer Hill Road, we find the Pebble Beach pub. This quintessentially local pub and lounge in the heart of Conquer Hill was originally Verling's grocery and butcher shop. The actual pub licence dates from the mid-1950s. It was named The Pebble Beach by the first publican to operate the premises as a pub, Tim Kinsella, who named it after a golf course in California. As the years went by, it was operated in turn by Leo Fitzgerald, Tom Maguire, Michael Grace, Kelly and Gleeson and now by the Grainger family.

As we move northwards along the Clontarf Road, an establishment called Clontarf Court Hotel used to exist at number 225, just past Fortview Avenue. A record exists of a licenced premises and restaurant on this site being purchased by a Mr John Flanagan in February 1899. Later adopting the name Fingal House, from the north Dublin district of that name and owned by the Bresnan family, it earned quite a reputation for itself as an upmarket restaurant and guest house with a full bar licence. The actual site of the building, beside Fingal Avenue, was once known as 'Fingal'. It operated as the Bram Stoker Hotel for a short time.

Further along, at 366 Clontarf Road between the old Albert Terrace and Byrne's Lane – just before Dollymount Park – Dollymount House once stood. It was a commodious pub and restaurant with a nautical air and ambiance. It was first licenced in 1782, as a regular fisherman's tavern by James Keogh. Later, Patrick O'Rourke ran it as Dollymount Tavern, with a fresh oyster restaurant attached. In the middle of the 19th century, Michael Byrne operated the establishment as Dollymount Hotel and Tavern. At the turn of the 20th century, it was known as Doyle's Dollymount Hotel and Tavern. Around 1914, the Monaghan family were in charge of the premises. Then, for many years, the Connolly family ran the business as the Dollymount Inn. From 1988, the Fitzgerald family operated the magnificent and very popular pub and restaurant known as Dollymount House. However, the end came in 2013 when it closed. It was demolished and its site is now occupied by Seascape Apartments.

In Kilbarrack, we find Madigan's pub in Kilbarrack Shopping Centre on Grange Park Walk. Many will recall that when this premises first opened, in 1971, it was called the Zodiac Lounge.

Also in Kilbarrack, the Foxhound pub opened in the 1970s at Greendale Shopping Centre on Greendale Road. This is a very traditional pub and scenes for *The Van* film were recorded here.

We find the Bayside Inn in Bayside Square. It was opened by the Lynch family in 1974. It is a little oasis of peace, at a safe distance from the busy Dublin to Howth Road.

Now back on the seafront, we turn left onto Baldoyle Road and at number 36 stands the Elphin pub, built on the site of an old inn called Warren House. Patrick J Brady was the first licensee here, in 1949 with Pat McKiernan as manager. McKiernan became the owner when Brady died in 1960. He named the premises The Elphin. The Fitzgerald family purchased the premises from the McKiernan's and run a thriving popular bar and lounge/restaurant. The name, Elphin, may come from a racehorse or from the town and Catholic diocese of that name in County Roscommon.

Following on to Warrenhouse Road, we reach Baldoyle Village and on Main Street, we come to The White House pub and restaurant at numbers 12-13 in the centre of the village. The premises dates from 1840 and has had numerous owners. Thomas Tallon, who named the place Baldoyle House, was the first owner followed by Elizbeth Tallon and then, Elizabeth Rathcliffe. A Mr Hoey acquired it in 1900 and a Mr Nixon succeeded him. The next owner, J Doyle named the place 'Courthill House'. He sold it to Edward Brennan in 1924, who disposed of it to Nora Leonard in 1932. She named it 'The Tringo', after a winning horse at Baldoyle Racecourse. At this time, another pub in the village called 'The Cyclists' House' came into the same ownership as The Tringo.

The Cyclist's House, first named 'Seaview House', stood on College Street, Baldoyle where the postal sorting office was located later. The pub had been licenced since about 1885.

The next proprietor of both premises was Patrick J Reynolds. He was succeeded by Paddy Carroll, who closed The Cyclist's House permanently. In 1965, Pat McKiernan (the aforementioned owner of The Elphin) bought The Tringo, painted it in brilliant white and called it the White House. In 1980, Mark Grainger became proprietor and named it 'Baldoyle House'. After Grainger moved on, the pub once again began to trade as the White House, under Ray and Mary Meehan.

The Racecourse Inn on Grange Road, Baldoyle is the area's 'baby' pub. It was opened in March 1980 by the Taylor family.

The large, company-run Donaghmede Inn, at the Donaghmede Shopping Centre on Grange Road was originally part of the Madigan chain of pubs.

Back to the coast and seafront one more time and we come to Sutton Cross and Village. The only bar in the village is The Schooner Bar, in the Marine Hotel at Greenfield Road. The hotel dates from 1897. Now the

Howth Road leads us into Howth and we will end our odyssey by visiting the pubs of Howth.

The Bloody Stream pub and restaurant is part of Howth DART Station. It is named after a stream of that name, which flows under the building.

Wright's Findlater cafe bar and restaurant on Harbour Road, Howth opened in 2003 and is thus a relative newcomer to Howth's licenced premises. It is on the site of the once thriving St Laurence Hotel, which was first established in 1840 and for many years, Saints nightclub operated here, later known as Good Time Charlies, which featured in *The Snapper* film.

Further along Harbour Road is the Waterside and Fisherman's Bar. It is a traditional 'early house'. It dates back to the 1800s, when it operated in a former boat house building on the harbour front. It previously operated under the names 'Cassidy's Waterside Lounge' and 'The Evora Lounge'. It has the El Paso Mexican restaurant attached.

O'Connell's traditional Irish pub is at 4 East Pier, Howth. From 1900, it operated as Buston's Hotel Luncheon and Tea Room. It first opened as a pub in 1971 and traded as The Pier House, which contained The Cibo Bar. It was named O'Connell's in 2012.

The Abbey Tavern on Abbey Street was formerly part of the Old Abbey monastery and part of the building dates back to the 15th century. It contains The Loft Restaurant, with the Abbot Restaurant attached and the whole establishment is in an old world cum nautical setting. Run by the Scott-Lennon family since 1945 it has achieved worldwide fame for its Irish-themed, traditional evening entertainment.

The Harbour Bar at 18 Church Street dates back to the 1700s. It traded as The Cock Tavern for many years then reverted back to the Harbour Bar name. It is a very atmospheric bar with the Gráinne Mhaol/Pirates' Wishing Well nearby.

McNeill's Top House bar and restaurant sits at 19 Main Street. For many years, it traded as Kruger's Top House until the name changed to McNeill's in 2016.

The highest pub in Howth – and on our entire North Bay trail – is the Summit Inn at the summit (actually 13 Thormanby Road), Howth Head. It first opened about 1850 and has been named The Summit Inn since 1950. A bar and restaurant, it is run by the Gaffney family.

Cleary's (Amiens Street)

Clonliffe House

The Sheds

Cusack's (North Strand)

The Elphin

Gaffney's

Summit Inn

Harry Byrne's

The White House

The Manhattan

Gill's Corner House

Kavanagh's (Malahide Road)

Meagher's

Abbey Tavern

The Beachcomber

Dollymount House

CHAPTER TEN

Bloody Sunday and the St Laurence O'Toole GAA Club

Many people, not fully 'au fait' with Irish history, are of the opinion that Irish independence was won with the 1916 Easter Rising. However, that pivotal rebellion was only the start. It was to take five more eventful and often bloody years of conflict before independence came, with the signing of the Anglo-Irish Treaty on 6 December 1921. For two-and-a-half years before that signing – January 1919 to July 1921 – the IRA fought British crown forces in the bitter and savage War of Independence. On Sunday, 21 November 1920, the War of Independence came to Croke Park and that day is forever remembered as Bloody Sunday.

This day is not to be confused with two other Bloody Sundays in Irish history. The first Bloody Sunday occurred on Sunday, 13 August 1913, when the Dublin Metropolitan Police (DMP) charged a Jim Larkin-organised ITGWU meeting in Sackville Street (now O'Connell Street), killing three people and injuring scores. The event took place during the William Martin Murphy-orchestrated great lockout of workers in 1913. In more recent times, the third Irish Bloody Sunday came on the 30 January 1972, when British Paratroopers shot dead fourteen civilians during a civil rights march in Derry.

On Sunday, 21 November 1920, a senior Gaelic football challenge match was organised between Dublin and Tipperary, two of the top teams in the country at the time. The throw-in was set for 2.45pm at Croke Park. Earlier that morning, in a meticulously planned operation, thirteen British intelligence officers and two auxiliary police were shot dead in Dublin by IRA Volunteers, lead by Michael Collins' 'Squad' of elite assassins (his counter-intelligence service). These assassinations were to almost destroy the British intelligence network in Dublin.

Revolutionary freedom fighter, Collins' real strength lay in his understanding of the murky waters between politics and intelligence work. He had his own sophisticated web of informers. These were men and women infiltrating the wickerwork of spies, lies and subterfuge in Britain's Irish governmental system in Dublin Castle and the notorious police 'G -division' of the DMP, with headquarters at Great Brunswick Street (now Pearse Street Garda Station). Four key men who passed on crucial information to him were Eamon (Ned) Broy, Joe Kavanagh, David Neligan and James MacNamara.

The 'G Division' was the police section detailed to survey, monitor and gather intelligence on the activities of leading republicans. In plain clothes and armed, their intelligence gathering included operating a network of spies in IRA circles. Among those spying on Collins and his men were the 'Cairo Gang', so named because they frequently held meetings in the Cafe Cairo at 59 Grafton Street. Many of these were British Intelligence operators brought over from England to track down Collins and top IRA men, 'take them out' and, effectively destroy the IRA. The Cairo Gang consisted mainly of officers posing as commercial travellers. Collins was aware that these agents were on the trail of himself and his men and were closing in. So, he moved first and those Sunday morning killings meant that key British agents and many of the Cairo Gang were wiped out. It was a major coup for Collins and in all, probably sixty IRA men were involved.

There was always going to be repercussions for those Sunday morning killings. The British military in Dublin were enraged and planned vengeful retaliation. However, nobody could have predicted the way and the place that retaliation would come. One British auxiliary allegedly stated that they tossed a coin to decide whether to go on a murder rampage in Croke Park or, to loot all of Sackville Street (now O'Connell Street). The scene was set for bloody happenings on what became known as Bloody Sunday.

The O'Toole's GAA Club, based at 100 Seville Place in the heart of Dublin's north inner city and close to Croke Park, were kingpins of Dublin GAA football at the time. The club was also very nationalistic and the clubhouse was a Michael Collins' 'nerve centre'. O'Toole's were very involved in the events of Bloody Sunday. So, it is appropriate to reflect on the club's history.

The St Laurence O'Toole GAA Club – known as O'Toole's and nicknamed 'The Larriers' – was founded in 1901, although earlier clubs of that name existed in 1888 and 1895. The club was spawned from the St Laurence O'Toole branch of the Gaelic League and also included a branch of the Irish Republican Brotherhood (IRB).

Also associated with the club from its beginning was the St Laurence O'Toole Pipe (Fife) band. The band was officially part of the club for many years. The band was formed in 1910, with Tom Clarke its first president, and Sean O'Casey its first secretary. It was the official band of the Irish Volunteers, a body that eventually became the IRA.

O'Toole's clubhouse was the band's headquarters and the band often played in Croke Park on All-Ireland Final days.

The St Laurence O'Toole in question, or Lorcán Ua Tuathail (c.1128-1180), was born at Castledermot in County Kildare and educated at Glendalough

Monastery, where he became abbot in 1158. He was consecrated Dublin's first Archbishop in 1162. At the time of the Norman invasion of Ireland in 1170, he first organised resistance but, on realising the strength of the Norman forces, he parlayed for peace with Strongbow and with King Henry II. He encouraged Strongbow to build Christ Church Cathedral – where the saint's heart is preserved. He died at Eu in Normandy, France in 1180 and is remembered there as St Laurent d'Eu. Canonised a saint in 1226, he is Dublin's patron saint and is one of only two Irish people to be canonised.

The parish of St Laurence O'Toole recalls him, as does the Gothic-style Catholic church opened in 1850, which stands on the corner where Sheriff Street meets Seville Place. A little shrine in the church embosoms a relic of the saint. The entire area of the sprawling parish of St Laurence O'Toole was reclaimed from the sea in the 18th century and this is where O'Toole's GAA Club came of age. First formed as a hurling club and with the iconic Five Lamps as its logo, it thrived from the beginning, with new members and players joining from a network of streets in the heart of the north inner city. From the start, the club was political and militant, in a very nationalistic area with a passionately nationalistic people.

Figures vary but as many as eighty-three O'Toole club members took part in the 1916 Rising. Among them were Tom Clarke and Seán Mac Diarmada, signatories of the proclamation declaring the Irish Republic. Many other prominent names were club members, including the above-mentioned playwright, Sean O'Casey.

The club had premises variously at Leinster Avenue and at Oriel Hall, Oriel Street. Then, in March 1920, the club bought 100 Seville Place as a clubhouse and it became an oasis of everything culturally Irish – language, dancing, music, storytelling, etc. The ruthless, pragmatic revolutionary that was Michael Collins and his famous 'squad' used the premises almost daily as a type of military headquarters, always wary of British forces who regularly ransacked the premises.

With no home pitch in the confined inner-city space, O'Toole's, played their matches at various venues, including the Phoenix Park. On the playing fields, the club enjoyed tremendous success. The senior footballers were the kingpins of Dublin football either side of 1920. They won eleven Dublin titles in all, their first at Croke Park in 1918, going on to make it 3-in-a row by winning the title again in 1919 and 1920. They had some outstanding players whose names have gone into club and county hero territory. They included team captain, Paddy McDonnell and his brother, Johnny, the goalkeeper while three Synott brothers – Joe, John and Stephen – were magnificent team players. In those days, the Dublin football team usually lined out with about ten players from the O'Toole's club. In fact, as county champions, they picked the Dublin team.

Here is a very interesting article taken from the official match programme for the 1974 Dublin v Galway All-Ireland Senior Football Final, played on 22 September 1974. The article is titled *Dublin's Long and Proud Tradition*:

> *Then in the 1920s from the docks area of the north side of the city in the parish of St. Laurence O'Toole (where young lads learned their football in 'The Blocks') an area from which sprang two outstanding clubs – St. Laurence O'Toole and St. Marys and between them won three All-Irelands in a row for Dublin – 1921, '22 and '23 and failed by one point to Kerry in the memorable 1924 final, having lost to Tipperary in 1920. So it could have easily been an all-time record of five-in-a-row.*

> *The McDonnell brothers, Paddy, a commanding leader of men, Johnny, that ageless goalie in the black felt hat ... the Careys ... the Synotts ... these were some of the names that will always be linked with the days of O'Toole's greatness. There were eight Synott brothers: Tom, Stephen, Jim, Josie, John, Patrick, Leo and Peter and they all played football with the exception of Tom and Patrick. Four of them – Stephen, Joe, John and Peter played for Dublin. The three most famous of them were Stephen, John and Josie.*

> *Men who fought in the G.P.O. and in Jacobs in 1916 were together on the Dublin team as the struggle for independence was being finally won in the twenties. Frank Burke, hailing from Carbury, five miles from Edenderry in Co. Kildare, was with Pearse in the G.P.O.*

> *And Frank Burke (still sprightly enough, incidentally, to watch this year's Hurling Final from the Hogan Stand) was in Croke Park on 'Bloody Sunday', marking Mick Hogan of Grangemockler as the bullets began to fly on that fateful day, November 21st, 1920.*

> *Dublin started their three-in-a-row run in the twenties with a victory over Mayo in the 1921 All-Ireland and Galway fell the following season by two points. By 1923 when they won a memorable clash with Kerry (1-5 to 1-3), they had fashioned themselves into a great side with strength in all the vital positions. No greater*

*halfback line has represented the metropolis than the
Josie Synott–Joe Norris–Jack Reilly line and at full-
back was Paddy Carey, flanked by Paddy O'Beirne
and Jim Sherlock. Keeping goal was Johnny McDonnell,
who would still be there in 1934 when Dublin lost to
Galway – indeed, he was captain of the Leinster team
that won the Railway Cup in 1935 and with Paddy, was
honoured by the Ireland selectors in 1924 and 1928.
Dublin's midfield partnership was Johnny Murphy and
Paddy McDonnell. The immortal Larry Stanley, later
to play with Kildare in the tremendous classic game
and replay with Kerry in 1926, was at centre-forward,
partnered by Frank Burke with another stylish Kildare
man, Joe Stynes.*

Over the years, that very vibrant St Mary's Club – based mainly in the Church Road area of the St Laurence O'Toole parish – went out of existence. Another local club, Shamrocks, amalgamated with O'Toole's. The other big GAA club in the area was St Joseph's. Founded in 1918, they beat their neighbours and great rivals, O'Toole's, in the 1930 Dublin Senior Football Championship final. The club declined over the years but, a revival began in 1989 when they amalgamated with O'Connell Boys (founded in 1964) to become St Joseph's OCB GAA Club. The club plays its games in Fairview Park.

The O'Toole senior hurlers had to wait somewhat longer than the footballers to win the Dublin Championship, finally making the breakthrough by winning the 1969 title. They have won 7 Dublin hurling crowns in all, including their own 3-in-a-row in 1995, 1996 and 1997. The hurlers too had some outstanding players, including the captain of the '69 side, Noel Doolin and Joey Morris, who won six Senior County Championship medals. Both of these and well-known author/artist, Jimmy Wren, among many others, played senior inter-county hurling for Dublin.

The O'Toole club moved its base from the north inner city to pastures new at Blunden Drive, Ayrfield, Malahide Road in the early 1980s. The club opened a very fitting and comfortable new clubhouse there for their centenary year in 2001.

In the wake of the Sunday morning's assassinations on that fateful day in November 1920, the British military were infuriated. They were large in number and consisted of a combination of the regular British army based in Dublin, the Royal Irish Constabulary (RIC) and the Dublin Metropolitan

Police (DMP). With the War of Independence raging, further Crown forces were sent to Ireland during 1920 to augment forces already there. The regular army was boosted with new battalions.

Then, from March 1920 on, reinforcements for the RIC began to arrive. Because of their uniform colours, which apparently resembled the colours of a hound pack in County Tipperary, they were immediately labelled 'The Black and Tans'. Recruited with indecent haste, they were of extremely dubious pedigree and their activities in Ireland showed them to be little short of drunken thugs, with scant regard for human dignity or life itself. Heavily armed and without discipline, they were beyond RIC control and operating independently, ruthlessly, illegally and with a criminal bent, they mercilessly inflicted the severest forms of brutality on a decent, innocent and somewhat defenceless Irish civilian population.

Then, from July 1920, more RIC back-up 'troops' filtered into Ireland as an auxiliary division. These came to be known as the 'Auxies' and were very identifiable with their Glengarry caps. They were allegedly ex-soldiers of the officer class. However, they soon showed themselves to be even more bloodthirsty than the 'Tans'. Both names became synonyms for terror. This combination was what the poorly armed IRA were fighting.

With about 10,000 people in attendance for the occasion, the ball was thrown in for the start of the Tipperary/Dublin match at about 3.15 pm by referee, Mick Sammon of Kildare. Of the Dublin panel of twenty players, twelve were from the O'Toole's Club, nine of whom started the game. With play in progress for just about fifteen minutes, a military plane flew overhead and Croke Park was, suddenly, almost totally surrounded by a convoy of British forces. Unlike the modern stadium, Croke Park was then just an open sports ground with no stands. Nobody is, or can be, sure what mixture of British military descended on Croke Park that day but, it is certain the Black and Tans were in the vanguard and certainly not a few were under the influence of alcohol. There was an obvious total lack of discipline in the ranks of the Crown forces. And there can be no doubt that the attack on the terrified spectators that followed was a cold, calculated revengeful retribution for the IRA actions that morning.

Suddenly bursts of machine-gun and rifle fire sprayed randomly and indiscriminately into the crowd and playing field. Fourteen people were killed and sixty-two wounded. Most of the victims were shot in the back. It is perplexingly chilling to note that the intention was to murder the entire Tipperary team. One of the dead was a Tipperary player, the right full-back and captain, Michael Hogan from the Grangemockler club.

For whatever reason, certain elements believed, especially the 'Tans; and the Auxies, that the arrival of the Tipperary team to Dublin for the match was linked to or, even responsible for the earlier murder of the British agents. Indeed, the Tipperary players were lined up along the wall at the railway end of the ground to be shot. They were held there for hours and, only for the intervention of the Auxiliary Commander, Major Mills, they would all have been shot dead.

Reports vary as to how long the actual shooting lasted but for whatever length it went on, it is something of a miracle that there were not far more deaths. Both sets of players had their watches, money, cigarettes and other belongings stolen. This was petty in the extreme, despicable behaviour and, unworthy of and unacceptable from any military personnel. Indeed, in any military conflict, surely a sporting event should be sacrosanct and be observed as out of bounds.

Five of those who lost their lives on Bloody Sunday were from our North Dublin Bay area. Two lived in Buckingham Street. Michael Feery (40) was a former British soldier who had served in World War I, with the same army that now ended his life. Sadly, he was to lie in the morgue at Jervis Street hospital for five days before he was formally identified. The other Buckingham Street resident was Patrick O'Dowd, a labourer who worked in Fairview. He left a wife and two children. James Matthews (38) was a tenement dweller in North Cumberland Street. A labourer, he was married with four daughters. John William Smith (14) was from Fitzroy Avenue. A pupil at St Patrick's School in Drumcondra, he was one of three schoolboys killed on Bloody Sunday. Many players and supporters repaired to O'Toole's clubhouse that evening and the Tipperary players, who had been robbed of their possessions, were helped by their Dublin counterparts.

The killings did not end at Croke Park. On the Saturday night/early Sunday morning before the game, two top-ranking IRA officers were arrested and taken to Dublin Castle, along with an Irish language student called Conor Clune, who appears to have been 'guilty' of no more than being in the wrong place at the wrong time. The two IRA men, Brigadier Dick McKee and Vice Brigadier Peadar Clancy, were taken to the guardroom in Dublin Castle with Clune, where they were savagely tortured and then shot dead by the Auxiliary division of the RIC, in the early hours of Bloody Sunday.

The Croke Park massacre only further invoked the hatred of the Irish people for the Crown forces in Ireland because of the brutal acts of cruelty and murder that they perpetrated and inflicted on the population. The 'Tans' and the Auxies especially had acted with callous indifference. However, Bloody Sunday was a public relations disaster and very damaging for the British Government. What happened made international headlines.

Indeed, that fateful day marked a watershed point between British forces and the IRA. More and more people turned to full support for the IRA and a stronger push towards an independent Ireland emerged. And it did help the notion of a truce and negotiations.

Well respected moderate and peacemaker, County Clare-born Archbishop of Perth in Western Australia, Patrick Joseph Clune (1864-1935) arrived in Ireland in 1920 after the events of Bloody Sunday. He spent a few weeks travelling between Dublin and London, negotiating between the British Government and the IRA. He had face to face talks with Michael Collins and Arthur Griffith as well as with British Prime Minister, Lloyd George. His efforts failed and in Paris, en route back to Australia, he stated that Lloyd George was in favour of a temporary truce but, some cabinet members were not, particularly Bonar-Law and Winston Churchill. Churchill was then British Minister of Munitions and Secretary of State for War. The archbishop described the IRA as 'the cream of their race'.

On his arrival back in Australia, he spoke openly and frankly about the terrible situation in Ireland. The archbishop's comments were carried by the world press and greatly raised public awareness as to the Irish situation, especially in America and in Australia. His praise for the insurgents in Ireland, who were demonised by the British, greatly embarrassed Britain and its reputation worldwide. Much public opinion swung towards the Irish cause.

However, there was yet much blood to be spilled as the longed-for truce did not materialise until twelve o'clock noon on 11 July 1921.

- Bloody Sunday, or *Domhnach na Fola*, will always be recalled as one of the saddest and most shocking days of the Irish War of Independence.

- In all, thirty-two people died in the Bloody Sunday atrocities. Fifteen died as a result of IRA operations that morning. Three men, Dick McKee, Peadar Clancy and Conor Clune were tortured and shot in Dublin Castle. Fourteen people were killed in Croke Park and eighty injured.

- A whitewash cover-up inquiry afterwards – which was held in camera – infuriated Irish people even more. No one was ever charged, held responsible, prosecuted or disciplined.

- While the GAA, at the time, had members who were also members of the IRA, the organisation itself was non-political and had not taken part in the 1916 Rising.

- In 1926, the GAA named the then newly built (original) Hogan Stand in Croke Park after the murdered Tipperary player, Michael Hogan.

- Two members of the Dublin squad on Bloody Sunday, Christy (who started the game) and Joe Joyce were sons of Martin Joyce, the sole family survivor of the notorious Maamtrasna murders. The murders took place in Connemara on 8 August 1882. In a bitter dispute involving 'Ribbonism' and embittered disagreements concerning grazing rights, five members of the Joyce family were killed. Martin later came to live in the Coolock area. He is buried in Kilbarrack Cemetery. The Joyce brothers were members of the Parnell GAA Club.

- Someone who had a lucky escape on Bloody Sunday was Christopher 'Yarra' Duffy, a 15-year-old schoolboy who was in attendance at the Dublin/Tipperary match on that day. A bullet penetrated him and lodged in the back of his neck where the base of the head and the top of the spine meet. In his flesh the bullet divided into two parts. It was feared that he would not live or that paralysis for life might be his lot. However, Yarra did survive the operation to remove the bullet and amazingly, went on to have a wonderful footballing career, for close on 20 years, with his club, the above-mentioned St Joseph's north inner-city club. He became their star player and spearheaded their winning of the Dublin Senior Football Championship, for the first and only time, in 1930. That was especially sweet as they beat their neighbours and great rivals, O'Toole's, in the final after a replay. Yarra won two Leinster senior football medals playing for Dublin in 1932 and 1933. With Lena, his wife, they reared their nine children in Ballybough House flats complex. Yarra Liked to swim in the sea at the Bull Wall and enjoy a pint afterwards in the old Wine Lodge or in Gaffney's pub, both in Fairview.

- Joe Norris, a regular Dublin player who won three All-Ireland medals with Dublin and ten Dublin senior football championships with O'Toole's and was at his footballing best at the time of Bloody Sunday, did not appear for Dublin on the day. Many people wondered why. The reason is that the night before the match, he (maybe fortuitously) fell among thieves and partied well into the early hours of that Sunday morning ... not wisely but, too well! He did show up for the match but with a somewhat dishevelled look! The Dublin captain wisely sent him home to recuperate!

- On Sunday, 22 November 2020, Tipperary beat Cork to win their first Munster title since 1935. On that occasion, instead of their normal blue and gold jerseys, the Tipperary team sported commemorative green and white jerseys, the colours the Tipperary team wore on Bloody Sunday and also the colours of the club of murdered player, Michael Hogan – the Grangemockler/Ballyneale Club. The last football All-Ireland title won by Tipperary was in 1920.

- On the actual 100th anniversary date of Bloody Sunday, the GAA held a very touching ceremony involving the lighting of fourteen memorial candles. The special event, in memory of the fourteen people killed on Bloody Sunday, was held on Hill 16 in Croke Park.

- In a gesture of remembrance to the fourteen dead, Dublin City Council, in 2020, voted to rename the bridge over the Royal Canal, at Croke Park's Canal End, Bloody Sunday Bridge. The official name of the Bridge had been Clonliffe Bridge but, it has been better known locally as Jones' Road Bridge or Russell Street Bridge.

- At 36 Seán McDermott Street, there is a plaque to the memory of Brigadier Dick McKee and Vice-Brigadier Peadar Clancy, Dublin Brigade IRA. At this house (then 36 Gloucester Street) they were arrested by British forces in the early hours of Sunday 21 November 1920. Both were severely tortured and murdered, with IRA Volunteer Conor Clune (as already stated) in the Guardroom of Dublin Castle. Conor Clune was not a nephew of the Cardinal Clune referenced above. All three martyrs are commemorated by a plaque at Dublin Castle, on the outside wall of the Guard Room, where they were tortured, while a memorial to McKee stands in Finglas Village. McKee Avenue and Road in Finglas, McKee Park and McKee Barracks (Blackhorse Avenue) in Cabra, also recall Dick McKee. Conor Clancy is recalled by Clancy Avenue and Clancy Road in Finglas, as is Conor Clune by Clune Road.

- The Irish Volunteers, formed in November 1913, became the Irish Republican Army (IRA) in January 1919.

- One of the saddest aspects of the whole War of Independence era is that many of the atrocities carried out by the Tans and Auxies, might have been avoided if they had not the full cooperation and total backing of the RIC and the DMP. These latter bodies were, after all, Irish and their role was to police and protect the people. Instead, they were little short of traitors and informers and even perpetrated and planned many of the shameful events that occurred. They supplied vital local intelligence (directions, maps, etc) and generally aided and abetted the marauding Tans and Auxies. The records they kept (if any) during the period were less than factual and often, totally misleading.

O'Toole's club crest

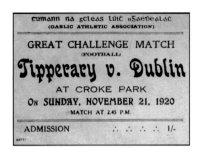

Match ticket

Michael Hogan

McKee/Clancy/Clune plaque, Dublin Castle

CHAPTER ELEVEN

Transport: Horse drawn, Canals, Railways, Trams, the Hill of Howth Tram

Shanks Mare was our earliest form of transport! If you 'rose' in the world, you might own a donkey or even a donkey and cart! The better-off folk travelled by horse.

Before the advent of railways in Ireland, transport within the country was by road and internal waterways. There was a reasonably good network of roads by the end of the 18th century but, they were poor and difficult to travel on. They were only suitable for light traffic of the time and not fit to carry heavy loads. In winter, many roads were impassable. Thus, in pre-railway days, water transport was the mode of transport used for heavy goods.

The canals, in their relatively short prime days, replaced the roads as a means of transport for passengers to the interior of Ireland. By 1817, both the Grand and Royal canals linked Dublin with the River Shannon. Barges and tow horses were the order of the day. The main items carried on the canals were agricultural products, such as corn and flour ferried to Dublin for exporting and, manufactured goods sent from Dublin to the country. Guinness Brewery at St James's Gate, Dublin made extensive use of the canals to supply their product throughout the country.

The Grand and Royal Canal networks revolutionised Irish travel in the 18th century. Nowadays, the canals are an attraction as a reminder of days that have been and serve as an amenity for fishing and cruising and for bank walking and cycling.

Since the years before the Act of Union in 1800, passenger and goods service between the larger towns in Ireland was provided by horse drawn mail coaches. Ireland has had a 'postal service' since 1660 but letter delivery, for example, was extremely slow as travelling by coach from, say, Dublin to Cork could take as long as 3 or 4 days. The very first regular stagecoach service between Dublin and Belfast began in 1752. And slow coach travel carried the extra risk of being held up by highwaymen and brigands, who quickly relieved you of your valuables. The introduction of Bianconi's stagecoach cars, beginning in 1815, did greatly improve the services, as he challenged all existing operators with his faster and cheaper service. Bianconi's coach system peaked in the mid 1840s (when he had one hundred cars on the roads) as the railways gradually took over.

Roads, canals and railways greatly helped communication and helped to unite the country by networking its length and breath. Generally, the development of transport and, an organised regular transport system altered the countryside and helped in its development and evolution. The railways, in particular, helped change, drive and improve the economy and had a huge social impact in contributing to many benefits, as well as making travelling easier and more accessible. The coming of the railways definitely spelt the end for all horse-drawn transport. However, it took many years to develop a railway network in Ireland.

The first railway to open in the country was a six-mile suburban stretch between Dublin, Westland Row (now Pearse Street Station) and Dún Laoghaire (then Kingstown) in 1834. Then, for about six years after the passing of the Railway Regulation Act in 1844 (there were a number of Railway Acts passed after 1840) new lines were laid connecting Cork, Galway and Belfast with Dublin. As further lines were laid, the interior of the country was opened up more and more and, made accessible. Railways had a major influence, generally, on life in Ireland in the second half of the 19th century after the famine.

From the mid 1840s, the railroad system began properly and changed public transport forever. On 24 May 1844, the 'Iron Horse' began running on the Dublin-Drogheda line, which in March 1875 became part of the Great Northern Railway Line. Eventually, seven railway lines came together to form the GNRC (Great Northern Railway Company). Since the opening of the Dublin-Drogheda line, plans were laid to organise a branch line to Howth. The project was overseen by William Dargen (the father of Irish railways) and a single line from Howth Junction (Donaghmede) to Howth was duly opened on 30 July 1846. And the trams were coming too!

On the island of Ireland, horse drawn trams were first used in Fintona, in County Tyrone in 1854. The first horse drawn trams in Dublin began operating between College Green and Rathgar in 1872. Prior to this, there was a stagecoach service between Dublin and Howth – which needed an armed escort for its passage through Ballybough! The first tram service from the city towards Howth began in 1873 and first served only as far as Annesley Bridge, later extending to Dollymount. These early trams were pulled by a team of horses with (a) race or tip horse(s) helping on hills, like Newcomen Bridge. From the mid-1900s, horse drawn trams began to be replaced by electric-powered trams, operated by the Dublin United Tramway Company (DUTC).

Clontarf had a tramshed or stable on the site of the present-day bus garage. The first section of this track to be electrified was between Annesley Bridge and Dollymount and the first electric tram ran on it on 11 November 1897. Soon, the rest of the Clontarf track to the city centre was also electrified and the first electric car to the city centre – Nelson's Pillar (The Spire today) – from any suburb was from Dollymount, which arrived at the pillar at 7.10am on 19 March 1898!

The Clontarf line was a pioneer in both Ireland and Britain for the use of high-tension electric current on overhead wires with substations. The route from the city centre to Clontarf was operated by the staff of DUTC. In 1898, the Clontarf and Hill of Howth Tramshed Company Ltd (CHHTC) was established and an agreement was made with DUTC to run trams from the city to Howth. The Clontarf-Howth line eventually came into operation in July 1900 (it ran via Blackbanks and Sutton) and it proved to be a smooth, fast and efficient service. It was to last until 1941.

The trams or "galleons of the street", as the poet, AE (George Russell) called them were surely part of what was Dublin 'in the rare oul' times'. They were objects of genuine interest and love for generations of Dubliners. The trams became part of the social life and scene of the then smaller and more close-kit local communities. The trams were not all alike. There were four-wheeled trams and trams with eight wheels. There were open top trams, covered-top trams with balcony ends, trams with completely covered saloons and some luxury trams. Trams had 'decency boards' fitted, to spare ladies alighting the steps from any would be 'peeping Toms' downstairs! As well as ferrying people, the trams offered a freight service also – including two from Howth, carrying sand and fish!

For a time, trams were the fastest vehicles on the road but, their demise began with the arrival of the motor bus and later, the motor car. It can be stated that the coming of the internal combustion engine ended the era of the tram. The big advantage that the buses had was their manoeuvrability. They could leave the main roads and struggle around all developing streets and housing estates, while the tram was stuck to its tracks.

Open competition raged from the mid 1920s, until Córas Iompair Éireann (CIE) was formed in January 1945. Later, in May 1959, CIE amalgamated with the GNRC and the last tram left Nelson's Pillar on 9 July 1949. The reasons for all tram closures was the fact that the trams had become antiquated and, somewhat shoddy and rundown. Above all, they were no longer profitable.

Just one tram was to survive for another 10 years. This was the most famous of all Dublin trams – the Hill of Howth Tram, of fond and iconic memory. It began operating in June 1901 and the five-and-a-quarter mile route was from Sutton depot to Howth Summit – among the most picturesque tram rides in the world. The line which the Great Northern Railway built and operated was, at Howth Summit, 365 feet above sea level. It was used by residents and tourists but never made a profit. It was taken over by CIE in October 1958 and on 31 May 1959, CIE, 'pulled the plug' and services ceased. This was the last tram to run anywhere in Ireland – the last of its type in Ireland's first tram era.

The Hill of Howth Tram consistently proves to be a lively topic of conversation, with great general interest. Indeed, it has been the subject of many booklets and articles. Many will recall broadcaster, Gay Byrne interviewing fellow broadcaster, Jo Linnane on that last journey as the tram – the number 9 from the 'Hill Fleet' – wound its way from Sutton through and over Howth Village, up the hill around the summit and back down again, with driver, Christy Hanway and conductor Alfie Reilly.

The tram actually had a predecessor! John O'Brien, a farmer on East Mountain had O'Brien's Vis-a-Vis operating on the Hill of Howth since 1867. This was a horse drawn bus with a capacity for fourteen passengers and it operated between Sutton and Howth Summit.

Addendum... Did you know?

- The invention of the bicycle, which began to come into common use in the late 19th and early 20th centuries, helped make places more accessible. The bike gave a certain freedom and you could meander off the main thoroughfares. It also meant that you were not stuck to rail times or indeed, with stabling and feeding a donkey or a horse!

- Road and railway engineer, William Dargan (1799-1867) oversaw the construction of the Dublin to Drogheda railway. In October 1840, construction of the Clontarf Railway embankment began. With Sir John McNeill (1793-1880) as director of operations, the familiar Clontarf landmark known as the 'stone arch', 'double arch' or 'skew' bridge, on the Clontarf Road was constructed as part of the embankment in 1843 and was, at the time, regarded as an engineering triumph. It is noteworthy that both Dargan and Mc Neill (MacNeill) assisted Thomas Telford with the construction of the Howth Road. Without this triumvirate, we may never have found our way to Howth! In the 1850s, Dargan lived in Maryville House near St Paul's College, Raheny. A statue to his memory stands on the lawn of the National Gallery at Merrion Square.

Killester bus

Old Dublin trams (c. 1913)

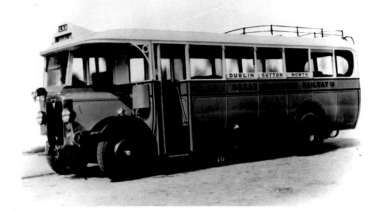

Dublin-Sutton-Howth bus

The Hill of Howth Tramway, 1907

Modern Dublin Luas

- Between 1844 and 1850, Clontarf had a railway station. In 1898, on a site known as the 'Black Quarry' on the Howth Road, Clontarf Railway Station proper, known as Clontarf Halt, was opened. Today's number 94 Howth Road, beside the railway bridge, was the station building and the adjoining number 96 was the station master's residence. The little gate on the city side of number 94 was the entrance that led to the platform. The station was closed in September 1956.

- The coming of the railway system changed so much – even time itself! Before the arrival of the railways, there was no standard time. Each area – town or village – kept its own time and Irish time was about half an hour behind English time. Railway time was the standard time, first introduced in England in November 1840. This was the first known occasion when various local times were synchronised and a common standard time adopted. Railway time was necessary to keep timetables on schedule and, for some time, a clock was regularly sent from London to Dublin's Ballast Office.

- A poignant memory from the early years of the trams was that because of widespread illiteracy, the Dublin Tramway Company used symbols to indicate the destination of trams. For example, the Dollymount trams daytime sign was a green shield while at night, two green lights were used.

- In 1925 Dublin's first official bus route – City Centre to Killester – was established. It was a single decker, number 43.

- Between 1980 and 1984, the railway line between Howth and Bray was modernised and electrified to herald the arrival of the DART (Dublin Area Rapid Transit), which began operating in 1984.

- Trams finally had their second coming and came back on Dublin streets in 2004. The carriages are very different and the system – the Luas (Dublin Light Rail System) – is modern, fast and efficient.

CHAPTER TWELVE

Dublin North Bay Writers

Dublin was designated a City of Literature on 26 July 2010 by the Cultural Department of the United Nations. When we look at Dublin's literary heritage, we might well proclaim, 'sure 'twas no wonder'! Dublin can challenge to be ranked as the world's most prominent City of Literature as, considering its size, it has produced a substantial body of writers of achievement. Indeed, the city has begotten more writers of renown than cities of comparable size around the world. These writers have emerged from a cornucopia of backgrounds with diverse styles, interests and genres. Indeed, collectively, Dublin's writers combine to give the city the rank, pedigree, status and recognition of a real City of Literature!

It is fair to observe that one of Dublin's more identifiable contributions to European evolvement has been its literary heritage in the areas of poetry, drama and song writing. Among Dublin's most eminent literary figures are its four winners of the Nobel Prize for Literature, three of them native born Dubliners – WB Yeats (1923), GB Shaw (1924), Samuel Beckett (1969).

Derry born Seamus Heaney, who lived most of his adult life in Dublin, won the prize in 1995.

In 1967, as part of the Ireland Commemorative Stamps Service, a set of stamps were issued by the Post Office, depicting scenes from *Gulliver's Travels*, commemorating the 300th anniversary of the birth of Jonathan Swift. Portraits of GB Shaw, WB Yeats and Samuel Beckett featured on stamp collections on Irish playwrights in 1980, 1994 and 2000. Shaw and Oscar Wilde were included in the Europa stamp series in 1980. The Europa series highlighted Wilde on four separate stamps on the occasion of the 100th anniversary of his death, in 2000. An Post issued a series of Stoker/Dracula stamps in 1997, to mark the centenary of the publication of *Dracula*. In 2004, Ireland and Sweden jointly issued postage stamps featuring Ireland's four winners of the Nobel Prize for Literature on separate stamps. The £20 and £10 Irish currency notes for the period 1982-1993 featured WB Yeats and Swift respectively. The £10 note for the 1993-2000 period carried Joyce's portrait and in February 1922, An Post issued two new stamps to celebrate the centenary of the publication of *Ulysses*.

Our North Bay Area has been and is, home to a plethora of writers. Some were born here; others came to live here and, a number are associated with the area in some way – some even wrote about the locality! Our list is by no means exhaustive or comprehensive. It is, however, confined to writers who have passed away and the subjects are dealt with in chronological order.

And it is important to remember that Dublin has on ongoing vibrant literary life!

Jonathan Swift, 1667-1745

Jonathan Swift was born on the 30 November 1667 in the now non-existing Hoey's Court off Werburgh Street in Dublin City Centre. Of Anglo-Irish stock, he grew up to be ordained in the Church of Ireland. He spent a number of years in London, where he was part of the Scriblerus Club, with many writers including Joseph Addison, William Congreve, John Gay and Alexander Pope. He strongly supported the Tory party against the Whigs and expected to be rewarded with a bishopric. Instead, he became Dean of St Patrick's Cathedral, Dublin in 1713 and remained so until his death in 1745.

He was a novelist, a poet, an essayist, a political pamphleteer and a political journalist. He was a conversationalist and above all, a lively wit and an acidic satirist. He was the best writer of his era, with strength and clarity in his output and was followed by many great Anglo-Irish writers. He was the first Dublin writer to gain a notable international reputation.

In his very original, satirical and witty writings, he targeted the hypocrisy of the Church of Ireland, suggesting that there was a yawning gap between what the church taught and real Christianity. Other targets of his were dishonesty, corruption, human misery and depravity and, England's ill treatment of the Irish. He always advocated justice for Ireland. Known generally as 'Dean Swift', his outstanding work was *Gulliver's Travels*, a runaway success after it was published in 1726. A satirical novel relating an adventure story, it is essentially mocking the English customs and politics of the time.

In his personal life, Swift appears to have been in something of a ménage-à-trois situation with Stella (Ester Johnson) and Vanessa (Hester Vanhomrigh).

In Swift's time, a regular spot for Dubliners to visit, for recreational purposes was a stretch of sand and shingle emanating from Fairview Strand towards Clontarf, known as 'The Strand'. This was before the reclamation that gave us Fairview Park, the area now covered by Clontarf DART Station and the East Point Business Park, as well as Clontarf Promenade. Here (as alluded to in the main text) the lords, ladies and aristocracy in general promenaded in their stylish carriages, pulled by their decorated horses. Regular citizens came to admire the style but, in equal measure criticize the grandeur of the horses and carriages. Swift loved to ride The Strand on his regular visits to the St Lawrence family at Howth Castle, where a full-length portrait of him by Francis Binden hangs to this day. Swift rode with two servants, one in front and one behind. He regularly visited Rev Mr Webber, a vicar at Howth Church of Ireland and Mrs Acherson at Grange House, Baldoyle. He also habitually walked along the Santry river, which enters the sea close to Watermill Road.

St Patrick's Hospital in Bow Lane (off Jones' Street) was founded in 1745, at Swift's bequest, for the treatment of mental illness in Ireland. Swift donated £8,000 to the hospital and wrote:

> He gave the little wealth he had,
> To build a house for fools and mad,
> And showed by one satiric touch
> No nation needed it so much.

Swift is buried in St Patrick's Cathedral, alongside Stella, where a marble sculpture by Patrick Cunningham, dating from 1766, commemorates him, as does a wall plaque in the cathedral. Another wall plaque recalls Stella.

Other plaques in memory of Swift are on Little Ship Street and in the Literary Parade in St Patrick's Park, beside the Cathedral. The good Dean is also recalled by Dean Street, Dean Swift Square and Swift's Alley, all in Dublin City Centre, as well as Swift's Row off Ormond Quay and Dean Swift

Green and Road in Glasnevin. Drapier Road recalls his *Drapier Letters*. Dean Swift Bridge on Mobhi Road is in his memory while the good Dean is reputed to have completed a number of his pamphlets at Deloitte House on Iona Park.

He is also recalled by the Irish Ferries' ship, *The Jonathan Swift*, which operated for the company from 1999-2018, when it was sold on.

Stella is recalled in Stella Avenue in Glasnevin,

Joseph Addison, 1672-1719

Addison Road and Addison Terrace in Fairview recall the English statesman, writer, politician and poet, Joseph Addison. In 1708 he was appointed Secretary of State to the then Lord Deputy for Ireland, the Marquis of Wharton. His stay in Dublin was short (a matter of months) and during that time, he represented Cavan in the old Irish Parliament. He is best remembered for essays in the *Tatler* and *Spectator* publications – the latter of which, he co-founded with his friend, Richard Steele.

His writings are mainly concerned with the propensity and disposition of the middle class, tales from his early years and a little philosophy. He wrote with a style that embodied humour and satire. He was a friend of Jonathan Swift.

Charles Lucas, 1713-1771

The celebrated writer, poet, apothecary, physician and politician, Charles Lucas was born in County Clare. For a time, he lived in a big house, known as 'Pennyville', at the Fairview Park end of Fairview Avenue.

A chemist by profession, he was the personal physician of Lord Charlemont. He contributed articles to The *Freeman's Journal* and penned several political pamphlets. He translated and printed *The Great Charter of the City of Dublin* in 1749 and served as MP for Dublin from 1761 to 1771.

Known as the 'Irish Wilkes' because of his often radical views, he was forever denouncing policies, systems or practices that he perceived as unfair. Even though, with Lord Charlemont, he supported independence for the Irish Parliament, like Charlemont, very hypocritically, he opposed Catholic Emancipation. Considering his stance, it is somewhat amazing that he is sometimes remembered as a patriot:

> *Lucas, Hibernia's friend, her love and pride,*
> *Her powerful bulwark and her skilful guide:*
> *Firm in the Senate, steady to his thrust,*
> *Unmoved by fear and obstinately just.*

Lucas is buried at St Michan's Graveyard, Church Street. A statue of him stands in Dublin City Hall.

Edmund Burke, 1729-1797

Dublin-born, Anglo-Irish Whig politician, orator, political theorist, philosopher and writer, Edmund Burke was a regular visitor to the domain of Lord Charlemont in Marino – to his Marino mansion and to the Casino.

At Trinity College in 1744, Burke founded a club that today exists as the College Historical Society. In 1763 in Britain, with other literary and artistic people including Dr Samuel Johnson and Oliver Goldsmith, he founded 'The Club', later known as the Literary Club.

From 1761 to 1763, he was posted to Dublin as secretary to William Hamilton, who was Chief Secretary for Ireland. He served as an MP with the Whig Party from 1765 to 1784 and became an eloquent, persuasive orator.

Many in the British Conservative Party still acknowledge him as their best ever political theorist. His advice to the British government was to follow a path of reconciliation in Ireland and the granting to Ireland of Catholic Emancipation and legislative independence.

Burke supported the rights of the American colonists to seek their liberties but, not their desire for total independence. He totally opposed the French Revolution. Many regard him as the instigator of conservatism. His best recalled work is *Reflections on the Revolution in France*, which was published in 1780.

A bronze statue of Burke, by John Henry Foley, stands in front of Trinity College since 1868. He is also remembered by the Edmund Burke Theatre at the Trinity Conference Centre, in the Arts Building in Trinity College.

Lady Sydney Morgan (née Owenson), 1780-1859

Novelist, Sydney Owenson, better known as Lady Morgan, was born in Dublin and sent to a Huguenot boarding school in Clontarf for three years. A miniature figure, just four feet tall, she worked as a governess, most notably with the Crofton family at Longford House in County Sligo, where she wrote most of her best work, a novel entitled *The Wild Irish Girl*. Published in 1806, this is a nationalistic novel highlighting Irish scenery and traditions, with echoes of the defunct old Gaelic civilisation.

In her work as a governess, she was familiar with the upstairs-downstairs nature of Irish life, with its privileged elite, aristocracy and the landless peasantry. In her novels, she wrote about Ireland in a very positive manner, about the country's history, culture and traditions and she strongly advocated Catholic Emancipation.

She married Thomas Charles Morgan in 1812 and over the years, her literary salon at 35 Kildare Street – the first of note in Dublin – had a brilliant circle, embracing the top socialites and literary personalities of the day. Visitors to her soirees included poet, Thomas Moore and writers, Charles Maturin and Samuel Lover. Italian violinist, Nicolo Paganini was also an attendee.

Lady Morgan travelled, on many occasions, to continental Europe and published books about her travels in France and Italy. Her portrait is displayed at the Royal Irish Academy in Dawson Street and there is a plaque to her memory at Setanta House, Kildare Street. A marble bust of Lady Morgan, by David d'Angers, is in place at the Victoria and Albert Museum in London. She is buried at Brompton Cemetery, Fulham Road, London.

William Carleton, 1794-1869

Novelist and storyteller, William Carleton, commonly known as the 'Poor Scholar', was born in Prolusk (or Prillisk), near Clogher in County Tyrone. As it was the era of the Penal Laws, there were no schools for Catholics, so he was educated in a number of hedge schools. In 1818, at 24 years of age, he walked to Dublin, where he remained for the rest of his life. He married Jane Anderson in 1882 and he converted to Protestantism.

He lived at the infamous Sheds at Clontarf, from where he liked to go on shooting trips to Howth. In the 1840s and early '50s, he resided at 3 Crescent Place beside The Crescent in Clontarf. He moved to the south side of Dublin in 1853. Carleton Road and Carlton Hall commemorate him in Marino.

A very tall, athletic figure with a grey beard, he presented a distinctive, striking presence around a then smaller Dublin. In later life he was something of a Tolstoian figure, very prominent and recognisable. He was something of a sportsman, a daredevil and a drinker – and the drinking helped keep him on the breadline all his life.

He wrote prolifically and profusely as a novelist, an essayist and a short-story writer. He spent much time studying and writing in Marsh's Library in St Patrick's Close. His work was published in various periodicals, magazines and newspapers. His great legacy is the way that he chronicled Irish peasant life before and during the Great Famine of the 1840s.

Essentially social history, his work is invaluable to anyone studying Irish social, political and religious history in the first half of the nineteenth century. He records Ireland's mud cabin days and depicts its artisans and peasants – from farmers and labourers to craftsmen. As a master storyteller, he meticulously details the very character of these inhabitants of nineteenth century rural Ireland – their culture and traits, their work, superstitions and crimes. He deals with the then everyday issues of the land war, tenants' rights, evictions, secret societies and emigration. His pen documents faction fights, dances, weddings, wakes and funerals and, of course, he catalogues too the awful time of the Great Famine. He sought to identify a national identity and his voice is that of the Irish peasant. Many regard him as Ireland's Walter Scott.

Carleton's greatest work is his two-volume, short-story publication, *Traits and Stories of the Irish Peasantry*, published in 1830 and 1833. His best-known novel is *Fardorougha the Miser* from 1839. WB Yeats said of Carleton, "He is the greatest novelist of Ireland by right of the most Celtic eyes that ever gazed from under the brows of a storyteller."

Oscar Wilde's mother, Lady 'Speranza' Wilde, told him, "You give meaning to the Irish character no other writer could."

In his biography of Carleton – *Poor Scholar*, published in 1947 – Benedict Kiely remarked that Carleton was "the greatest novelist that Ireland, in the nineteenth century, gave to the English language."

Writer and political activist, Darrell Figgis, writing under the pen name Michael Ireland, published a study of Carleton.

Clontarf-born, Barbara Hayley published a very comprehensive *A Bibliography of the Writings of William Carleton* in 1985.

An obelisk marks his grave in Mount Jerome Cemetery, Harold's Cross, Dublin.

Charles Lever, 1806-1872

Novelist and doctor, Charles Lever was born at 34 Amiens Street. This house, next door to Cleary's pub, was knocked down in 1844 to make way for Amiens Street Railway Station or, more specifically to facilitate the building of Amiens Street Railway Bridge.

His father, an English architect called James Lever, built a house on the site where today's Cadbury's factory stands on the Old Malahide Road in Coolock. He named the house Moatfield, after a moat or mound, which is still visible in the factory grounds. It was in this house that Charles was reared. He also lived, for some time, on Philipsburgh Avenue, Fairview.

He qualified as a physician in 1831, at Trinity College and practiced as a doctor during the dreadful cholera epidemic of 1832.

Something of a wit and raconteur, his stories are colourful and, mostly rural. They tend to be light-hearted, humorous and very entertaining. He helped create the image of the irreverent, daring and carefree character of the young Irishman.

Some critics accused him of 'stage Irishness' and failing to condemn British rule in Ireland. Conversely, in his later novels, he points to England's total ignorance of Ireland and its failure to differentiate between their own attitudes and that of Celtic Ireland. Unionists accused him of being anti-British.

He introduces many features of northeast Dublin into his books. In *The O'Donoghue*, he devoted a chapter to Clontarf, describing it as "the then fashionable watering place" and Bull Island also features. In *That Boy of Norcott's*, he introduces the Green Lanes of Clontarf.

His best works are *Harry Lorrequer* (1840) and *Charles O'Malley, the Irish Dragoon* (1841). In all he wrote thirty novels and five books of essays and short stories. All his work is characterised by rollicking and anecdotes.

Lever died in Trieste, Italy and is buried in the English cemetery in Florence.

Martin Haverty, 1809-1887

Martin Haverty was born in County Mayo. A journalist and historian, he lived for many years at 21 The Crescent, Marino. He wrote for the *Freeman's Journal* newspaper, mainly as a foreign correspondent, as he travelled extensively on mainland Europe.

He is best remembered for his long and thorough history of Ireland, published in 1860 and entitled, *History of Ireland, Ancient and Modern, for use in Schools and Colleges*. It is the history of Ireland from Celtic times to the Act of Union of 1800.

Haverty died in January 1887 at 40 St Alphonsus Road, Drumcondra. He is buried in Glasnevin Cemetery. Haverty Road in Marino is named in his memory.

Sir Samuel Ferguson, 1810-1886

Belfast-born poet, barrister and antiquarian, Samuel Ferguson married Mary Catherine of the Guinness dynasty in 1848 and went to live in Howth. Ferguson loved the Howth promontory stating, "I know of no more healthful or agreeable place during the summer months."

He moved to Dublin City Centre and settled at 20 North Great George's Street. At this premises, – an 'open house' – being of a gregarious nature, he held soirees for lovers of art, music and literature. His salon became noted for intelligent conversation and so generous and wonderful was the hospitality shown to all who visited, that it became known as the 'Ferguson

Arms'. Among those entertained there were Joseph Sheridan Le Fanu, Lady Morgan and Charles Lever.

He was appointed Deputy Keeper of the Irish Public Records in 1867 and his impressively diligent work here earned him a knighthood in 1878. In 1882, he was elected first president of the Royal Irish Academy, founded by Lord Charlemont of Marino. When his health began to fail in 1886, he returned to Howth and lived in Strand Lodge House on Claremont Road until his death.

Of his large body of work, his epic poems, *Congal, Aideen's Grave (The Cromlech of Howth)* and *Lament for Thomas Davies* are probably his best recalled works. He is commemorated with plaques in St Patrick's Cathedral and at the house he occupied at 20 North Great George's Street. He is buried in Donegore near Templepatrick in County Antrim.

John O'Leary, 1830-1907

Young Irelander, Fenian, journalist and writer, John O'Leary, a conspicuous man with full beard and piercing eyes, was born in County Tipperary. He became editor of the Fenian newspaper the *Irish People* but he and his co-editors, Thomas Clarke Luby and Charles Kickham, were betrayed by Pierce Nagle and he was sent to jail for a period of 9 years for his 'nationalistic activities'. After his release, O'Leary lived, for some time, in a boarding house called Lonsdale House at St Laurence Road in Clontarf.

He was very friendly with WB Yeats and while the Yeats' family lived in London, WB regularly stayed with O'Leary when visiting Dublin, to converse with him. Yeats admired the sheer romanticism in O'Leary's ideas for Ireland – as opposed to the materialism all around him. Thus, O'Leary inspired Yeats for his Irish and nationalistic-themed poetry. Yeats also sought his advice when editing some of his work.

After O'Leary's death, in his poem, *September 1913*, Yeats included the lines:

> *Romantic Ireland's dead and gone*
> *It's with O'Leary in the grave*

These and other lines by Yeats greatly inspired the men of 1916 to rise up.

O'Leary's main work is the two-volume, *Recollections of Fenians and Fenianism*.

Bram Stoker, 1847-1912

Writer and theatrical manager, Bram (Abraham) Stoker was born at 15 The Crescent, Marino. He is probably the best known and most successful of all North Bay writers. A sickly child, he was not expected to live and did not walk until he was almost eight years of age. We do not know the nature of his illness – was it physical, psychological or both?

After The Crescent, the family lived on Collins Avenue and Upper Buckingham Street. Later, Bram himself lived at several addresses around St Stephen's Green. In Autumn 1864, he entered Trinity College and, from a small, delicate boy, he grew to be a 6'2" very strong man and athlete and became college sports champion in a few disciplines. He was one of a very select few to become President of the College Philosophical Society and Auditor of the Historical Society. He had an exceptional academic career.

He followed his father into the old imperial Civil Service at Dublin Castle but, he was an unhappy civil servant. He found desk life dull and boring and, he did not like the way that Britain ruled Ireland. He began to write and to attend the theatre (his first love) to gain release from a monotonous job. He became obsessed with the stage and with drama. He saw the famous British Victorian actor, Henry Irving, in action in 1876 at the Theatre Royal on Dublin's Hawkins Street. He was to meet Irving a number of times and Irving asked him to come to London and become part of the Lyceum Theatre and Players.

In December 1878, Bram married Florence Balcombe, one of society's beauties who had been courted by the redoubtable Oscar Wilde. Florence had lived at 1 The Crescent and her family were involved with the Clontarf Town Commissioners. Ironically, Wilde introduced Florence to Bram and he regretted doing so when she went on to marry him.

Stoker resigned his job in the Civil Service and they moved to London, where Stoker became Irving's secretary and manager of the Lyceum Theatre. Bram and Florence had one child, Noel, born in 1879. He was to remain with Irving until the actor's death 25 years later in 1905. During that time, Stoker organised eight tours of America and Irving became the first actor to be knighted. After Irving's death, Stoker's own health began to fail and he died in April 1912. His ashes lie with those of his son, Noel Thornley Stoker, in the columbarium at Golders Green Cemetery, London.

Stoker wrote in his spare time. He wrote seventeen books, a myriad of short stores and numerous other works of fiction and non-fiction. His masterpiece was the book, story and character *Dracula*, published in 1897. *Dracula* is the classic, pure Gothic vampire story with the prototype eternal vampire. It is a blood-curdling, spine chilling tale, lurid and creepy, full of gloom, horror and mystery. Over time, people were led to believe that Dracula was based on Vlad the Impaler (Vlad Tapes Dracula), the 15th century Romanian prince and originated in Transylvania. This is not the case! Vlad was a sadist who did not drink blood while Dracula is a vampire who cannot survive without drinking blood. In any case, we now know that the true origins of Dracula lie in Ireland and Stoker's Irishness – Stoker never travelled to Transylvania in his life. Irish history – political, social, cultural and religious – Irish mythology, lore and legend all coalesced in Stoker's mind to create the other worldly story and the immortal fiend that is Dracula.

Stoker is commemorated by Stoker Park at The Crescent, which has a (ground) memorial plaque to him. The Stoker Dracula Organisation organise an annual Stoker commemorative event in Clontarf, as well as providing ongoing Stoker/Dracula tours and walks. In the north inner city, a mural memorial to Bram and Dracula is painted on the walls of the corner house at the Kilkenny Street/Buckingham Street junction.

(For the real genesis of Dracula, researchers and aficionados should read Dennis McIntyre's *Bram Stoker and the Irishness of Dracula*, published by The Shara Press in 2013.)

Lafcadio Hearn, 1850-1904

Lafcadio Hearn was a writer, translator, teacher and orientalist. He had a complex identity. He was born in Greece of an Irish father and a Greek mother. A slightly figure of just five foot, three inches tall, he spent most of his youth in Dublin, including some time in Fairview. His childhood home was at 47-48 Lower Gardiner Street. Number 47 was also the home of actor and dramatist Dion Boucicault (1820-1890).

He worked in America before settling in Japan. His output of writings was greatly influenced by those years in Dublin. He became fascinated by Irish mythology, superstitions, folklore and ghost and fairy stories. He was deeply interested in supernatural fiction and the weird. His work, often Gothic, embodied much folk belief and the macabre.

Living in Japan and becoming a Japanese citizen, he came to love Japanese culture, Japanese writing and the Japanese lifestyle. He chose the fresh, new exotic east, as yet untouched by industrialism, over the more industrial and capitalist west. From 1890, he made Japan his home. He adopted the name Koizumi Yakumo and became appreciated as one of the country's most revered writers. Hearn changed from Catholicism to Pantheism. He lectured on the English language, on literature, on culture and on folklore at the Imperial University in Tokyo. He became an interpreter and mediator of Japan and Japanese culture and philosophy for the west. His best-known works are *Kwaidan*, a collection of ghost stories and *Japan: An Attempt at Interpretation*. Some schools in Japan have writings by Hearn on the curriculum.

His ashes are buried in Zoshigaya Cemetery in Tokyo. He is commemorated by a monument at Metsve in Japan, where he lived for some time and his home there is preserved. Both Lefkada and Fort-de-France on Martinique Island in the eastern Caribbean Sea have streets named after him. In America, his one-time home is maintained as a historical house.

In Ireland, he was remembered by the Lafcadio Hearn Museum and Library at the now defunct Sundoi Ireland International School near Newbridge in County Kildare. In Dublin, there are wall plaques to his memory at 21 Leinster Square, Rathmines and at 73 Upper Leeson Street. In Tramore, in County Waterford, the Lafcadio Hearn Japanese Gardens, opened in 2016, are extensive and beautiful. Ulick O'Connor's writings about Hearn were first published in Seamus O'Sullivan's *The Dublin Magazine* and later in book form.

Oscar Wilde, 1854-1900

Oscar Wilde is surely one of the most quoted people ever. A witty dramatist, poet and author, he was born in Dublin and grew up to become one of the most flamboyant writers and conversationalists that ever lived. He became notorious for his flippant quips and epigrams of every kind. Some observed that he bore a certain air of condescension, which others referred to as 'well-bred arrogance'.

At one time, he would have been a regular visitor to the Clontarf area, as he courted a beautiful young lady named Florence Balcombe, who resided at 1 The Crescent. Her family were involved with the Clontarf Town Commissioners. Oscar introduced Florence to Bram Stoker, who had also resided at The Crescent and was a regular visitor to the Wilde family residence. Both Oscar and Bram visited the local pub, Carolan's on the Hill, now Harry Byrnes. While Bram might have been satisfied with a 'pint of plain', Oscar's tipple would be a more refined 'gin and supplement'! To the chagrin of Oscar, Florence went on to marry Bram, while he himself emigrated to London and married Constance Lloyd in 1884.

Oscar's other North Bay connection involved Greek scholar, Professor John Pentland Mahaffy, who was one of Oscar's tutors at Trinity College. They spent the Summer of 1874 at Mahaffy's home in Earlscliff in Howth. With Mahaffy, Oscar worked on proofs and helped edit Mahaffy's book, *Social Life in Greece from Homer to Menander*.

Wilde founded the 'aesthetic cult' encouraging 'art for art's sake' and was lionised by high society, Victorian London. He wrote plays, essays, letters, criticisms and one novel, *The Picture of Dorian Gray*, published in 1890. All bear the hallmark of his remarkably ornate phraseology. His plays, which are of the social comedy genre, are laden with wicked and cutting wit, paradox, satire and irreverence. In his writings and lifestyle, he spotlighted the comic topics of social injustices deep rooted in Victorian London.

Full of verve, Wilde was tall and distinctive with his own special charisma. He dressed in a somewhat eccentric manner and came across as a very intelligent dandy with effeminate ways but, he was Lord of the English language and was the leading figure in literary, cultural and social circles in Victorian society.

His masterpiece was the play, *The Importance of Being Earnest*. This is pure satire, mocking the superficiality, hypocrisy, artificiality and money mindedness of the Victorian aristocracy. But, the Victorians could only take so much and desired revenge. Their chance came when Oscar was charged with homosexual activity, then illegal. In 1895, he was given a two-year prison sentence with hard labour. This ruined his reputation. Broken by the severe and humiliating prison environment in Reading Gaol, on release, he spent his final years in exile in France, using the name Sebastian Melmoth. So, a very unique and enviable life lived 'up in the stars' ended in a chaotic shambles in the gutters. He himself commented, "The Gods had given me almost everything. I had genius, a distinguished name, high social position, brilliancy, intellectual daring ... now I am completely penniless and absolutely homeless."

Wilde converted to Catholicism and died of cerebral meningitis at the Hotel d'Alsace in Paris, in November 1900. He is buried in Père Lachaise Cemetery (Cimetière de l'Est) in Paris. His grave is marked by a monument by Jacob Epstein. Noted for his immortal quotes, his last is one of his best. When presented with his medical bill on his deathbed he remarked, "I shall die as I lived – beyond my means."

Plaques to commemorate Wilde are to be found at his birthplace, 21 Westland Row and at St Patrick's Park, Dublin 8. There is a memorial statue, a colourful sculpture of Wilde by Danny Osborne, put in place in 1997 in Merrion Square. It is in three parts, featuring a reclining Oscar with two stone pillars adorned with his quotations. One pillar has a female torso on top, representing Oscar's wife, Constance. The other pillar has a male torso on top. These are directly across from 1 Merrion Square North, the house where he grew up and where the Wilde family lived between 1855 and 1879.

In Galway, on William Street, there is a statue of Wilde in conversation with Estonian writer, Eduard Vilde. In London, a windowpane in Poet's Corner in Westminster Abbey is inscribed to him. On Adelaide Street in Central London, there is an Oscar Wilde statue by Maggi Hambling, dating from

1998. It is in the form of a green bench-like sarcophagus with a bust of Wilde at one end.

Two of Wilde's outstanding works were published towards the end of his life. *De Profundis*, written while he was in prison, is a monologue addressed to Bosie (Lord Alfred Douglas), his one-time lover who effectively betrayed Oscar. *The Ballad of Reading Gaol*, published after his release from prison in 1897, highlights the inhuman condition of prison life at the time. The Irish Ferries' vessel, *The Oscar Wilde*, also recalls Oscar. It was acquired by the company in 2007 and sold later.

Jane Barlow, 1857-1917

The Barlow family's connection with Clontarf and Raheny goes back to 1801, when James Barlow (Jane's grandfather) bought some land in Raheny and later acquired Sybil Hill house and farm. His son, John and his wife, Jane Disney, lived there for over 50 years. John died in 1874 and Lord Ardilaun bought the Sybil Hill property to expand his St Anne's Estate. Rev James W Barlow (Jane's father), who was vice-provost at Trinity College, came to live at 'The Cottage', Ballyhoy – a secluded, quiet place on the Howth Road beside Raheny Village – in 1865. His family had lived in Dollymount, where Jane was born in 1857.

Author and poet, Jane Barlow was to live most of her life at The Cottage. Later known as 'Ballyhoy', the house is now a retirement nursing home called 'Raheny House'. Her name is recorded on a plaque at the house. Jane became a very popular writer and poet, mainly concerning herself with matters such as landlords, the peasantry and the Great Famine.

In The Cottage, serene and idyllic with a somewhat romantic winding avenue and an old-fashioned garden, she lived a quiet, introverted life, away from worldly attractions. Visitors remarked on the treasury of books and paintings in The Cottage.

She romanticised peasant life in poetry of a melodramatic nature. Her novels are somewhat slow moving. The peasant life she portrays is of the humble, romantic and humorous type. Critics have pointed out that living such a secluded life and not being 'out there', her concept of peasant life is somewhat superficial. Her work has themes similar to John Synge's writing but, his overshadows Jane's because he was more talented and he had a more full and rounded understanding of rural life in Ireland.

Jane Barlow was a contemporary of WB Yeats and she was involved in the Irish Literary Renaissance. Although she had a firm unionist background, she considered herself a nationalist. In 1904, she became the first woman to be conferred with an Honorary Doctorate in Literature by Trinity College.

Her friend, Katherine Tynan, visited her regularly and observed that Jane possessed "a thoroughly cultivated mind."

Her best known works include *Irish Idylls*, *Bog-Land Studies* and a collection of poetry.

Katherine Tynan, 1861-1931

Poet, novelist and journalist, Katherine Tynan was born in Dublin. As well as her great output of poetry, she wrote over one hundred novels, a five-volume autobiography and contributed many articles to various periodicals. She mixed in the same social circles as Padraic and Mary Colum, WB Yeats, AE (George Russell), George Sigerson, Michael Davitt, John O'Leary, Maud Gonne and Douglas Hyde. Many of these and other well known literary and historical figures visited her salon at the family farm, White Hall in Clondalkin. She visited Charles Stewart Parnell when he was imprisoned in Kilmainham Gaol in 1881 and joined the Ladies Land League, founded by Anne Parnell at that time (1881).

She loved mother nature and the outdoors generally and loved her frequent visits to the countryside and the sea at Clontarf and Raheny, on visits to her writer friend, Jane Barlow. While much of her poetry is of a religious bent, it is also very much about her natural surroundings. Her best loved poem is *Sheep and Lambs*, which ends

All in the April evening
April airs were abroad
I saw the sheep with their little lambs
And thought on the Lamb of God

WB Yeats, 1865-1939

The poet and playwright, William Butler Yeats, was born in Sandymount, Dublin but spent much of his youth in his mother's (Susan Mary Pollexfen) childhood home, Merville, in Sligo town. He was the greatest poet of his era and one of the greatest ever in the English language. His themes were broad, embracing mysticism, the occult, spiritualism, theosophy, oriental philosophy and Irish mythology and nationalism. He left an outstanding body of poetry and plays, which is simply beautiful, brilliant and exquisite.

Much of his poetry is not easy. It is, in fact, somewhat obscure and a challenge to the reader. His words are strung together with craft and finesse, with fluency and with a lovely delicate touch. In his Irish themes, he poignantly portrays the Irish landscape and its people. He still maintains a huge international profile.

Yeats regarded Sligo as his spiritual home. He referred to County Sligo as "the land of heart's desire". Indeed, he is synonymous with the county, which is affectionately known as 'The Yeats County'. Yeats welcoming signs polka dot the county, where there is a whole industry of activity built around his legacy. Sligo's natural beauty and enchanting landscape, including Knocknarea, Ben Bulben and Lough Gill, together with the folklore and legends of the area, inspired some of his best poetry.

In the late 1880s, the Yeats family came to live in Balscadden Cottage, a house on the cliffs on Kilrock Road, overlooking Balscadden Bay in Howth. Six months later, they moved to a house called Island View on Harbour Road, Howth and lived there until 1884. The then teenage Yeats (from 16 to 18 years old) took the tram to and from the Erasmus Smith High School in Harcourt Street for two years – October 1881 to December 1883. Like Sligo, Howth was an explorative area for Yeats and, he reconnoitred the area and its special charms – the sea, the mountains, the valleys, streams and woods. He had begun writing poetry and many critics argue that it was while in Howth that he began to incubate the aesthetic theories that manifested themselves later in his poetry.

Yeats was greatly influenced in his Irish mythological and nationalistic themes by Standish O'Grady and Katherine Tynan but, in the main, by the old Fenian, John O'Leary. When the Yeats family lived in London, the poet often stayed with O'Leary at his Lonsdale House lodgings at St Laurence Road, Clontarf, on his frequent visits to Dublin. He admired the beauty of O'Leary's patriotic and romantic dream for a free Ireland, as distinct from the narrow-mindedness, the pettiness and the begrudgery then so rampant in Irish politics.

Yeats also despised the materialism and the vulgar greed of the rich. This is the theme of his poem, *September 1913*. Yeats identified with the Irish cause for freedom and justice and, he was a member of the IRB but, his views stopped short of independence. He belonged to the Anglo-Irish ascendency and he never forgot that. As an Anglo-Irish Protestant, he liked the elitist family lifestyle enjoyed by the gentry but conversely, he was envious of comparison to his own family status, in that they had not the means to live in the 'Big House' ways. He was somewhat jealous of the big houses around him, like those in Sligo, including Lissadell, Hazelwood and Marquee House.

Although he did not really support the 1916 Rising (it took him by surprise) the event deeply impressed him – the idealism, the sacrifice, the bravery and nobleness demonstrated, especially by the leaders. Indeed, he felt the nationalism evident in his writings, particularly in his play *Cathleen ni Houlihan*, might be responsible for what happened in 1916 and he asked himself in later life, "Did that play of mine send out certain men the English shot?"

Some regard this comment as arrogant, even boastful. Others say it fitted into his overall deportment – the way that he portrayed a self-image as an artist with something of a brazen manner, which marked him as, at heart, of privileged aristocratic stock. Nevertheless, his poem, *Easter 1916* is essentially written in admiration of all involved with the 1916 Rising.

Yeats lifelong muse was the nationalist and revolutionary, Maud Gonne. The tall and beautiful Gonne was an actress and an Irish republican revolutionary. He first met her when he was 23 years old and over many years, she rejected his marriage proposals. Many critics say it was good that she never married him as, in his attempts to 'woo' her, she motivated him to compose many wonderful poems. He married George Hyde Lees in October 1917.

Yeats was involved in founding The Irish Literary Theatre in 1899 and the National Theatre Society in 1902 and the opening of our National Theatre – The Abbey Theatre – in 1904. He was a director of the Abbey from 1904 up to his death.

In 1922, Yeats – who never attended university – received honorary degrees from both Trinity College Dublin and Queen's University Belfast. He was a senator in Seanad Éireann from 1922 to 1928. In 1923, his literary genius was recognised when he became the first Irish recipient of the Nobel Prize for Literature, the citation for which read, "For his always inspiring poetry, which gives expression to the spirit of a whole nation."

He did capture Ireland and the Irish landscape in words nobody else ever did, in a very Yeatsian way but, many argue that he did not and could not know Ireland and its people intimately, as he never frequented the public houses! They maintain that he could not write definitively on Ireland and its people without knowing pub life and lore, which was at the very heart's core of Irish life, society and culture. He was once lured into a pub on Baggot Street but asked to be escorted off the premises immediately!

Yeats died in January 1939 at Roquebrune-Cap-Martin on the French Riviera and, as World War II was raging, he was buried there but, he had frequently requested that he be laid to rest in the graveyard at St Columba's Parish Church, Drumcliffe, County Sligo – the parish where his great-grandfather had once been rector. That wish was fulfilled when, in September 1948, his body was exhumed, repatriated to Ireland and buried in Drumcliffe Graveyard.

His self-written epitaph on his grave has become world famous:

> *Cast a cold eye*
> *On life, on death.*
> *Horseman, pass by!*

The lines are the last three lines of his final poem *Under Ben Bulben*, written in 1938, one year before his death. Scholars constantly debate the true meaning of these words. His grave has become a shrine, a place of pilgrimage for thousands of writers annually.

There are many memorials to WB Yeats. A bust of Yeats by Albert Power is in place at Sandymount Green, Dublin since 1925. It is not far from where he was born at 5 Sandymount Avenue. On St Stephen's Green, there is a *Knife Edge* sculpture memorial to Yeats by Henry Moore, dating from 1967. There is a Yeats plaque at 82 Merrion Square, Yeats' first Irish home with his wife and children – a house he bought in 1922. Another Yeats plaque can be viewed at St Patrick's Park, Dublin 8. In Howth, there is a Yeats plaque at Balscadden House, Balscadden Road.

The Yeats' Society Sligo host an annual international summer school in honour of the poet. The Yeats Museum and Library, established in 1958, is located in a striking former bank building at Hyde Bridge over the Garavogue river in Sligo. Outside the building is a statue sculpture of Yeats, created by Ronan Gillespie in 1989. All of this 'Yeats Corner' is at the junction of Stephen Street and Markievicz Road.

An Irish Navy patrol vessel and an Irish Ferries' ship are named *William Butler Yeats*.

Stephen Gwynn, 1864-1950

A somewhat forgotten writer, journalist and political figure associated with Raheny is Stephen Gwynn. A Protestant, born in Dublin, he became a moderate cultural nationalist. He was a grandson of Irish nationalist and Young Irelander, William Smith O'Brien. As a member of the old Irish Parliamentary Party, he represented Galway as an MP from 1906 to 1918 and supported John Redmond. He became involved with the Irish Literary revival and, for a time, was Secretary to the Irish Literary Society. He was a member of the Gaelic League. He was also a soldier and served in World War I as an officer of the Connaught Rangers.

He lived in Raheny Park House from 1905 to 1910. In his book, *For Second Reading*, he recounts his farming experiences on the house's ten-acre estate – typical Irish mixed farming. At the house, he received many of the leading political figures of the time as visitors. These included Roger Casement, Douglas Hyde, Tom Kettle, Eoin MacNeill and Pádraic Pearse. He wrote prolifically – political, literary, biographical and general history.

He also wrote poetry and personal memoirs. He became an authority on 18th century Ireland. One of his best remembered books is *Irish Literature and Drama*. Also remembered is his vigorous historical poem, *A Song of Defeat*, which is a synopsis of Irish history from Brian Boru to the Manchester Martyrs.

Eoin MacNeill, 1867-1945

Politician and scholar, Eoin MacNeill, is buried in Kilbarrack Cemetery. Born in Glenarm in County Antrim, he had a deep interest in Irish history and the Irish language. He was a founder member of the Gaelic League in 1893 and was editor of its official publication, The *Gaelic Journal*.

He was Chairman of the group that established the Irish Volunteers in 1913 and became Chief of Staff. He became something of a fall guy when his countermanding order to Pearse, Connolly and the other organisers of the 1916 Rising caused confusion and effectively stopped the 1916 Rising taking place on Easter Sunday, as planned.

MacNeill became Minister for Education in the first Irish Free State government, having previously served as Minister for Industry and Minister for Finance under the auspices of the first Dáil. He was also, for a time, Ceann Comhairle of the Dáil. He represented the Free State on the disastrous Boundary Commission in 1924 but later resigned from that body, after some of its findings and deliberations were leaked. When the border with the six northern counties was confirmed in December 1925, MacNeill was heavily criticised. He subsequently had to resign from his ministry and lost his Dáil seat in 1927, prompting him to retire from politics.

His place in Irish history is unsure and many regard him as not being of a real political bent, rather more suited to scholarship. He had many publications but is mostly remembered for *Phases of Irish History* (1919) and *Celtic Ireland* (1921).

Arthur Griffith, 1871-1922

Politician, political thinker and journalist/writer, Arthur Griffith, was born in Upper Dominic Street, Dublin in 1871. He lived at 122 St Lawrence Road in Clontarf from 1911 until his death, in 1922.

A nationalist, he joined both the Gaelic League and the IRB. A scholarly man, he became a gallant agitator for Irish freedom and independence. He was very impressed by the Boers in South Africa – their self-sufficient lifestyle and their drive for independence. Likewise, he was motivated by Hungary's fight for independence from Austria and felt that their type of struggle could work in Ireland. He edited the *United Irishman* newspaper from 1898.

He founded the Sinn Féin organisation in 1905 and a new newspaper in 1906 called Sinn Féin. He used the newspaper and organisation to popularise his ideas towards achieving Irish independence. In a series of articles, he basically advocated withdrawing all contact with and, support for, all British institutions and withdrawing Irish MPs from the parliament at Westminster. His method would be passive, involving civil resistance.

His articles and writings, in general, certainly greatly rejuvenated the national spirit of the Irish people. The pamphlet, *The Resurrection of Hungary: A Parallel for Ireland* contained all his essential doctrines: self-reliance, self-determination and parliamentary and general non-cooperation with British authorities.

In the aftermath of the 1916 Rising, when all the detainees (internees) were released from Frongoch and other places of detention and returned to Ireland, they all joined together under the umbrella name of Sinn Féin. Already an organisation and a slogan, Sinn Féin now became a republican party and, under the Sinn Féin banner the 1918 General Election was won in landslide fashion. Griffith himself was elected TD for East Cavan. Sinn Féin then set up Dáil Éireann and that led to the 1919-1921 War of Independence. Griffith was a key figure and leader of the Irish delegation that signed the Anglo-Irish Treaty in December 1921. He became the first President of the Irish Free State then established. He died in office of cerebral haemorrhage in 1922, barely 50 years old. He left a wife, whom he had married in 1912 and two children.

Griffith is normally associated with 'heavy' political writing and one of his better remembered works is *Thomas Davis – Thinker and Teacher* but, he did write some light-hearted stuff, such as his poem, *Pride of Pimlico*.

Griffith is not forgotten in Dublin. There is a wall plaque on his house in Clontarf. Griffith Park, along the Tolka river in Drumcondra recalls him. The broad, tree-lined crossover road, Griffith Avenue, linking Clontarf and Marino with Whitehall and Glasnevin, is named after him, as is the Griffith housing estate in Glasnevin. The modern, dominating mass of apartments, Griffith Wood, on Griffith Avenue, also recalls him. Griffith Court, Griffith Downs and Griffith Lawns all at, or near, Griffith Avenue are in his memory. On the south side of Dublin City, in the Dolphin's Barn area, Griffith Square and Griffith College commemorate him and on the lawn outside Leinster House on Merrion Square West is a type of obelisk by Raymond McGrath, dated from 1950, dedicated to Griffith, Michael Collins and Kevin O'Higgins.

Sean O'Casey, 1880-1964

Playwright and memoirist, Sean O'Casey, was born John Casey, the youngest of thirteen children at 85 Upper Dorset Street, Dublin 1. He was to live at four other addresses in the North Bay area, including 25 Hawthorn Terrace and 18 Abercorn Road, both in the East Wall area. The name 'Hawthorn' is derived from the thorny tree, the fruit of which is the little red haw. In 1868, Abercorn Road was named after the Duke of Abercorn, who served two terms as Lord Deputy: 1866-1868 and 1874-1876.

He lived at 35 Mountjoy Square, where he did much of his writing. His last Dublin address was 422 North Circular Road, where he composed his best works.

He received little formal education but became self-educated from his experiences on Dublin's north city streets. Despite poor eyesight, he was an avid reader. People are often surprised that O'Casey, a Protestant, should be of such humble origins and actually work as a newspaper boy and a labourer but, the Dublin of that era did have a substantial number of 'artisan Protestants'.

He spent 21 years of his life, 1889-1910, living in the East Wall area and for a time, attended St Barnabas' School there. These were formative years in his life and greatly influenced his later writings. He became both swayed and motivated by the socialism preached by James Connolly and especially Jim Larkin. Thus, his political orientation became socialist and left wing. He involved himself in the Irish political scene, seeking independence and a fair deal for the poor. He rallied against capitalism and British domination of Ireland. He became a member of Conradh na Gaeilge (The Gaelic League), the ITGWU and the St Laurence O'Toole GAA Club. He was secretary of the Irish Citizen Army for some time.

O'Casey was deeply troubled by the exploitation and the sad dilemma of the working-class fraternity. He fought for social reform and was the first writer to give a voice to Dublin's working class. He highlighted the real heroes of tenement life – the strong women who played a central role by 'keeping the home fires burning' in difficult circumstances. He immortalised his native Dublin – particularly tenement Dublin – in his output of writings, especially in his trilogy of Dublin plays, which became internationally renowned. These are *The Shadow of a Gunman*, *Juno and the Paycock* and *The Plough and the Stars*. These plays were first produced in the Abbey Theatre in Dublin respectively in 1923, 1924 and 1926. In *Juno and the Paycock* the 'Paycock' was played by Clontarf actor, William Joseph (Will) Shields, later known as Barry Fitzgerald, who also played Fluther Good in *The Plough and the Stars*.

The plays are essentially about poverty-ridden, tenement, working-class Dublin, as well as revolution and civil war in the turbulent years of 1916 and afterwards. He hit out against the horror and suffering caused by rebellion and civil war when often, the wrong people, poor civilians, suffered most. His socialism shines through as he brilliantly captures and portrays the quick wit, quip and humour, the plain deadpan philosophy of Dublin's inner-city dwellers, with colourful phraseology. He ingeniously captures the inventive spontaneity of the phrases, sentences and sayings spoken by the slum dwellers. A Protestant, he was as poor as any of the Catholics who inhabited Dublin's notorious slums, dominated by grim experiences, poor health and high infant mortality. He lays bare the squalor and degradation in which the inhabitants of the tenements lived and his descriptions of them are affectionate and accurate. He also admired their devotion to the church.

He had been fully involved with the poor, the artisans, during the bitter dispute that was the infamous Dublin lockout of workers in 1913. O'Casey's writing is powerful and original, creative and intense. He could be blunt, outspoken and difficult, annoying many who called him a crank. Many were unhappy about the way that he portrayed the Dublin of the early 20th century, especially 'official' Ireland. Likewise, the insinuation in his plays that the true revolutionary heroes were not the gunmen but rather, the courageous, non-violent people and the vigour of stalwart women was not well received in nationalistic circles. In *The Shadow of a Gunman* (set in 35 Mountjoy Square) he disputes the status of the IRA, hits at their activities and attempts to dislodge the 'hero' gunman off his perch.

The Plough and the Stars caused protesting riots at the Abbey Theatre, as he again challenges the kudos bestowed on the gunmen. Many felt O'Casey was distorting history. The play was less than supportive of the 1916 Rising, which O'Casey regarded as a failure, as it did not deliver the socialism so dear to him. He felt that, in the new Irish Free State, nationalism and Catholicism were the winners. The play also had the character of a prostitute, which a church-ridden new state was not ready for. During the Abbey riots, suffragette and nationalist, Hanna Sheehy-Skeffington made a speech declaring that the protests were against the defamation of the rebels of Easter Week 1916. WB Yeats hit back, declaring that "O'Casey's fame is born tonight."

O'Casey's myriad of other plays never reached the dizzy heights or had the same energy as the trilogy. His anti-war play, *The Silver Tassie* was rejected by the Abbey and especially by Abbey director, WB Yeats. The two men, until now firm friends, quarrelled bitterly over the play – many that say Yeats' treatment of O'Casey smacked of professional jealousy. This rejection was part of the reason O'Casey moved to England permanently, in March 1926. He married Eileen Carey in Cheyne Row, Chelsea in September 1927. He lived in London for some time, then moved to Devon in the southwest of England, settling first in Totnes and then Torquay. He died in September 1964 in St Marychurch, Torquay. He was cremated at Golders Green Crematorium in London and his ashes were scattered there.

Like JM Synge and later Frank McCourt and Christy Brown, O'Casey portrayed life too real, too raw, too close to the bone for many people's liking. Like Yeats, James Joyce and GB Shaw, he was central to the Irish literary revival. Although he left Ireland disillusioned, his triumph was his writing. He published some books under the Irish version of his name, Seán Ó Cathasaigh.

O'Casey is commemorated in Dublin by two plaques: one at St Patrick's Park, Dublin 8 and the other at 85 Upper Dorset Street. A Sean O'Casey pedestrian bridge, dating from 2005, across the River Liffey joins Custom House Quay with City Quay. He is also remembered in East Wall by the Sean O'Casey Theatre and Centre at St Mary's Place. The former Upper Rutland Street, which joins North Great Charles Street with Summerhill is now called Sean O'Casey Avenue.

O'Casey's life story is told in the film, *Young Cassidy*, in which Rod Taylor plays Sean. Both *Juno and the Paycock* and *The Plough and the Stars* were made into films, while *The Shadow of a Gunman* was adapted for television. However, perhaps the greatest memory of him are the characters that he created, such as Joxer Daly and Fluther Good, that are legends in Irish theatrical circles. He left us an autobiography in six volumes. O'Casey is often quoted and a favourite O'Casey quote is "A pound in the pocket is good for the nerves"!

Padraic Colum, 1881-1972

Padraic Colum, a short, stocky figure, was born Padraic Columb in Longford Town in 1881. He was a playwright, a novelist, a biographer, a folklorist and a storyteller but above all, he was a poet. His first 8 years were spent in Longford, then 3 years in Cavan and the rest of his youth in Glasthule, near Dún Laoghaire in Dublin.

He joined the Gaelic League and, with Douglas Hyde and many others, he was central to the Celtic Revival, the Literary Revival and the Irish Renaissance. He also joined the Volunteers. He was friendly with James Joyce and Oliver St John Gogarty. He was central part of a group of writers that included WB Yeats, AE, Lady Gregory and JM Synge that put so much effort into establishing Irish theatre. In that, they were following in the wake of the great efforts that Bram Stoker had made to promote drama in Dublin, in the 1870s.

In 1912 Colum married suffragette and teacher, Mary Maguire and they lived in a cottage in Howth, before emigrating to America in 1914. They both taught comparative literature at Columbia University in New York City. Colum also wrote and edited in America and lectured on Irish literature at several universities. During his long life, Colum wrote much verse, many children's books and prose, including works on James Joyce and Arthur Griffith. He was one of Ireland's most versatile writers.

Things rural and country-life were central to Colum's work and he deals with the actuality of country life, especially around the turn of the 20th century. He wrote about wandering folk – travelling artisans, fiddlers, shanachies and ballad singers – all of whom he observed in his growing up years and much of his language was the language of the peasants. Many of his children's stories and books re-tell traditional tales of folklore, legends and traditions, which he loved. He was one of the first to dramatise rural life. It is as a lyric poet that he gained worldwide fame and his Irish ballad-style poems are much loved.

In 1923, Hawaiian authorities invited him to the Sandwich Islands, to survey and record their traditional folklore and myths and to revive the literary heritage of the ancient civilisation of Polynesian people. He published two volumes of their stories for Hawaiian posterity.

Colum's huge literary legacy includes plays, novels, poetry and literary criticism. There is a tenderness and gentleness as well as a richness – soft sounding words – evident in much of his poetry and three of his best known are *An Old Woman of the Roads*, *She Moved Through the Fair* and *A Cradle Song*. He died in Enfield, Connecticut in January 1972. His body was brought back to Ireland and buried in St Fintan's Cemetery in Sutton.

In Dublin, Padraic Colum is commemorated by plaques at Eden Road, Glasthule, Dún Laoghaire and at 11 Edenvale Road, Ranelagh. In Longford, Colum is remembered by a stone memorial on Dublin Road, Longford, on the site of the workshop where he was born and where his father was Master. A Padraic Colum gathering takes place annually in Longford Library since 2017.

James Joyce 1882 – 1941

Novelist, poet, playwright and quintessential Dubliner, James Joyce, was born at 41 Brighton Square, Rathgar, Dublin in February 1882. Celebrated as probably Dublin's most famous writer, his work became very influential.

Due to his father's inability to manage his own and the family's financial affairs, his squandering, drinking ways and general fecklessness, James and his family were destined to live a somewhat nomadic life, close to the breadline. They moved address regularly, for non-payment of or, to avoid paying rent. About 1893, they came to the north side of Dublin and James was to live at 11 different addresses, including 29 Hardwick Street, 14 Fitzgibbon Street (now number 34) and 2 Millbourne Avenue in Drumcondra. He lived at six separate addresses in the Fairview area: 17 North Richmond Street, 29 Windsor Avenue, Convent Avenue, 13 Richmond Avenue, 8 Royal Terrace (now Inverness Road) and 103 North Strand Road. He also lived at Glengariff Parade and at St Peter's Terrace (now St Peter's Road) in Phibsborough.

Joyce attended O'Connell Schools in North Richmond Street for a short time but, his father moved him to nearby Belvedere College, as he did not want James mixing with 'Paddy Stink' and 'Mickey Mud'. Joyce loved the North Dublin Bay area, especially the Bull Island, the North Bull Wall and Dollymount Strand. Indeed, he once stated that a very early writing inspiration for him was the effects a nubile young girl had on him on an occasion at Dollymount Strand. This is described in the scene in his semi-autobiographical *A Portrait of the Artist as a Young Man*, where Stephen Dedalus (Joyce's alter ego) watches a girl and is "touched with wonder" and smitten by the sheer and endless wonder of mortal beauty.

As he wrote, Joyce felt ill at ease in Dublin even though the city is prominent in all of his writings and, he is indelibly linked to it. He was to leave Dublin forever in 1912. He especially disliked the overbearing power that the Catholic Church had over people's lives. He hated the domineering oppression of the church, its icy-breath, staunch conservatism and the manner in which it expected conformity. Perhaps, most of all, he could not tolerate how, in his view, the Church choked creative thinking. Joyce also felt very uncomfortable with his family situation and with the Irish political scene at the time.

In 1904, he met Nora Barnacle, a chambermaid from Galway and on 8 October of that year, they eloped to continental Europe and settled for some time in Trieste on the Adriatic Sea in northeast Italy. He was to marry Nora in 1931. They had two children, George and Lucia.

Soon, his life on the continent was to resemble the nomadic style he had experienced with his family in Dublin. He and Nora were to move around quite a bit and live frugally, close to destitution. They lived in both Zurich and Paris and depended on borrowings and allowances from friends and acquaintances. Joyce had serious problems with his eyesight, suffering from iritis glaucoma and cataract problems. At times, in between operations on his eyes, he was totally blind.

Despite difficulties, Joyce kept writing, prose, drama and some lovely, lyric-style, love poems – he was very musical. He found continental Europe, especially Paris, cosmopolitan and tolerant of – even encouraging for – freethinkers. He felt stimulated by "the reality of experience" and free to express himself. His prose could be very incisive, very penetrating and very powerful. *Ulysses* is his masterpiece, even if he himself regarded *Finnegans Wake* as his 'magnum opus'.

Ulysses was first published on 2 February 1922 (Joyce's fortieth birthday) in Paris by Sylvia Beach, an American lady who owned a bookshop in the city called Shakespeare and Company. The book was to announce him on the international stage. He began writing it in 1914 and based it on Homer's *The Odyssey of Odysseus*, which deals with the massive human disaster occasioned by the disastrous ten-year Trojan war. It was written for his muse, Nora Barnacle, who was central to much of his output of writings. It was in memory of their first date, on 16 June 1904.

Ulysses came to represent something of a watershed in modern English literature and both influenced and stimulated greatly many later writers, even if some 50 years passed before the book found its footing in Ireland. It is accepted as a standard work in western literature. The three main characters in *Ulysses* are the cuckolded Leopold Bloom, his wife Molly (Nora Barnacle) and Stephen Dedalus (Joyce himself) but maybe the real and main character is Dublin itself. All the events in the book, which has no real central plot, take place in 18 hours in Dublin on 16 June 1904.

Many critics regard *Ulysses* as the great Irish novel but many others disagree, claiming that while it is a great Dublin/urban book and did put Dublin and, consequently, Ireland on the world literary map, it does not reflect the Ireland of Joyce's era. Ireland was then and for long years afterwards, rural and agricultural – an agricultural, farming-based society, economy and country – totally dependent on the land for sustenance. That reality is not evident in *Ulysses*. Where is the country and countryside/landscape described by Padraic Colum, who was born the year before Joyce?

> *Wet winding roads, brown bogs with black water ... the*
> *smell of the beasts, the wet wind in the morn; and the*
> *proud and hard earth.*

Ulysses is characterised by Joyce's use of third-party narrative, by his 'stream of consciousness' style and ironic humour. Throughout the book, he displays total mastery of the English language. *Ulysses* has, perhaps, received more attention than any other 20th century book, being praised and ridiculed in turn, in countless critical studies. With imaginative fiction, he immortalised what he saw as a shabby-genteel Dublin. His technique, including the use of silent monologue, was daring and revolutionary, even if some critics declared his work unintelligible and ungrammatical. Joyce experimented with and teased the English language and was not afraid to try new literary methods. Censors in Britain and America banned the book on the grounds that its contents were indecent, erotic, obscene and pornographic. Many were outraged by its iconoclasm and its explicit, even raw references to the human body. Some viewed it as morally corrupt and even saw it as a possible source of social anarchy. The book did not become freely available until 1936.

Ulysses has a daunting, forbidden reputation for the reader. Many view it as simply inaccessible. Then along came *Finnegans Wake*, published in 1939. It took Joyce 17 years to complete. Only the most studious and patient of intellectual scholars can come to terms with his rhythmic flow in this work, with words and phrases from other languages interwoven with English. Many readers admit to simply being unable to decipher and understand a work that is almost baffling!

In Dublin, Joyce, who sang with a light tenor voice, is remembered by an annual summer school and an annual Bloomsday celebration on 16 June. Fourteen Robin Buick brass pavement plaques form a Joyce/Ulysses walk, beginning in Middle Abbey Street and leading through O'Connell Street to Kildare Street. The 'sirens' episode in *Ulysses* is recalled by a wall plaque in the Ormond Hotel on Ormond Quay. Joyce characterises the River Liffey as Anna Livia Plurabelle and there is a Joyce bridge across the river at Usher's Island.

There are two Joyce sculptures in Dublin by Marjorie Fitzgibbon. One (a bust) is at St Stephen's Green (south) since 1982. The other is on North Earl Street since Bloomsday 1990. There is a James Joyce Centre at 35 North Great George Street, which was first opened in 1996. A James Joyce Museum operates at the Martello Tower, now known as the Joyce Tower, in Sandycove. Joyce actually lived in the tower for a short time in 1904. It was officially opened, fittingly enough, by Sylvia Beach in 1962 – she was the original publisher of *Ulysses*. On Beach Road in Sandymount is *An Gallán Gréine Do James Joyce* by Clíodna Cussen and it dates from 1983.

There are wall plaques commemorating Joyce at 41 Brighton Square, Rathgar; 23 Carysford Avenue, Blackrock; 1 Martello Terrace, Bray; Mullingar House, Chapelizod; Newman House, 86 St Stephen's Green (South) and St Patrick's Road, Dublin 8. Number 52 Upper Clanbrassil Street, Dublin 8 has a plaque recalling the character Leopold Bloom, and there is a publishing company called The Leopold Bloom Press on Grafton Street. Corporation Street was renamed James Joyce Street in the 1990s. This was originally Mabbot Street, which Joyce notes as the entrance to Nightown (Monto) in the 'Circe' section of *Ulysses*. Also in the Joyce 'theme' are the sprawling Ulysses House on Foley Street and Bloom House at the intersection of Sean Mac Dermott Street with Gloucester Place. A pathway at Liberty Park (off Foley Street) is called James Joyce Walk. There is a Joyce Avenue in Foxrock, a James Joyce Court in Bayside and a Joyce Road in Drumcondra. In University College Dublin (UCD), the James Joyce Library is on four levels in the Library Building.

In Trieste, Italy, there is a Joyce sculpture at Porte Rosso, a small Joyce Museum on Via Madonna de Mare and the Joycean Laboratory at the University of Trieste.

Irish Ferries have the *MV Ulysses* as a RORO car ferry ship, which was launched in September 2000.

And who can forget the song *Finnegan's Wake*, especially as performed by Ronnie Drew and The Dubliners!

Joyce is buried in the Cementerio de Fluntern in Zurich, Switzerland, where there is a statue to him. It is a major tourist attraction and the city has a Joyce foundation.

Frank Gallagher, 1898-1962

Frank Gallagher was born in Cork City but lived, for a time, at Raheny House, the retirement home once occupied by author, Jane Barlow. His name is mentioned on a plaque at the house.

He became the first editor of the *Irish Press*, founded by Éamon de Valera in 1931. He worked in Radio Éireann as a director and as director of the Government Information Bureau under De Valera. He wrote many short stories, biographies and interesting historical articles. His main publication are *Days of Fear* and *The Four Glorious Years*. He also wrote under the pseudonym, David Hogan.

He lived in Sutton after leaving Raheny.

Brendan Behan, 1923-1964

Writer, playwright, poet and talker, Brendan Behan lived, as a child, at 14 Russell Street off the North Circular Road near Croke Park Stadium in Dublin's north inner city. Behan's family resided in a one-roomed, basement flat in a house that was one of five tenement houses on the street owned by Brendan's grandmother, Christine English, known as 'Grannie'. For good measure, Grannie owned another house on nearby Fitzgibbon Street.

In 1928 he went to school at St Vincent's Primary School, run by the Daughters of Charity of St Vincent de Paul on North William Street. He later attended Bolton Street Technical School. He left school at 14 years of age and followed his father's trade as a house painter.

About 1935, the family moved to better accommodation in a new house at 70 Kildare Road in Crumlin. Being very proud of his northside roots, Brendan felt unhappy and alienated in what he regarded as being out in the country in "cow and culchie land"!

Behan's family were republican and socialist – he declared himself a communist. He joined Fianna Éireann as a teenager and later became a member of the IRA. He was caught in possession of explosives in Liverpool as a sixteen-year-old and sent to Walton Jail, Liverpool but because of his age, he was moved to serve three years in Hollesley Bay borstal institution, Woodbridge, Suffolk in England. He was to spend several spells in jail in Ireland, in Mountjoy, Arbour Hill and the Curragh Prison, due to his republican activities. While in prison, he learned to speak Irish and subsequently wrote in English and Irish.

Brendan Behan is best known for three publications – two plays and his autobiographical book, *Borstal Boy*. The first play is *The Quare Fellow*, published in 1954. It gained him international acclaim when it was produced at the Stafford Theatre in London, in 1956. It is set in Mountjoy Prison, where Behan became acquainted with murderer, Bernard Kirwan and the tragic comedy is based on him. The play provokes us to consider the morality of capital punishment. The play has a gay character and also includes the song, *The Auld Triangle*, which has ever since been a celebrated song and a nostalgic Behan memory. The well known, traditional local pub, The Auld Triangle at 28 Lower Dorset Street recalls Behan, the play and the song.

The second play, *An Giall*, written in Irish, was later translated and performed in English as *The Hostage*. The play's setting is a brothel in Dublin's Nelson Street and it examines the circumstances of a would-be political execution – a young soldier awaiting retaliatory execution. The play also examines the Anglo-Irish political situation. Like *The Quare Fellow*, it too, was a great success.

Borstal Boy recounts Brendan's borstal confinement. The book was banned in Ireland because of its content with regard to Irish Republicanism and to the Catholic Church, as well as its portrayal of teenagers being involved in sexual acts.

In 1955, Brendan married Beatrice Ffrench-Salkeld. Their only child, Blanaid, a daughter was born in 1963.

Behan was notorious and, in his pomp, was known to expound boisterously and tempestuously in 'wild Irishman' fashion on a plethora of topics. He was a larger-than-life individual with a somewhat unpredictable nature. He exhibited the drunken Paddy to the world and it certainly did him no favours. He described himself as 'a drinker with a writing problem'! His lifestyle eclipsed his writing as the undoubted literary talent and creativity that he possessed were, sadly, over-shadowed by his tendency towards self-destruction. He lacked the self-discipline to fulfil his true potential as a writer. He was a diabetic and his drinking, coupled with his tendency towards invective, made him unwelcome in many social situations and in many of his favourite pubs and bars. He loved an audience and he could be a nuisance and a bowsie, truculent and repetitive as he tended to celebrate his reputation as a boisterous boozer and a jailbird. The Behan myth often marred his work but his overall generosity and bonhomie, together with his disregard for convention, were enough to maintain a certain popularity.

He did challenge Ireland's political, social and sexual conventions. He did achieve great success at home and abroad but, many critics argue that he never reached his full potential as a writer. Perhaps he was unable to cope with fame? He died, aged forty-one, in March 1964 and is buried in Glasnevin Cemetery. His excessive drinking coupled with jaundice and diabetes were the cause of death. And surely, his life is as engrossing as anything that he wrote!

Peadar Kearney, author of our national anthem, *The Soldier's Song*, was Brendan Behan's uncle and brother of Brendan's mother, the celebrated Kathleen Behan.

Much like Sean O'Casey, many regarded Brendan Behan as a character from the Dublin slums who worked his way through life by natural ability and grit, despite his circumstances. Others view both Behan and O'Casey as from a class often referred to as the 'shabbygenteel'.

Behan is remembered by a life-size statue, sitting in conversational mode on a bench by the Royal Canal at Binns Bridge, Lower Drumcondra Road. There is a Behan wall plaque in St Patrick's Park, Dublin 8. The old houses on Russell Street where he lived have been replaced by the Brendan Behan Court of modern dwellings – with a commemorative wall plaque – and across the road, on the opposite side of Russell Street, is the Behan Square of apartments.

An old adage maintains that there is no such thing as bad publicity. Behan said there is – your own obituary.

Christy Brown, 1932-1981

Although almost totally spastic in his limbs, due to cerebral palsy, Christy Brown became an accomplished poet, author and painter through the only body parts he could control – the toes of his left foot. He was the tenth of 22 children in a family that lived in poverty at 54 Stannaway Road, Kimmage in South Dublin.

Christy had little formal education, except for some time spent at St Brendan's School/Clinic in Sandymount. Christy's most recognised work is the book, *My Left Foot*, first published in 1954. This was made into a film directed by Jim Sheridan in 1989. It starred Daniel Day Lewis and Brenda Fricker and won two Oscars. This turned Christy into a celebrity and over the years, he became very dependent on alcohol. His masterpiece, a book called *Down All the Days*, was published in 1970. It was very successful and was translated into many languages.

In 1972, Christy Brown married Mary Carr and their wedding reception was held in Sutton Castle Hotel. They lived for some time in Shielmartin in Sutton. They then moved to live in Rathcoole in south County Dublin and later resided in Ballyheigue in County Kerry. Finally, in 1978, they moved to Parbrook, near Glastonbury in Somerset, in the southeast of England.

Christy became something of a recluse and he died in Parbrook in September 1981, aged 49 years. He is buried in Glasnevin Cemetery, Dublin.

John McGahern, 1934-2006

County Leitrim born John McGahern was one of Ireland's best and most important writers of the second half of the 20th century. In all, he wrote six novels, four collections of short stories, plays and a brilliant autobiographical *Memoir*. Essentially, he was a chronicler of rural life in Ireland, so much of his work is actually good social history. He wrote about an Ireland that was, thankfully, vanishing – a stultifying, parochial Ireland. He portrays an Ireland that was moving from being a repressed, insular state to one morphing into freedom and self-confidence. It is an Ireland over-flowing with secrecy and deception – a dreary, priest-ridden countryside.

McGahern's second book (his first was *The Barracks*, 1963) *The Dark* (1965) was to change his life forever. The book was banned by the Irish Censorship Board shortly after its publication for obscenity or, as one critic put it, for 'pornographic depravity'. This, together with the fact that he had married a Finnish theatre director, Annikki Laaksi, in a registry office – 'a foreign divorcee' – led to his dismissal from his primary school teaching post at St John the Baptist Boys School in Clontarf, Dublin. The school's patron, the redoubtable Archbishop of Dublin at the time, John Charles McQuaid, left no room for debate or any form of compromise on the matter. It was an action that would not be tolerated a generation later and had nothing to do with his ability or performance as a teacher. A puzzling aspect of a teacher being sacked by the Church is the fact that the Church does not pay the teacher's salary, the state does, so who is the employer and who should have the power to 'hire or fire'? He was forsaken too by the self-righteous but also church-fearing teacher's union, the INTO.

Remarkably, McGahern bore no grudge although he had to endure a certain social and cultural stigma for a time as a 'proscribed' author and, it was no fun being out of work in the Ireland of the 1960s. In the long term, his career blossomed with his output of writings, international recognition (especially in France), lecturing tours, literary awards and a happy writing/farming life in his native Leitrim. Of course, when a 'new' Ireland crystallised, he was given the status he and his work deserved and he now occupies an exalted position among Irish writers.

What is the essence of McGahern's comparatively small but brilliantly intimate output of writings? He looked for transparency – the truth. He could be very explicit in his portrayal of the truth. Perhaps above any other writer, he captured and detailed the Irish psyche and what it is to be Irish in his wonderful storytelling manner. His fountain of inspiration stems from real life events. His was an enviable vision of the countryside, a vision that only a person moulded in the countryside could have. He chronicled very insightfully and his prose, describing everyday events, is often lyrically beautiful and very (often minutely) detailed. He did not harbour or condone "hypocrisy and cant". In fact, the honesty permeating from his work plays a major role in making him the excellent and best-read author he is. His appeal is universal; he has no pretension or indeed, contrivance. Anyone can read McGahern, ordinary folk as well as the intellectuals. Indeed, he had much to offer social historians.

Often referred to as the Irish Chekhov, McGahern asks fundamental questions with regard to how post-independence Ireland evolved and the values and culture that dominated, the constraints people lived with and under. However, far from condemning, he is all empathy. He includes the better side, such as neighbourliness, self-reliance, the parish network (the Meitheal), the family unit and the humour in his observations. What is often called his 'landscape literature' is splendidly crafted as he regularly shines a light into dark corners, often depicting a dark Ireland. Much of his writings could be regarded as considered exactness, his language often simple but very subtle and loaded with feeling. He is non-judgemental, happy to just state the facts and he shows no bitterness for his own childhood of trauma and the obvious physiological scars that he carried as a result of the words and actions of his somewhat brutal father.

His critics will point out that there is a sameness about his work – much of it drawn from the same source and well – the Irish countryside. This, however, is disingenuous. He did not spend his entire life in the countryside. He lived abroad and lived in Dublin as a student and, for nine years, as a teacher. He included all these experiences in his work – especially Dublin.

One of McGahern's short stories, *Korea*, became a feature film in 1995, directed by Cathal Black. His masterpiece, *Amongst Women*, was made into a four-part television series.

John McGahern died of cancer in the Mater Hospital, Dublin in March 2006. He is buried beside his mother in the graveyard at St Patrick's Church, Aughawillan, County Leitrim.

Gaffney's public house in Fairview has a plaque, with a commendation, in memory of McGahern.

Jonathan Swift

Edmund Burke

Lady Sydney Morgan

Bram Stoker

William Carleton's tombstone

Brendan Behan (with Jackie Gleeson)

Oscar Wilde

Padraic Colum

John O'Leary

WB Yeats

Christy Brown commemorated in his home place

Sean O'Casey

John McGahern commemorated in Ballinamore, Co. Leitrim

Jane Barlow

Acknowledgements

Photographs and images used in this volume under Creative Commons licence include:

The Custom House in Dublin Seen Early in the Morning by Bjørn Christian Tørrissen (Creative Commons 4.0) – http://bjornfree.com/travel/galleries/

Baily Lighthouse, Howth Harbour. Photographer: Prasanna Kumar Mamidala. (Creative Commons 4.0)

Dublin Bay Dublin Ireland Aerial Photography by Giuseppe Milo (Creative Commons 3.0) – https://500px.com/p/pixael?view=photos

The Custom House in Dublin at Night by Jimmy Harris (Creative Commons 3.0) – https://www.flickr.com/photos/jimmyharris/2259405960/in/set-72157606827651351/

Custom House Quay, The Famine Memorial by David Dixon (Creative Commons 2.0) – https://www.geograph.ie/photo/7292957

Universal Links on Human Rights. 1995 sculpture by Tony O'Malley photographed by William Murphy – https://www.flickr.com/photos/infomatique/23983101810

Chariot of Life sculpture by Oisin Kelly in grounds of Irish Life Centre, Abbey Street, Dublin. Unveiled in 1982. Photograph by UtDicitur on Wikimedia Commons

Easter Weekend in Dublin (James Connolly, 5 June 1868 - 12 May 1916). Photograph by William Murphy – https://www.flickr.com/people/80824546@N00

Busaras, from north side of Talbot Memorial Bridge by Jnestorius on Wikimedia Commons

Connolly Railway Station (Amiens Street) by William Murphy (Creative Commons 2.0) – https://www.flickr.com/photos/infomatique/24574559941/

Front side of a monument to the victims of the Dublin and Monaghan bombings in Talbot Street, Dublin. Photography by Keresaspa on

Wikimedia Commons – https://commons.wikimedia.org/wiki/ File:Dublin_and_Monaghan_front.png

The Convention Centre in the Dublin Docklands by J.-H. Janßen on Wikimedia Commons

Raheny GAA Clubhouse, All Saints Drive by SeoR on Wikimedia Commons

St. Fintan's Cemetery, Sutton by William Murphy from Dublin, Ireland (Creative Commons 2.0) – https://www.flickr.com/photos/ infomatique/8000123438/

Irish Goat by Steve Ford Elliott (Creative Commons 2.0) – https:// www.flickr.com/people/69669465@N00/

Statue of Grainne Mhaol Ni Mhaille (Grace O'Malley, 1530-1603), the Irish Pirate, located at Westport House, Co. Mayo, Ireland by Suzanne Mischyshyn (Creative Commons 2.0) – https://www. geograph.org.uk/profile/34287

Ireland's Eye from Howth Harbour © 2008, Pilise Gábor

Howth Castle in Dublin viewed from a rocky outcrop on Howth Hill by O'Dea on Wikimedia Commons

County Dublin, Howth Martello Tower by Jonjobaker on Wikimedia Commons

Plaque remembering Thomas Telford at the corner of Bayside and the Coast Road by Dwmalone on Wikimedia Commons

The LUAS - Dublin City Centre (180mm) by William Murphy (Creative Commons 2.0) – https://www.flickr.com/photos/ infomatique/1507653387/

**Other Books by Dennis McIntyre
published by The Shara Press**

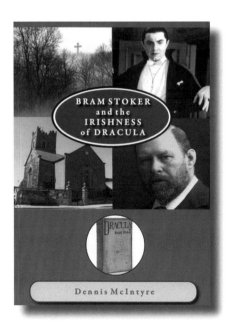

Bram Stoker and the Irishness of Dracula

Bram Stoker has long been recognised as a true master of the horror genre and has rightly won acclaim for his creation, *Dracula*, the world's most enduring vampire story. However, the inspiration and origin of Stoker's masterpiece has long bedevilled scholars and devotees alike and many theories abound, including the plethora of possible Irish influences.

> *"This is a most welcome volume for both scholars and readers."*
> *– John Moore (International Stoker scholar, connoisseur and bibliophile)*

Once in a while, a book comes along that is definitive in its subject matter – this is such a book. The author has unearthed many slants and angles on Dracula's origin but, of particular interest is the revelations concerning Stoker's mother's connections with Longford House and those winding Ox Mountain roads.

First published in Ireland, in 2013, by The Shara Press
ISBN: 978-0-9527311-1-5

Available to buy online. See inside back cover for further information.

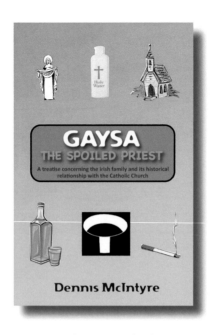

Gaysa, the Spoiled Priest

A treatise concerning the Irish family and its historical relationship with the Catholic Church

This treatise delves deep into the matter of how religion (priests and the Catholic Church) infiltrated and wove itself into the very fabric of Irish society and Irish life. It relates the almost unbelievably sad story of the pathetic, fictitious, Gaysa (the principal character in this narrative and a spoilt priest) and the repercussions that his rejection had for his life and the lives of those around him.

It is a book that is rich in social history and will be of interest to anyone curious about just how Ireland and Irish society, dominated by the Catholic Church, developed in the way that it did.

"There was and is little wrong with the church that Our Lord, Jesus left to us. It has stood and will continue to stand the test of time. There was and is no cause for anyone to throw out the baby with the bathwater."

First published in Ireland, in 2020, by The Shara Press
ISBN: 978-0-9527311-5-3

Available to buy online. See inside back cover for further information.

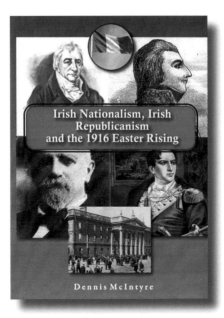

Irish Nationalism, Irish Republicanism and the 1916 Easter Rising

This is the fascinating story (or stories) of Irish nationalism and republicanism, as well as the history of the 1916 Rebellion – commonly known as the Easter Rising – with some associated writings, poems and songs.

It spans an amazing array of captivating events and personalities in a short and concise manner but, very thoroughly researched with acute attention to detail. It is very readable, fascinatingly interesting, most informative and copiously illustrated.

It is a factual account (yes, warts and all) of all matters covered, presented in a non-interpretative, non-judgemental way. There has been no publication of its kind covering similar ground. It even unearths information that, for some, will be new.

If you want to know about the history of Irish nationalism and Irish republicanism and the story of Easter 1916, then this is the book for you.

First published in Ireland, in 2016, by The Shara Press
ISBN: 978-0-9527311-3-9

Available to buy online. See inside back cover for further information.

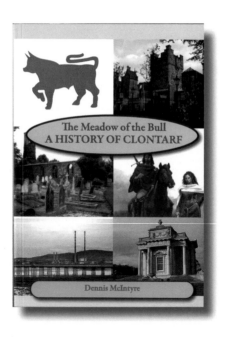

The Meadow of the Bull: A History of Clontarf

This book is the result of a detailed study of the Clontarf area in all its aspects. The author, Dennis McIntyre, in painstaking research, has captured the mood and the heart of Clontarf. Chapter by chapter, the story is told in an unrushed and thorough manner, tracing the area's fascinating history, from the arrival of the first inhabitants through the coming of Christianity and the intrusions of the Vikings and the Normans, Daniel O'Connell and the 'Monster Meeting that never was', Lord Charlemont and the Casino, the Howth gun running episode, Clontarf Town Hall and the Easter Rising of 1916, the churches, the schools, the clubs as well as contemporary events all feature, making this book a must for all Clontarfites, teachers, students and anyone in any way interested in Irish and local history.

A well-chosen selection of old and new illustrations delightfully adorns this book.

First published in Ireland, in 1987, by The Shara Press. Second edition published in 2014.
ISBN: 978-0-9527311-2-2

Available to buy online. See inside back cover for further information.

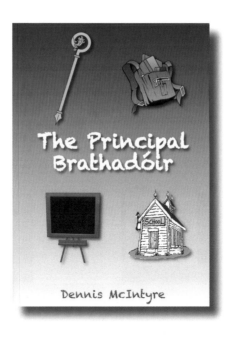

The Principal Brathadóir

This publication is pioneering stuff of a new whistleblowing nature, as the author critically portrays the behind-the-scenes goings-on he perceived to be part of the Irish primary school system. It explores much that has been hidden under the carpet for far too long, as it dismantles any notion that people have held (or hold) of every school institution being a cosy place of harmonious learning.

As an obviously judicious insider in the primary school scene and system, there is a certain anger as the author spits out what many have been choking on for years and exposes a dirty underbelly, which no doubt some will find unpalatably unpleasant. It contains some very profound comments on topics such as fear, power, religion and the clergy, equality, fairness, the community, teachers and teaching and, of course, education itself.

This treatise may come to represent a watershed in Irish primary school history and, is as loud as calls come for major changes in the governance of our primary schools. Nobody is above the law or sacrosanct as far as the author is concerned.

First published in Ireland, in 2018, by The Shara Press

ISBN: 978-0-9527311-4-6

Available to buy online. See inside back cover for further information.